APOCALYPSE

APOCALYPSE

A NATURAL HISTORY OF GLOBAL DISASTERS

Bill McGuire

CASSELL

LONDON

First published in the United Kingdom in 1999 by Cassell & Co.

Text copyright © 1999 Bill McGuire
Design and layout copyright © 1999 Cassell & Co.

Distributed in the United States of America by Sterling Publishing Co. Inc.
387 Park Avenue South, New York, NY 10016–8810

A CIP catalogue record for this book is available from the British Library

ISBN 0-304-35209-8

Edited by Maggie O'Hanlon
Illustrations by Richard Garratt

Printed and bound in Great Britain
by MPG Books Ltd, Bodmin, Cornwall

Cassell & Co.
The Orion Publishing Group
Wellington House
125 Strand
London WC2R 0BB

*This book is dedicated to
the memory of Janet Heath*

CONTENTS

PREFACE

It is perhaps entirely appropriate that the first words of this book should be penned amid the ruins of Rabaul town on the island of New Britain, Papua New Guinea. Devastated in September 1994 by the simultaneous eruption of its two local volcanoes – Vulcan and Tavurvur – this once beautiful South Pacific town and its people struggle to recover from the near-lethal blow that Nature has struck them. As I write, Tavurvur continues to blast out clouds of ash every few minutes, and these settle over the battered remains of the town, adding to the metre of ash already accumulated and making everyday life a dirty, dreary ordeal.

What has happened here, in this tropical paradise on the lovely Gazelle Peninsula, is a lesson to us all. As a race, we survive on planet Earth purely by geological consent. Nature is all-powerful, as demonstrated by the mayhem here in Rabaul and similar, almost daily, episodes of destruction across the planet. Over the last few thousand years, however, she has been remarkably serene, dealing none of the literally Earth-shattering blows of which she is capable. While primitive societies have metamorphosed extraordinarily rapidly into the single, technology-based global village that many of us take so much for granted, she has slept – or at least dozed – and now we await the legacy of her awakening – global disaster. Beware!

Bill McGuire
RABAUL VOLCANO OBSERVATORY
6 October 1998

CHAPTER 1

WAITING FOR ARMAGEDDON

And he gathered them together into a place called
in the Hebrew tongue Armageddon.
And the seventh angel poured out his vial into the air;
and there came a great voice out of the temple of heaven,
from the throne, saying, 'It is done'.

Revelation 16–17

---

*Imagine, if you will, the following terrifying scenario. A race of 'intelligent'
beings clings precariously to the surface of a tiny, rapidly spinning ball of rock
as it hurtles through space. The skin of the rock is broken into pieces that jostle and scrape against one another as they float erratically on a semi-molten
stratum. Here and there molten material bursts through onto the surface,
while some of the pieces founder and slide down into the hot interior. The
rocky sphere is periodically pounded by other rocks and icy fragments as it
flashes through a universe filled with debris. Only a frail gaseous envelope
allows the beings to breathe while, at the same time, providing a last shield
against some of the smaller rocks and the intense cosmic radiation coming
from the Sun and other stars, but even this is in constant turmoil as it speeds
across the rock's stormy, water-covered exterior.*

Can the Earth really be such a fragile and perilous place? Perhaps to the
comfortably off inhabitant of a small town in England or the USA it
may not seem so, but to a poor villager in the Philippines, whose house
is destroyed by typhoons every year and who has already had to move
his family twice following eruption and earthquake, the picture painted
may approach reality. The truth actually lies somewhere between the
two perceptions. Without question the Earth is a menacing place, but
not uniformly so, either in space or time. At least over the span of

modern human society, some parts of the planet have survived little touched by the destructive forces of Nature, while others have succumbed time and time again to the worst the Earth can throw at them. Looking back in time, a similar situation is encountered, with episodes of devastation interspersed with quiet periods when Nature adopted a benign stance.

Whichever view we have of Mother Earth, as a loving and caring parent or our ultimate nemesis, we can be sure of one thing: she is a survivor; a middle-aged veteran who has hurtled through the universe for 4.6 billion years, with a similar length journey remaining. We are relative upstarts, arrogant newcomers who have yet to prove ourselves on Nature's battlefield and who may, in fact, not have what it takes to survive in the long term. The planet we live on and the space it travels through may simply be too hazardous for us. Meanwhile the war for the continued existence of the race goes on. So far we have prospered, but the greatest battles with Nature are yet to be fought, and the final outcome remains in the balance.

Life on a dynamic planet

The Earth is far from being alone in our neighbourhood of the galaxy, which we call the Milky Way. It is part of a family orbiting a rather unspectacular star – the Sun – that consists of nine planets, dozens of moons, and countless asteroids, comets and smaller fragments of debris left over from the formation of the solar system 4.6 billion years ago. The Earth, however, is very different from its planetary siblings, both geologically and biologically. As far as we know, only the Earth has an outer layer that is broken up into huge rocky plates that slowly move relative to one another across the surface of the planet, reflecting the turmoil in the hot interior.

Notwithstanding the recent debate over the validity of evidence for ancient microbial life on Mars, and the potential for life on some of the moons of the outer planets, the Earth remains the only place in the entire universe where we are certain that life exists. Our home planet is in a constant state of flux, with both the surface and the life that exists upon it constantly evolving over time. It is this dynamic nature that makes the Earth so unique and also makes it so hazardous. In order to appreciate how and why Nature poses such a constant threat to our race, we must learn something about the Earth and its environment.

Although there is much we still do not understand about the planet we live on, the explosion of geophysical research this century, particularly in the 1960s and 1970s, has ensured that we now have a reasonably sound knowledge of the Earth's structure and the way it operates. Much of what our planet looks like today reflects how it was constructed so long ago, from debris left over from the Sun's formation, and how it has evolved since.

Earth: the early years

Compared with the age of the universe, currently estimated to be around 14 billion years, the Sun and its entourage, including the Earth, are relatively new on the scene. The Sun is one of a younger generation of stars that formed from the atoms of much older stars that blasted themselves apart in titanic explosions millions, or even billions, of years earlier. This younger-generation status is critical for the Earth and neighbouring planets, because many of the most important elements of which they are composed, particularly iron, silicon, aluminium and oxygen, were cooked up by nuclear wizardry in the later stages of the life cycles of these older stars, before they were hurtled into space during their violent death throes.

Our solar system began to form some 4.6 billion years ago from the condensation of a particularly dense cloud of interstellar gas and dust, perhaps, according to some, as a result of shock-waves generated by a nearby exploding star, or *supernova*. Within a million years or so a weakly shining *proto-Sun* was formed as gravity took a hand and began to pull the debris together into a central mass. Once the density became high enough, nuclear reactions became possible in the early Sun, and it began to resemble much more the bright, blazing object we are all familiar with today. Although the Sun's formation scavenged over 99 per cent of the available mass from the original debris cloud, much material remained to form a disc around the new star, rather like the rings that still exist around Saturn and, to a less dramatic extent, around Jupiter and Uranus. While the individual particles within this debris disc travelled around the Sun, they repeatedly collided, at times coalescing to form larger particles and at others fragmenting due to the energy of the collisions. Gradually, however, material gathered itself into larger fragments, first of all metres across, then into kilometre-sized bodies known as *planetesimals*. This slow, incremental growth process is known as *accretion*, and it is the mechanism by which the Earth and all her sibling bodies in the solar system came into being.

As the debris disc continued to accrete, a few of the larger bodies began to dominate the process, their greater masses generating gravitational fields that enabled them to attract and sweep up more and more of the smaller fragments. This process occurred rapidly, perhaps taking only a few tens of thousands of years, and resulted in the formation of 'embryo' planets, known as *planetoids*, which were large enough to contain sufficient radioactive isotopes to heat up and partially melt their interiors. These hot, partially molten objects underwent a process known as *differentiation*, which saw the heavy metallic elements, such as iron, sink to form a core, while the lighter, rocky materials formed an outer carapace. The debris disc now consisted of many fewer, but larger, objects hurtling around the Sun – often on collision courses. Impacts between objects were common, and these sometimes, where they were of similar dimensions, ended in spectacular mutual destruction but also, where one was significantly larger, in the growth of one body at the expense of the other. While the destructive events led to the break-up of some of the early, differentiated planetoids to form the swarms of iron and rocky meteorites that continue to rain down upon the Earth, the bodies that survived grew larger and larger while their numbers became smaller and smaller.

After 100 million years or so the sweeping-up process was almost complete. The final stages of accretion were, however, very much a lottery for the surviving planetoids. Because of the smaller numbers of objects, collisions between two bodies became less likely, but because of their larger size, collisions were much more likely to result in mutual destruction. In fact, such destruction proved to be the fate of all but a few of the surviving planetoids. Only nine made it to true 'planethood' while the rest perished; their legacy was to be captured as moons by the newly formed planets, or to roam space as asteroids, perhaps waiting to vent their jealousy on their more successful competitors by a collision in their distant future.

Fortunately for us, the Earth made the grade and, despite some serious pounding, managed to survive into quieter and safer times. Along the way it also managed to gain a companion. During the late stages of the bombardment a chunk of rock as big as the planet Mars smashed into the Earth with sufficient force almost to split the fledgling planet apart. Luckily it didn't, but it did eject enormous quantities of debris, which formed a ring around the young planet, rather like the original solar-system debris disc. In the same manner, this material rapidly collected itself together, some suggest within a few months, to form our celestial neighbour, the Moon. At the same time, the great impact may have tilted the Earth off its axis, the feature of our planet that even today gives us our seasons. Like the roaming asteroids, the Moon also has a major role to play in the Earth's hazardous present and future, with its tidal influences not only affecting the oceans but also pulling at the Earth's crust with, on occasion, sufficient strength to trigger earthquakes and volcanic eruptions.

Following the end of the accretion process and the sweeping-up of most of the major debris in the solar system, the Earth had a chance to evolve without too much violent interference from extraterrestrial visitors, although smaller collisions remained common. By now the planet was proving to be a particularly effective heat engine, with the high concentrations of radioactive elements in the interior, augmented by heat energy generated by collisions, raising temperatures to levels sufficient to ensure that the Earth developed a molten magma ocean possibly 400km deep. Like the planetoids that collided to form our planet, the molten mass began to differentiate, with the more dense components, such as iron and nickel, sinking to form a metallic core within a rocky exterior.

At this time much of the Earth would have experienced temperatures not much different from the exteriors of some of the cooler stars, certainly in excess of 2,000°C and perhaps even approaching 5,000°C. Inevitably, where it made contact with the icy vacuum of space, the baking Earth began to cool and solidify, somewhere around 3.8 billion years ago, forming a thin crust that constantly broke up and reformed in response to impacts from above and molten outbursts from below.

Gradually, however, this crust began to adopt more coherent behaviour in response to the forces operating beneath in the still-molten interior. There are two ways to transfer heat from the interior of a planet into space: the first is by *conduction*, in which heat energy is transferred from atom to atom until the surface of the planet is reached. This is the same mechanism that transfers heat from a cooker hotplate to a saucepan full of soup resting upon it. A second way is by *convection*, which involves the rise of deeper, hotter, and therefore lower density, molten material toward the surface, while the cooler, higher density material already at the surface is displaced and sinks to take its place. The result is the formation of continuous currents, known as *convection cells*, which constantly churn up the interior as they go about the business of transferring heat from the hot centre of a planet to the cold of space. Using a culinary analogy once again, similar convection patterns may be seen operating in the aforementioned pan of soup, with hotter liquid from below rising in the interior of the pan, moving to the edge, cooling and increasing in density as it goes, before sliding back beneath the surface.

The effect of the underlying convection cells on the thin surface crust of the early Earth was to cause it to break into fragments and pull apart where new hot magma was rising from below, and to sink back into the inferno where two fragments collided. Gradually, as the Earth cooled and crystallized, the solid crustal fragments became larger and thicker until they took the form of *plates* thousands of kilometres across (see figure below). Such plates, the earliest of which may have formed as long as 2.7 billion years ago, form the basis of the concept of *plate tectonics*, which we use today to explain how our planet operates geologically (see p. 20).

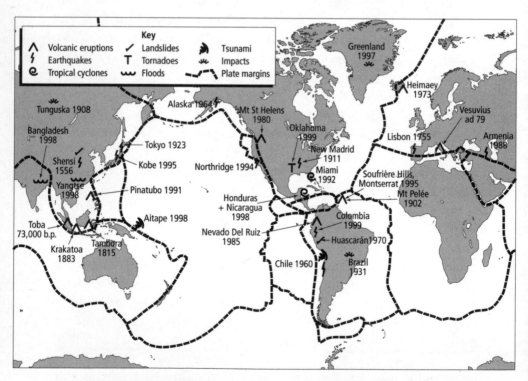

The Earth's outermost brittle layer – the lithosphere – is broken up into a dozen or so huge, rigid plates and a number of smaller platelets. Most geological hazards, particularly earthquakes and volcanic eruptions, are confined to the margins of the plates.

If the entire history of the Earth were likened to a team of international athletes running 1,500m then they would, by this time, be somewhere over half-way round the second of a total of 3½ laps. During their next lap the planet would continue to cool, allowing oceans to develop, and the first simple life forms would begin to generate the oxygen needed to form a breathable atmosphere. The real explosion of life would not, however, begin until that period of geological time known as the Cambrian – well after the bell has rung and the athletes are on the home straight of the last lap. Dinosaurs make an appearance as the runners battle for the lead in the home straight and disappear again when the leaders are still 25m from the finish, while the human race arrives on the scene in the last split-second of the race when the winner is centimetres from breasting the tape.

In comparison with the age of the planet we live on, we are thus the newest of all the tenants on the block, and it is our short time on Earth that conditions the way we think about geological and geophysical processes and the potential threat they pose. We fear earthquakes, hurricanes and moderately large volcanic eruptions because we have seen them and experienced them, but we have yet to witness the devastation caused by an impacting asteroid the size of a minor city or to experience the blind terror of being faced with a sea-wave higher than a cathedral. Consequently these threats have no meaning for us on a daily basis; they are viewed merely as scientific curiosities – quirks of Nature that happened in the past but that can surely not happen again. The frequencies of such global mega-hazards (see p. 208) demonstrate that the threat they pose is not only real but also imminent.

The structure of the earth

Like a metaphorical onion, the Earth consists of layers (see figure on p. 18) which we can figuratively peel away to reveal more of the interior. Unlike an onion, however, the layers that make up our planet differ markedly from one another, not only in their composition but also in their structure and physical characteristics.

The crust

Although we are most familiar with the *crust*, the Earth's outermost layer, this makes up less than 1 per cent of the volume of the entire planet and barely 0.5 per cent of its mass. To the human race, however,

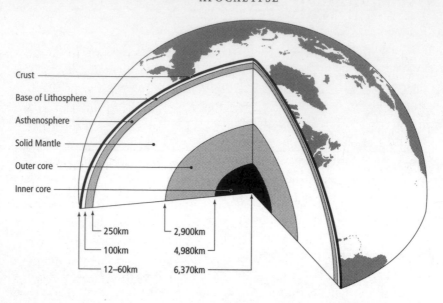

Crust

Base of Lithosphere

Asthenosphere

Solid Mantle

Outer core

Inner core

250km

100km

12–60km

2,900km

4,980km

6,370km

The Earth consists of three layers: the crust, the mantle and the core. The crust and the uppermost part of the mantle make up the brittle lithosphere from which the Earth's plates are constructed. Beneath the lithosphere, the partially molten asthenosphere is the source of the magma that reaches the surface at volcanoes.

it is all important, providing us, most of the time at least, with a stable platform on which to develop our civilization and supporting an amazing range of plant and animal life to feed and clothe us.

In simple terms, the Earth's crust can be divided into two types: that which floors the great basins that enclose the Atlantic, Pacific and Indian Oceans, and that which forms the continental landmasses, such as the Americas, Africa, Eurasia and Australia. Both types of crust were ultimately derived from molten magma, with the ocean basins being made up of the dark-coloured volcanic rock known as *basalt*, and the continents being constructed from paler coloured *granite*. The continents have, however, been much modified over time by geological and surface processes to produce a plethora of rock types, including sandstones, limestones, clays and marbles, to name but a very few. The crust is not of the same thickness across the planet and is, in fact, much thinner – typically less than 10km – beneath the oceans. In contrast, where collisions of the plates that make up the Earth's outer carapace have raised huge mountain ranges, such as the Himalayas, the energy of the impacts has also pushed the crust deeper into the interior, resulting in crustal thicknesses of 70km or more.

The mantle

Until this century we knew very little about what lay beneath the crust of our planet. Now, thanks in particular to the relatively new science of seismology, together with studies of the fragments of the Earth's deep interior ejected by volcanoes, and through observations of other bodies in the solar system, we are able to build up a broad picture of what lies deep beneath our feet. Immediately beneath the crust is the *mantle*. This layer makes up the bulk of the planet, comprising three-quarters of its volume and two-thirds of its mass. The mantle is generally solid, although it is molten in places, and it is the ultimate source of all the magma that breaches the overlying crust to reach the surface via volcanoes. It consists of both upper and lower layers, both of which have the same very simple composition. Although other components are present, the mantle is largely made up of the bright green mineral *olivine*, more commonly known as the semi-precious stone peridot.

The core

Studies of the seismic waves generated during earthquakes have enabled us to 'see' deep into the Earth, revealing that the mantle stops at a depth of not much under 3,000km where it comes into contact with the Earth's *core*. As mentioned on p. 15, it is in the core that iron and the other dense elements are concentrated, with the result that, although the core makes up only 15 per cent of the planet by volume, it comprises a third of its mass.

Most of what we know about the Earth's core is based on second-hand observations and is derived either from studying the compositions of meteorites left over from collisions of planetoids during the early history of the solar system or by theoretical modelling. Like the mantle, the core consists of two components: the inner core and outer core. Unlike the mantle, however, these differ considerably in that, while the inner core consists of a metallic sphere of solid iron and nickel, the outer core is made up of a mobile mass of liquid iron.

As in the hot-soup analogy (pp. 15–16), the outer core convects as it picks up heat from the solid inner core and transfers it upward to the lower mantle, generating the Earth's magnetic field as it does so. This is crucial to the development, and perhaps even the existence, of our species. Without a magnetic field, we would have had no reliable means of navigation during the pioneering episodes of our civilization and the growth of a global society is likely to have been much hindered. Even more importantly, the Earth and all life on it would have much less protection from the high-energy atomic and subatomic particles periodically emitted by stormy outbursts on the Sun, and the surface of the planet would be considerably more hostile to the development and survival of complex life forms.

The outer core is not the only part of the Earth's interior in turmoil. Although the mantle is essentially solid, most of it behaves like a viscous fluid that slowly convects, picking up heat from the outer core and transferring it onward, toward the surface. Despite the temperatures being extraordinarily high in the mantle, over 2,000°C at the boundary with the outer core, it does not generally melt because the predominant mineral, olivine, has a very high melting point at the huge pressures that exist within the mantle. Somewhat surprisingly, the mantle rocks melt at only quite shallow depths, often less than 150km beneath the surface. Although temperatures are lower here, so are the pressures, and the balance between the two is exactly right to cause the mantle to melt, if only partially. This uppermost, partially molten region of the mantle is known as the *asthenosphere* and is the source of all magma and therefore, ultimately, of all volcanoes.

Above the asthenosphere, the remaining mantle and the overlying crust are both solid, relatively cold and brittle. Together they constitute the *lithosphere*, which is broken up into about a dozen huge rigid plates and several smaller platelets, which creep slowly over the planet's surface at the rate of a few centimetres a year. The plates that make up the outer layer of the Earth do not, therefore, comprise just the crust; they consist of the crust and the thin brittle layer of the uppermost mantle, and they 'float' on the partially molten asthenosphere.

How the Earth works: plate tectonics

An appreciation of the concept of *plate tectonics* is crucial to our understanding of the nature and spatial distribution of many natural hazards. So what exactly is plate tectonics and how does it work? What drives these gigantic chunks of rock across the planet's surface, and what does plate movement have to do with earthquakes and volcanoes? Once again we must return to the idea of the Earth as an enormous heat engine that is constantly trying to cool itself down by transferring heat toward the surface and ultimately into space.

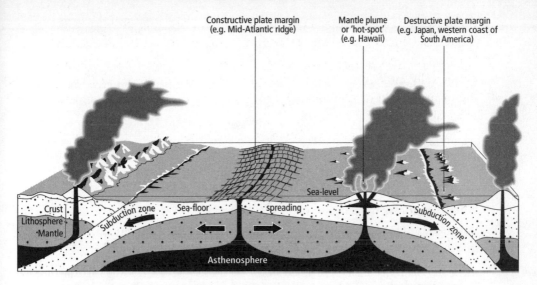

Constructive plate margin
(e.g. Mid-Atlantic ridge)

Mantle plume
or 'hot-spot'
(e.g. Hawaii)

Destructive plate margin
(e.g. Japan, western coast of
South America)

Sea-level

Crust
Lithosphere
Mantle

Subduction zone Sea-floor spreading Subduction zone

Asthenosphere

Earthquakes and volcanoes occur mainly where the Earth's plates are in contact with one another. The most explosive and therefore most dangerous volcanic eruptions occur at destructive plate margins where one plate is being subducted beneath another. Devastating earthquakes can occur either at destructive plate margins or at conservative margins where two plates are scraping past one another.

The great driving force behind this tendency to lose heat is convection (see figure above), which, as already explained, was responsible in the Earth's early history for breaking up the superficial crust into fragments. The same process is still going on today. Rising convection currents in the uppermost mantle bring hotter material from deeper within the Earth. As this hot mantle rock reaches the relatively shallow depths of the asthenosphere, the pressures exerted upon it fall, allowing it to start to melt. At the same time the rising current reaches the base of the rigid lithosphere and starts to move laterally, dragging the overlying rigid plate with it.

Constructive plate margins

Where two convection currents are moving laterally outward in opposite directions, the rigid lithosphere is pulled apart, allowing the magma generated by melting to rise toward the surface, and a *constructive plate margin* is formed. This takes the form of an often-irregular fracture, which may be many thousands of kilometres long and which repeatedly fills with magma as the two newly formed plates are progressively pulled apart. The process can go on for hundreds of millions of years, after which time the two plates may be separated by thousands of kilometres. The magma that rises to fill the space is basalt, a volcanic rock of high density. Because of its high density, the topography it forms is typically low-lying and, consequently, occupied by the oceans. Constructive plate margins are, therefore, typically submarine, forming a network of *mid-ocean ridges*, tens of thousands of kilometres long, that criss-cross the planet. Here new basaltic oceanic lithosphere is constantly being created and pushed away from constructive margins at rates of a few to several centimetres a year.

Subduction and destructive plate margins

If new lithosphere is being created at the mid-ocean ridges then either the Earth must be getting bigger or somewhere an equal amount of lithosphere must be being destroyed. As there is no evidence whatsoever for the former we need to hunt for lithospheric graveyards. In fact, these are easy to find and, once again, we must look beneath the oceans. Adjacent to many of the major continental landmasses are spectacular ocean trenches, some deep enough to swallow Mount Everest. Here the oceanic lithosphere ends its long journey from a mid-ocean ridge and plunges back into the Earth's interior. After a trip of many thousands of kilometres, which is likely to have taken hundreds of millions of years, the basaltic oceanic lithosphere has cooled considerably and is cold and very dense. When it comes into contact with another plate heading in the opposite direction, something has to give, and it is invariably the coldest and densest plate that is forced to slide underneath, returning to the hot interior of the planet from which it was formed. The process is called *subduction*, and the deep trenches where this occurs are known as *subduction zones*. For obvious reasons, these graveyards of the oceanic plates are also known as *destructive plate margins*.

Because the oceanic plates take only a few hundred million years to travel from mid-ocean ridge to subduction zone, the crust that floors the oceans is much younger than that which underlies the continents on which we live. These are often made up of rocks over 1 billion years old and sometimes, in the interiors, over 3 billion years old. Why, then, have the continents been around for so long? The continental plates also slowly move around the planet, so why are they not also subducted? The clue lies in the composition of the rocks that make up the continents: granite. This pale, spectacularly crystalline rock can be found as an ornamental facing stone on buildings around the world, which is a reflection of its ubiquitous occurrence. In addition to its colour and crystallinity, granite differs from the basalt that makes up the oceanic plates in having a significantly lower density. Because of this, whenever an oceanic plate and a continental plate meet it is always the dense oceanic plate that loses the battle for survival and disappears once again into the inferno. Rather like trying to push a beach ball beneath the surface of a swimming pool, subducting a continental plate is simply not possible. The granite plate is constantly buoyed up because of its low density and therefore survives. Because of this, many of the continents are almost as old as the Earth itself, slowly growing in size over the billions of years as volcanic activity and other geological processes gradually add material to the margins.

Conservative plate margins

All over the planet, then, plates are moving apart and colliding. In some places, however, two plates scrape past one another without the formation of new lithosphere and without old lithosphere being destroyed. These *conservative plate margins* are actually major active faults and, as such, are the home of some of the biggest earthquakes in history. Probably the best-known conservative plate margin is that marked in California by the San Andreas Fault, where the Pacific Plate to the west is scraping northward against the North American Continental Plate at around 5cm/year. Two of the planet's most famous cities, San Francisco and Los Angeles, sit directly on the fault, and the former was completely destroyed during the major earthquake of 1906. Despite moderate quakes in both 1989 and 1994, the inhabitants of both cities know that a really big one is due. But when?

If plates at conservative margins such as the San Andreas Fault moved slickly past one another there would be no such thing as large, destructive earthquakes in these areas. Unfortunately, this is not what happens. Scraping two gigantic chunks of rock past one another can never be smooth and easy. Rather like trying to scrape two cheese-graters against one another, the great rock masses stick periodically, causing the accumulation of enormous strains in the rocks on either side. Eventually these strains become so great that the fault between them jerks into life, displacing one of the plates laterally by several metres relative to the other as the accumulated strain of several decades, or even centuries, is released in a few tens of seconds. It is this sudden movement of the adjacent plates and the gigantic amount of energy generated as strains are released which trigger an earthquake and the characteristic shaking and rippling of the ground that causes so much damage in such a short space of time.

Earthquakes and volcanoes

Earthquakes are not solely confined to conservative plate margins such as the San Andreas Fault, but neither is their occurrence random. A trawl for reports of significant earthquakes in the press will keep bringing up the same countries and regions: Italy, Greece, Turkey, Iran, Afghanistan, China, Indonesia, Japan, Chile, Colombia, Mexico, Nicaragua, California, among others. Other parts of the globe, however, are notable for the general absence of destructive earthquakes, for example, the UK, most of western Europe, central Africa and Australia. Examination of a global earthquake map will reveal that most quakes occur within narrow bands, forming a network that coincides rather well with the positions of the major plate margins. Therefore, as well as periodically terrorizing the inhabitants of countries cut by conservative plate margins, earthquakes also constantly prey on the minds of those living in regions close to the subduction zones that mark the edges of destructive plates. Here, huge strains accumulate between the over-riding plate and the plate that is disappearing beneath it, until the pressures become great enough to cause them to slip suddenly and jerkily against one another, generating a quake. Although earthquakes also occur at constructive margins, the threat they pose here is relatively minor. This is partly because such quakes are relatively small compared with their conservative – and destructive – margin equivalents and partly because most constructive plate margins are submarine, with little in the way of major population centres nearby.

Not to be left out, wherever earthquakes occur volcanoes are rarely far away. Volcanoes are also largely confined to plate margins and, apart from a few examples in the heart of Africa and some isolated volcanic islands in the ocean basins, they are congregated above subduction zones and form strings of active vents along the mid-ocean ridge system where new oceanic lithosphere is constantly being created.

Volcanoes and earthquakes represent just two of the geophysical hazards that continue to make our planet such a risky place. Let me try then to evaluate just how dangerous the Earth remains at the end of the twentieth century, and look at the prospects for natural disasters in the coming millennium.

All you need to know about geophysical hazards but were afraid to ask

So far I have explained a little about how the Earth was born through violence, how it survived a rather troubled childhood and how it gained some degree of respectability and stability in its later years. Rather like an aging rock star attempting to relive a misspent youth by periodically trashing a hotel room, however, our home planet still contains considerable pent-up energy, which it feels the need to release on occasion. Like the hotel furniture, we are invariably on the receiving end. The role of plate tectonics in the fostering of geophysical hazards through its encouragement of earthquakes and volcanoes has already been touched upon. These phenomena will now be treated in a little more detail, alongside those other natural threats whose purpose seems to be to make life that much more unpleasant for the human race, namely wind-storms, floods, giant sea-waves and landslides. I will also take a broader look at the Earth's environment as a whole and try to answer the question: is life on Earth becoming more dangerous and, if so, is it of our own doing?

Geophysical hazards are not confined simply to the solid Earth beneath our feet. The oceans and the atmosphere seem to conspire to make life difficult, if not lethal, for us, and even our solar system reveals its animosity by periodically hurling chunks of rock and ice at the planet. For the purposes of this book, such potentially devastating cosmic hazards as the cataclysmic explosion of a nearby star, an event known as a *supernova*, or dramatic changes in the radiation output of our own Sun will be ignored. In broad terms, the geophysical hazards that we face can be conveniently categorized as: *geological* (earthquakes, volcanoes and landslides), *atmospheric* (wind-storms, such as tornadoes and tropical cyclones), *hydrological* (floods and the giant sea-waves known as tsunami) and *extraterrestrial* (asteroid and comet impacts). Let us examine each of these in turn, focusing on where the phenomena occur and what threat they pose rather than on their mechanics.

Geological hazards

As we have seen, earthquakes and volcanoes are intimately linked with the system of plates that form the outer carapace of the Earth, and they tend to be confined to the margins of these plates rather than their relatively stable interiors. As with many natural systems, however, this is something of an oversimplification and, to some extent, a dangerous one.

Earthquakes Although the vast majority of the world's earthquakes, and there are over 500,000 a year, do occur at plate margins, a few do not. Within the interiors of the plates there are deep faults that, although active, move only very occasionally. The problem is that, when they do move, perhaps after centuries of inactivity, the release of the huge accumulated strains can generate some of the largest and potentially most destructive earthquakes known. To compound the situation, because of the long gaps between movements along such faults, the local populations are typically not geared up to expect an earthquake; unlike the situation in Tokyo or San Francisco, buildings are rarely built to withstand the shocks, and the authorities are often unprepared for coping with the devastation.

The classic example of such an *intraplate* earthquake occurred almost 200 years ago, right in the heart of the USA. In 1811 what may have been the most energetic earthquake in the history of the country shocked the sparse population of New Madrid in Missouri. Although it is difficult to get an accurate estimate of the strength of the quake (or more accurately series of quakes), because there were too few buildings in the immediate area on which the effects could be measured, it was powerful enough to cause significant structural damage in Washington DC and Pittsburgh and on the coast of South Carolina, and it was even felt nearly 2,000km away in Boston. Unlike the San Andreas in California, no fault is visible at the surface in New Madrid. Clearly, however, one is lurking down there somewhere and, despite another smaller quake in 1895, has been accumulating strain over the past 190 years. Without question, there will be a major earthquake in this region again, and the impact will be devastating in urban areas made up of buildings that are simply not constructed to withstand the severe ground-shaking that will accompany the next activation of the hidden fault. The New Madrid case illustrates once again the false sense of security engendered in people who have never experienced a major disaster. Eight generations have lived and died since the last 'big one', and it is doubtful whether most of the population of Missouri now ever give a single thought to the idea that their lives may end in the rubble of their own house, shaken to bits by the next movement of the subterranean fault.

All over this planet earthquakes are occurring every minute of every day. The Earth can truly be called a restless planet, and the heat constantly seeping up from below keeps the rocky exterior constantly on the move. Fortunately for us, most earthquakes are so small as to be detectable only with *seismographs*: instruments specifically designed to detect the tiniest trembling of the planet. Larger quakes do, however, occur on a daily basis, and over 3,000 quakes of magnitude 5 or greater on the Richter Scale occur every year. When such events occur in a densely inhabited area, particularly one with poorly constructed buildings, big problems can arise.

In January 1999, as I was writing this, an earthquake registering magnitude 6 hit a mountainous region of western Colombia, completely flattening several towns and cities, including the city of Armenia. Television pictures revealed that the city had been reduced to rubble, with almost every building damaged or completely destroyed. Although at that time the final death toll remained undetermined, it turned out to have been over 2,000, with hundreds of thousands of others injured or homeless. The amazing thing about this Colombian quake is that, despite its enormous destruction, it was not a particularly big one.

The scale for measuring earthquake magnitudes was devised by Charles Richter in 1935 and, although open-ended, rarely extends above 8. The scale is *logarithmic*, meaning, in simple terms, that each point on the scale represents a quake 10 times more powerful than the point below. Thus the Colombian quake was 10 times stronger than a magnitude 5 (the size of the quake that triggered the collapse of the Mount St Helens volcano in 1980), and 10 times weaker than a magnitude 7 (approximately the strength of the Loma Prieta quake that hit San Francisco in October 1989). Extraordinarily, the San Francisco quake took only 64 lives and left the city looking pretty much as it had before the event. The contrast with the appearance of Armenia after a quake 10 times less powerful could not be greater.

Why is there such an enormous difference in destructive impact? Many factors determine the destructiveness of an earthquake, including the nature of the underlying geology – for example whether a town sits on solid bedrock or soft sediments – and the depth of the quake (see Chapter 4). The main determinant of earthquake destructiveness is, however, within our own control and involves the construction of buildings. As the saying goes among earthquake engineers: 'It is buildings not earthquakes that kill people.' In San Francisco the buildings were constructed from materials that were able to cope with even quite large earthquakes, and they were put together in such a way as to enable them to withstand strong ground motion without falling down. Unfortunately this was not the case in Colombia, where even emergency

27

service buildings were not earthquake proof. It remains a sad fact of life, but the sort of devastation seen in Colombia, and that recently caused by relatively small quakes in Turkey in 1992 (4,000 dead), Afghanistan in 1991 (1,200 dead) and the country of Armenia in 1988 (55,000 dead), will continue until something is done about improving building construction in quake-prone developing countries.

Volcanoes As the Earth is always shaking somewhere, so it is always erupting molten magma. Because it is not possible to say exactly when a volcano becomes extinct, however, it is not easy to estimate just how many volcanoes are currently active. Probably the best guess can be arrived at by adding up all those volcanoes that have erupted since the Earth started to warm up at the end of the last Ice Age, around 10,000 years ago. This gives us about 1,500 volcanoes that we can expect to burst into life at any moment. Some of these, such as Stromboli and Etna in Italy, or Kilauea in Hawaii, are erupting almost continuously, while others lie dormant for hundreds or thousands of years before blasting back into life. In any given year about 50 volcanoes will erupt, some mildly and others with a violence capable of sending shock-waves across the region, if not the planet.

As with intraplate earthquakes, volcanoes are not always confined to the margins of plates. Fortunately, however, intraplate volcanoes are rarely as dangerous as their seismic counterparts. Probably the best known of all intraplate volcanoes are those that make up the Hawaiian–Emperor chain of islands in the centre of the Pacific Ocean. These volcanoes have been generated by what is known as a *mantle plume*, or more simply as a *mantle hot-spot*: a finger of hot mantle that touches the cold, brittle lithosphere above it and effectively melts its way through. Although the hot-spot stays put in the same place, the Pacific plate moves across it at a rate of about 9cm/year. In fact, the plate has been trundling slowly over the hot-spot for the past 80 million years, leaving a chain of volcanic islands now 6,000km long. The chain even has a kink about half-way along where the plate changed direction around 43 million years ago.

At present the Big Island of Hawaii lies above the hot-spot, as indicated by its two currently active volcanoes, Mauna Loa and Kilauea, the latter being one of the most active in the world. Although occasionally burning parts of the local forest, bulldozing down a few houses and frightening the local wild pigs, however, the lava-dominated eruptions of the Hawaiian volcanoes are not a major hazard, and this is typical of most intraplate, hot-spot-related volcanoes.

Much more dangerous are the deadly explosive volcanoes formed at destructive plate margins, which stand as intimidating sentinels along the edges of the deep ocean trenches that mark the subduction zones where oceanic plates return to the hot mantle. Over 1,000 such volcanoes dominate South-East Asia, forming the Ring of Fire that encircles the Pacific Ocean, and many erupt every year to the terrible cost of their local populations. The magmas that feed subduction-zone volcanoes are formed in a rather interesting way. As the dense, cold, and rather soggy oceanic plate sinks back into the hot mantle, it is rapidly heated up, boiling off the seawater that has permeated the oceanic crust after a few hundred million years lying beneath several kilometres of ocean. As the water rises into the hot mantle rock above the subducting plate, it has the effect of causing the mantle to melt, forming basaltic magma that works its way back to the surface, eventually to be erupted, usually without too much violence, at a volcano. As the now dried-out oceanic plate slides even further into the Earth, it continues to heat up and eventually melts itself. This time, however, the magmas formed are sticky and gas-rich. They breach the surface with a bang, blasting onto the scene with the sort of explosive violence seen recently at Montserrat in the Caribbean, and earlier at Mount St Helens in the USA (1980) and Pinatubo in the Philippines (1991). When rated according to the *Volcanic Explosivity Index*, or VEI (see p. 74), subduction-zone volcanoes typically have eruptions meriting values of 4 and above on a scale ranging from 0 to 8.

The devastation of which subduction-zone volcanoes are capable has rarely been more graphically demonstrated than in 1902 on the French West Indian island of Martinique. During the early years of the twentieth century, volcanoes and their activity remained a mystery to most, and volcanology itself was a fledgling science, struggling to comprehend the most spectacular and frightening of all natural phenomena. Consequently, when the island's volcano, Mont Pelée, rumbled into life in February, after 50 years of slumber, neither the local inhabitants nor the authorities paid much attention. Concern increased over the next few months, however, as animals collapsed and died from the effects of noxious gases, up to 40cm of ash fell in the capital, St Pierre, and earthquakes shook the island. On 5 May a lake that filled the summit crater of the volcano breached its banks, and a boiling torrent of mud poured through the town and into the harbour, scalding and burying over 100 sugar-mill workers on the way. Major panic ensued, but the governor of the island, acting on the advice of a so-called 'committee of experts', assured the inhabitants that the volcano was safe and that the town was protected from lava flows by the shape of the land.

As a result of this pronouncement that St Pierre was not in danger, its population was swelled further by refugees from other parts of the island, and the governor and his family joined them from his residence elsewhere. Undoubtedly the governor's decision not to evacuate was influenced by the fact that an election was due on 10 May. Not only was the decision the wrong one, however, it was the last one he would ever make. At 8a.m. on the morning of 8 May the population of St Pierre was reduced from an inflated 30,000 to four – two of whom later died from their injuries. An avalanche of molten magma fragments and incandescent gases blasted into the town with the force of a hurricane, levelling every building, incinerating every living thing and even speeding out over the sea to destroy 18 ships anchored in the harbour. The governor's committee of experts had been wrong. They did not appreciate that lava flows are not a major problem on subduction-zone volcanoes and they had never seen or heard of the devastating phenomena that wiped them out. St Pierre had been annihilated by a *pyroclastic flow*, one of the most terrifying and destructive of all volcanic phenomena.

Now we know much more about these flows and the damage they can do, largely because of what happened on Martinique and, coincidentally, during a similar lethal eruption that took over 1,000 lives on the same day on the nearby island of St Vincent. We know, for example, that, unlike lava flows, pyroclastic flows do not always take account of the topography, and that the only way of protecting lives from their unimaginable temperatures and velocities is to evacuate the threatened area in time. As with most geophysical hazards, therefore, we learn from our mistakes – at least, sometimes. Deaths still occur from pyroclastic flows, and as recently as 1997 on Montserrat, the Soufrière Hills volcano took 19 lives in just such a way. Pyroclastic flows are only one of a whole spectrum of destructive phenomena associated with explosive volcanoes that will be examined in more detail in Chapter 2.

Landslides Compared with the power of earthquakes and the majesty of volcanic blasts, landslides, the third geological hazard, may appear to lack charisma. They are certainly often viewed as the poor relation of the geophysical-hazard family, despite causing devastation across the planet year after year. The problem with landslides is that they often take the form of a secondary hazardous phenomenon. In other words, they tend to be triggered by another event, such as an earthquake, a volcanic eruption or torrential rains associated with a hurricane. For example, much of the chaos caused in late 1998 by Hurricane Mitch in the Central American countries of Honduras and Nicaragua resulted from landslides triggered by a deluge that dropped 0.3m of rain a day on the region. Scientists from the US Geological Survey (USGS) have estimated that, in Honduras alone, rainfall associated with Mitch caused over 1 million landslides, blocking roads, inundating farmland and destroying entire communities.

Much of the damage and loss of life attributed to earthquakes can also be traced to landslides resulting from the intense shaking of the ground, and in some cases such *seismogenic* landslides are the main cause of death. In Japan, for example, it is estimated that landslides cause over half of all earthquake-related deaths. Furthermore, a landslide caused one of the greatest natural disasters ever when a large earthquake in the Shensi Province of China in 1556 triggered the collapse of hills that were made up of weak sediments formed by the action of ice during the last Ice Age. Many of the local inhabitants, who lived in cave systems within the hills, were buried alive, and the final death toll was estimated at over 800,000. An earthquake also triggered the greatest recent landslide disaster. In 1970 a quake of almost magnitude 8 caused the unstable and overhanging peak of the Nevados Huascaran Mountain in Peru to detach itself and crash down on the densely inhabited slopes below. Less than 4 minutes after the collapse, 18,000 people were dead, their towns and villages buried under a 30m-high pile of mud and rock.

Landslides can also be associated with volcanoes, with the Mount St Helens eruption of 1980 perhaps being the classic example. Here, after nearly a 150 years of inactivity, fresh magma began to rise into the volcano, pushing out the northern flank into a gigantic bulge almost 100m high. When the volcano was shaken by a magnitude 5 earthquake on 18 May, the bulge became detached and slid down the flanks as a huge landslide. The removal of the northern side of the volcano released the pressure on the magma underneath, which blasted out in a violent eruption that lasted for many hours. In the event only around 70 people died, but the situation could have been much worse if the area around the volcano had not been evacuated in time.

Atmospheric hazards

If this is the sort of damage the Earth can cause as it shakes, buckles, slides and explodes, what then of our atmosphere? Like the surface on which we live, the air we breathe is constantly in motion, driven by the heat of the Sun, the Earth's rotation and the constant exchange of energy with the oceans. Generally speaking, this motion takes the form of a benign and pleasant breeze. Sometimes, however, it can become a wailing banshee with the power to hurl straws through telegraph poles and wipe all evidence of human habitation from the surface of the planet.

Hurricanes Wind-storms, particularly hurricanes, constitute one of the most destructive of all geophysical hazards. Because they are particularly common in the affluent regions of the Caribbean and the Gulf and southeastern states of the USA, they have also caused some of the greatest economic losses of all natural disasters (see figure on p. 33).

The awesome power of a hurricane and its capacity for destruction on an epic scale made themselves known in all their glory to the inhabitants of Miami in August 1992, when Hurricane Andrew pounded the city into a pile of debris. Miami had previously suffered direct hits from hurricanes in 1926, 1928 and 1950, but it had never experienced anything on the scale of Andrew. As for earthquakes and volcanoes, a scale has been devised to record the strength of hurricanes. The *Saffir-Simpson Scale* classifies hurricanes in terms of categories ranging from 1 to 5, largely based upon the average and peak strengths of the winds. Because wind-speed recorders at the National Hurricane Centre in Miami were destroyed at the height of the storm, it was not possible to determine exactly what the wind velocities were when Andrew struck. Evidence from the extent of the damage caused suggested, however, that the storm bordered on a category 5, the top of the scale, with average wind speeds of over 250km/hour and peak gusts in excess of 300km/hour. Few buildings can withstand such winds, and the hurricane cut a 30km-wide swathe of complete destruction through the south of the city. Because it was travelling unusually rapidly for a hurricane, the worst of the storm had passed on within 7 hours, leaving up to 300,000 buildings completely destroyed or seriously damaged and over 150,000 people homeless. At a cost to the US economy of US$32 billion, Hurricane Andrew was the second-most expensive disaster in the history of the country, exceeded only by the bill arising from the earthquake at Northridge, California, in 1994. In terms of human impact, however, it

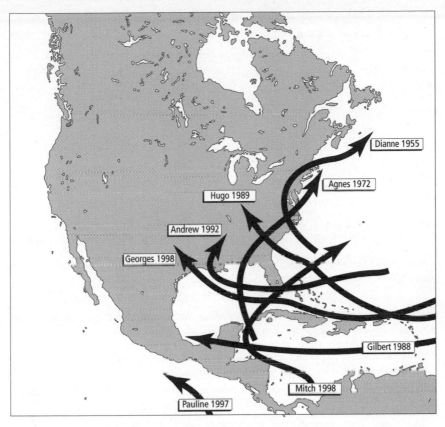

From early summer until autumn, the Caribbean region and the eastern and Gulf coasts of the USA are under threat from potentially devastating hurricanes. Hurricane Andrew, which struck Miami in 1992, caused the greatest natural disaster in US history, but with the numbers of large hurricanes on the increase this record is unlikely to last for long.

was by far the most destructive natural catastrophe ever to hit the USA. The last victims of the storm were not rehoused until 1995, and rebuilding continues today.

Hurricanes are not only confined to the tropical Atlantic Ocean, but also occur at comparable latitudes of the Indian and Pacific Oceans, where they are known as cyclones or typhoons. *Tropical cyclone* is the general term used for all these devastating wind-storms. For most of this century around 30–40 tropical cyclones have been generated each year, perhaps two-thirds of which occur in the Pacific. The majority of the storms blow themselves out over the sea, leaving only a few each year to make landfall. In addition to the Caribbean and southeastern USA, other particularly vulnerable regions include Bangladesh, Japan and the Philippines. Under certain conditions, however, tropical cyclones may travel beyond their traditional hunting grounds, and in 1938, in New England, 2,000 lives were lost as a rapidly moving hurricane headed north along the eastern seaboard of the USA. Hurricane or near-hurricane force winds may also accompany low-pressure weather systems at higher latitudes, and average wind speeds in the storm that caused so much devastation in southern England in October 1987 were not far short of those that characterize a category 1 hurricane.

In recent years, the numbers of hurricanes have been increasing, and there are now some 40 per cent more intense hurricanes than there were 30 years ago. Worryingly, this does not seem to be a blip, but part of a continuing trend caused by global warming. In order for a hurricane to form, the sea-surface temperature in the spawning grounds must be at least 26°C. However, recent scientific research has revealed not only that sea-surface temperatures are rising, but also that, for every 1°C rise, more hurricanes can be expected. In the eastern Atlantic, for example, sea-surface temperatures of 27°C will generate, on average, one or two hurricanes a year, while a rise to 28°C will result in seven or eight. With the global-warming trend set to continue for at least another 50 years, whatever we do today to reduce 'greenhouse gas' emissions, the prospects for hurricane-prone regions look increasingly bleak.

Tornadoes Sometimes spawned by tropical cyclones, tornadoes – terrifying rotating cylinders of solid wind – can be even more destructive, if on a smaller scale. Tornado funnels are generated during violent thunderstorms, appearing from the cloud base and eventually, in some cases, touching the ground. Most damaging tornadoes are confined to the USA, and particularly to the states of Oklahoma, Kansas and Texas, which constitute 'tornado alley'. Here tornadoes typically form in the contact zone between warm, moist air from the tropics and colder, drier air from the north.

The winds in a tornado vortex can often reach incredible velocities. On the *Fujita Scale* used to categorize tornado strength, an F5 tornado (the strongest yet known) is characterized by average wind speeds of between 400 and 500km/hour. No man-made structure can withstand such velocities, and a direct hit by a tornado funnel will rip any building apart. Even a close shave can be severely damaging, with the very low barometric pressures generated by the whirling vortex often being sufficient to cause nearby structures literally to explode. A particularly scary trait of tornadoes is that, if conditions are right for one to form, they are right for many to form. In other words, tornadoes often travel the countryside in swarms. In the first few days of April 1974, for example, nearly 150 tornadoes took over 300 lives in Alabama, Tennessee, Kentucky and neighbouring states.

Hydrological hazards

The power of water should never be underestimated, and flooding, whether inland or coastal, causes havoc, devastation and loss of life. Nevertheless, its effects may pale into insignificance when compared with the horror and destructive force of a major tsunami.

Floods Where there is wind there is often rain, and where that rain is torrential and persistent it will not be long before floods follow. In broad terms, flooding can be subdivided into two types: river and coastal. The former develops when a river catchment cannot cope with the degree of surface run-off during periods of heavy rainfall, while the latter results from high tides, storm surges or a combination of the two. The intensity of rainfall during a tropical storm can be almost un-believable. In 1970, on the island of Guadeloupe in the Caribbean, for example, nearly 4cm of rain fell in only 1 minute, while on the French island of Réunion in the Indian Ocean nearly 4m of rain fell in a single 24-hour period in March 1952. Given such statistics, it should not be surprising if some river systems periodically find it difficult to cope.

Flood disasters are on the increase world-wide. One reason for this is that precipitation during the current period of man-induced global warming appears to have become more concentrated, with more intense rain-storms dumping huge volumes of water over very short periods. At the same time, surface run-off into rivers is increasing as vegetation, particularly forests, is destroyed and less water is taken up by plants. Furthermore, flood plains are becoming more densely populated, particularly in developing countries, where the competition for agricultural land and living space becomes ever greater. In any single year, floods may affect upwards of 100 million people world-wide, killing up to 20,000. Many of those affected live in Bangladesh, a country that regularly finds two-thirds of its land area submerged, either by waters flooding down the Ganges river system or by cyclone-related storm surges pouring inland from the Bay of Bengal. Close neighbour China also has a long history of flood problems, with over 5 million flood-related deaths occurring since the middle of the last century. The 1990s have seen some spectacular and devastating floods in both the developed and developing world. In economic terms, the great US Mid-West floods of spring 1993 were probably the most destructive, with damage estimated at up to US$20 billion. At the height of the floods, nine states through which the Missouri and Mississippi rivers flowed were affected, with over 15 per cent of the country under water. Over 50,000 homes were damaged or destroyed and 325 million square kilometres of farmland submerged. More recently, 1998 saw major floods in both Bangladesh and China, with the numbers of people affected running into an extraordinary hundreds of millions.

Coastal flooding can be both sudden and devastating. One of the worst incidents led to the destruction of the Texas city of Galveston in September 1900, when a storm surge driven onto the coast by a hurricane took up to 8,000 lives, the worst natural disaster in the history of the USA. Galveston had been constructed on a barrier island off the mainland, a vulnerable location even in fine weather, with the land rising to barely 3m above sea-level. Serious flooding associated with tropical storms in 1871, 1875 and 1896 should have been enough to warn the authorities and population of the dangers, but no measures were taken to protect the city. When, in the opening year of the new century, a hurricane made a near-direct hit, Galveston virtually ceased to exist. Throughout the height of the storm the entire island was under 3m of water, with survival possible only for those who managed to cram into the few tall buildings left standing. When the storm subsided, the seaward third of the island had been scraped clean of all evidence of human habitation, and the remaining two-thirds survived only because it was protected from the giant waves by a huge wall of debris.

Tsunami Although, to the residents of Galveston, it may not have seemed possible for waves to get any more powerful, the impact of a storm surge pales into insignificance when compared with the terrifying power of the giant sea-waves known as tsunami. This Japanese word, which means, literally, 'harbour-wave', is often mistakenly translated into English as 'tidal wave'. In fact tides have no involvement in their formation, and this confusing term should be avoided wherever possible. Tsunami can be produced in a number of ways, for example by coastal or submarine landslides, or by the collapse or explosion of island volcanoes (see Chapters 2 and 3).

Most, however, result from submarine earthquakes in which the shock caused by a sudden movement along a fault in the sea-bed displaces a huge volume of water. Once generated, tsunami can travel at enormous velocities and for great distances. Somewhat disconcertingly, the waves are difficult to detect in deep water and may be little more than 1m high. As they approach a coastline, however, and enter shallow water, the waves begin to pile up, reaching heights of up to 30m or more. In deep water they can move at speeds in excess of 900km/hour, and they can cross the Pacific Ocean in only 20 hours.

Because the Ring of Fire is so seismically active, the Pacific is particularly prone to earthquake-generated tsunami, and 10 lethal waves have impacted on Japan, Hawaii, Alaska, Chile, Nicaragua and Papua New Guinea over the last 100 years. The second half of the nineteenth century seems, however, to be one of the most destructive periods in terms of tsunami. In 1868 10,000 people died when a tsunami powerful enough to carry a US warship 3km inland smashed into the coastline of Peru. Only 15 years later, in 1883, the island volcano of Krakatoa blew itself apart in one of the loudest explosions ever heard, at the same time forming a devastating wave that took the lives of 36,000 inhabitants of Sumatra and Java. After a pause of 15 years, Japanese deep-water fishing fleets, on returning to their home ports in 1896, found their homes destroyed and their families among the 26,000 victims of a tsunami that slipped beneath the keels of their ships without their even noticing.

Although the effects have often been locally devastating, all tsunami recorded during historic times are dwarfed into insignificance when compared with the gigantic tsunami of prehistory. Gigantic sea-waves over 300m high have occurred in the past when unstable volcanic islands have collapsed into the ocean (see Chapter 3). When this next occurs, and there is no question that it will, the consequences will be catastrophic for the entire ocean basin and all those who live within it.

Extraterrestrial hazards: comets and asteroids

So far I have looked at the geophysical hazards that the Earth itself spawns. We should never forget, however, that the greatest threat to our planet and our species comes from without. Despite the fact that the great bulk of the debris left over from the early history of the solar system has been swept up by the gravitational fields of the planets over the past 4.6 billion years, there are still alarming numbers of rocks out there looking for a spectacular way to end their existence. Without further research and observation they remain ballpark figures, but it is estimated that up to 1 billion rocks greater than 10m across have orbits that intersect that of the Earth. Although, on average, one object of this size will hit the Earth every year, most will break up and disintegrate in the atmosphere before they reach the surface. Of greater concern are objects of 50m or more across, which are large enough to penetrate the atmosphere and impact with sufficient energy to destroy a city and which can be expected to hit every century or even less. In 1908, at Tunguska in Siberia, a rock of this size devastated thousands of square kilometres of forest, but resulted in few deaths because of the remoteness of the impact site. Larger objects of 1km or more are much less common, although the effects of their impact would be devastating on a global scale (see Chapter 5). The next 1km impact – and we can expect, on average, one every 100,000 years – is likely to kill several hundred million people, either directly or as a result of dramatic changes to the planet's environment, including an *impact winter*, which may mean no growing season for months or years.

Geophysical hazards and the human race

We now have a more detailed picture of the different ways in which Nature can make life difficult for us here on planet Earth. What, however, is the cumulative impact of geophysical hazards on human society, and how much risk do we as individuals face every day from Nature's fickle moods? Exactly what events constitute a natural disaster, and how does their impact fare against other man-made or 'technological' disasters or the everyday personal threats that we all face, such as violent crime, road accidents and house fires? Let me now attempt to place geophysical hazards and the threat they pose in the context of the modern world.

As we enter the last few months of the second millennium AD, the population of our crowded planet has just breached the 6-billion level, with the vast majority concentrated in developing countries, situated in the most hazardous parts of our world. The last decade of the millennium also coincides with the International Decade for Natural Disaster Reduction, as designated by the United Nations (UN), but despite many initiatives designed to better understand geophysical hazards and their effect, natural disasters have not only continued unabated but have actually increased in both number and impact.

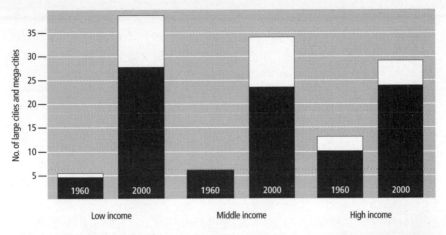

Not only is the Earth's population growing at an alarming rate, but more and more people are cramming themselves into large cities (3–8 million inhabitants) or mega-cities (over 8 million inhabitants). Many such concentrations of population are in developing countries, which are most vulnerable to natural disasters. (Source: Institution of Civil Engineers, UK, 1995)

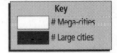

This is partly a function of the higher population densities in the most dangerous regions and partly the result of the increasingly detrimental impact of the human race on the environment. Population density is now becoming a critical factor in determining the scale of a natural disaster, particularly in southern and South-East Asia. In Bangladesh, for example, the population density is approaching 1,000/km², an extraordinarily high density for a country that is regularly two-thirds under flood water. This figure compares with 237/km² for the UK, 27/km² for the USA, and 37/km² for the planet as a whole.

A growing problem in recent decades has been the tendency for many of the Earth's inhabitants to cram themselves together into gigantic, sprawling agglomerations known as *mega-cities* (see figure above). Where these are located in hazardous regions and are made up primarily of poor accommodation with little in the way of a developed social and economic infrastructure, as at Mexico City and Dhaka in Bangladesh, a recipe for disaster is well and truly in the making. The next time a major earthquake strikes beneath Mexico City, or river floods, fed by rains in the Himalayas, coincide with a tropical cyclone in the Bay of Bengal, the recipe will be complete and tens or even hundreds of thousands will perish.

Mankind is not only aggravating the situation by placing more and more people in badly constructed homes in hazard-prone areas (often not out of choice), but also by toying with the environment at both local and global levels. The degree and impact of river flooding in Bangladesh, for example, is increasing due to greater surface run-off caused by deforestation in the Himalayan foothills that source the rivers. On the grandest scale of all, mankind is currently bang in the middle of a dangerous planetary experiment involving the heating up of the Earth through emissions of 'greenhouse gases' such as carbon dioxide and methane. Few scientists deny that the planet is warming as a result, and many feel that it is this rapid, human-induced change in the global climate that is feeding increasing numbers of natural disasters across the planet, particularly wind-storms and floods.

The concept of risk

So far I have happily used terms such as 'hazard', 'risk' and 'disaster' in a general context without explaining exactly what they mean. These are all specific terms with clear definitions and are in common use by social scientists, disaster managers and others in the 'catastrophe business'. Let us look at *hazard* first. A technical definition might be 'a naturally occurring or human-induced (anthropogenic) phenomenon, process or event that is capable of causing a loss (for example of life, property or infrastructure)'. In simpler terms, a hazard is therefore a source of danger or a potential threat to individuals or to part or all of society. On the other hand, *risk* is somewhat different and is perhaps best defined as 'the exposure of something of human value to a hazard'. The term 'risk' is closely bound up with probability and may also be thought of in terms of the probability, or likelihood, of a particular hazard taking place. It is worth noting here that geophysical hazards have always existed, but before humankind appeared on the scene they posed, at least from our anthropocentric viewpoint, no risk whatsoever. The term *disaster* is perhaps more difficult to pin down, primarily because it is much more subjective. In personal terms, the death of a loved one or the loss of a career might be disastrous to the small number of people affected, but can such events really be thought of as disasters in the same way as the 200,000 deaths resulting from the devastating 1923 Great Kanto Earthquake in Japan? Clearly not.

What then about the destruction of the space shuttle *Challenger* in 1986? This is constantly referred to as a disaster, despite the fact that it involved the loss of only seven lives. Undoubtedly the enormously high profile of a shuttle launch, together with the shock factor arising from the capture of the explosion live on television, contributed to its definition as a disaster. More importantly, however, the cost to the US National Aeronautics and Space Administration (NASA), in terms of both the craft and the setback to the entire manned spaceflight programme, ensured that this was an *economic* disaster.

A broad definition of disaster could thus be 'the realization of hazard' in terms of injury or loss of life, damage to property and goods or a detrimental impact on the environment. A more specific definition of a disaster or 'catastrophe' is used by some insurance companies and others. This definition recognizes that a disaster has occurred only if more than 50 people are seriously injured or 2,000 homes destroyed, or if the cost of the damage exceeds US\$58.6 million at 1992 prices; this is clearly a pretty meaningless definition in many circumstances. The terms 'disaster' and 'catastrophe' are highly subjective and are likely to remain so. We all know intuitively when a non-personal disaster has occurred, and we need no figures or statistics to confirm what we see and feel.

Just exactly how much at risk are we from geophysical hazards, and how much is the risk increasing as we prepare to enter the next millennium? Some idea of the current situation can be gained from examining average risks of death due to various causes for an individual living today, although this can be somewhat misleading. The table below, for example, shows that the chances of you or I dying in an asteroid impact

Average risk of death from various causes for US residents.

Cause of death	Probability	Cause of death	Probability
Car accident	1 in 100	Hurricane	1 in 25,000
Murder	1 in 300	Flood	1 in 30,000
Fire	1 in 800	Tornado	1 in 50,000
Accidental shooting	1 in 2,500	Snake bite or insect sting	1 in 100,000
Electrocution	1 in 5,000	Lightning	1 in 130,000
Asteroid or comet impact	1 in 10,000	Earthquake	1 in 200,000
Air crash	1 in 20,000	Firework accident	1 in 1,000,000

are actually twice as high as in an air crash. This is because, while the death toll associated with an air crash will normally be of the order of a few hundred, the impact of a 1km asteroid can be expected to take the lives of a billion or more. If then we could jump forward a million years and count the number of deaths due to air crashes and impacts over the intervening period, we should find asteroid-related deaths to be about twice as great. The principal reason why few people will be able to accept such figures is that, so far as we know, there have been no deaths due to an impact event in historical times. Once again the problem is one of perception. Because we have not experienced an impact event we find it difficult to imagine that, firstly, one will happen again, and secondly, that it can affect us as individuals.

Exactly how many people are affected by geophysical hazards every year, and is the situation getting worse? If we take a close look at the annual statistics kept by reinsurance companies such as Munich Reinsurance and Swiss Reinsurance we can get some idea. In the decade from 1960 to 1969, the Earth appears to have been a much safer place than it is now. Then geophysical hazards caused 16 major natural disasters, at an average economic cost of less than US$5 billion a year (at 1996 prices). In contrast, in the 10 years between 1987 and 1996, there were 64 natural disasters at an average economic cost of over US$40 billion a year. In other words, natural disasters in any single year during the late 1980s and early 1990s caused almost as much economic damage as in the whole of the 1960s.

It is worthwhile making some comparison with other disastrous events over the same period, such as technological disasters, wars and drought. Despite the dramatic rise in natural disasters over the period, more people were killed between the mid-1960s and 1990 in wars and more were affected by drought and famine. In fact, over this period, 90 per cent of all the disaster-related deaths that occurred on the African continent were due to drought-induced starvation. The numbers of people affected or killed by man-made (or technological) disasters, such as the 1964 Aberfan landslide in southern Wales or the chemical release in Bhopal, India, 20 years later, have remained, since the 1960s, at less than 25 per cent of the comparable natural-disaster figures, although the trend here is also upward.

Returning to natural disasters, the situation since 1996 has become even worse, and, at the time of writing, the figures for 1998 had just been issued, confirming just what a terrible year it was. As defined by

Top ten major natural disasters in 1998. (Information from Munich Reinsurance)

Month	Event	Country	Economic losses (US$ million)	Insured losses (US$ million)	Deaths
Jan.	Ice-storm	Canada, USA	2,500	1,150	23
Feb.	Earthquake	Afghanistan	Unknown	Unknown	4,600
May	Earthquake	Afghanistan	Unknown	Unknown	4,500
May–Aug.	Heat-wave and forest fires	USA	4,275	Unknown	130
May–Sept.	Floods	China	30,000	1,000	3,656
June	Cyclone	India	1,700	400	10,000
July–Sept.	Floods	India and Bangladesh	5,000	Unknown	4,500
Sept.	Hurricane	Caribbean & USA	10,000	3,300	4,000
Sept.	Typhoon	Japan	1,500	700	18
Nov.	Hurricane	Central America	5,000	150	14,000

the reinsurance companies, which, it must be admitted, are mostly concerned with economic and insured losses rather than loss of life, there
were over 700 natural disasters in 1998. Throughout the world 50,000
lives were lost to geophysical hazards that cost the global economy
around US$90 billion. Statistics relating to the 'top ten' worst natural
disasters of 1998 are shown in the table above. As is often the case, however, because most of the disasters occurred in poor, developing-world
countries where insurance is a very low priority, the international insurance industry only had to pay up US$15 billion, little more than 15 per
cent of the total economic cost.

It is said that, in disaster, the poor lose their lives and the rich their
money, and the enormous disparity between a natural disaster as defined
by lives lost and one defined in terms of the cost to the insurance
industry is particularly well demonstrated by a comparison of two of the

43

1998 events. While the terrible ice-storms that held much of eastern Canada and the USA in their grip during January cost insurers over US$1 billion, only 23 people died. In contrast, Hurricane Mitch, which devastated Central America in November, resulted in only US$150 million of insured losses, although the death toll approached 15,000 and the degree of disruption to the social fabric of both Honduras and Nicaragua was enormous.

It was particularly noticeable that most of the natural disasters during 1998 were related to wind-storms and floods, which caused 85 per cent of economic losses and 90 per cent of insured losses. The statistics of the most devastating event, the catastrophic floods that affected the Yangtse and other rivers in China, are mind-boggling. Over 56 million people – not far off the population of the UK – were flooded out of their homes as the rivers burst their banks, and 240 million were adversely affected in some way. The Chinese floods constituted the biggest economic disaster of the year, with damage estimated at around US$30 billion, three times more than that attributed to Hurricane Georges, which pounded the Caribbean in September.

The increases in floods and wind-storms in recent years go a long way toward explaining the worrying trend in the numbers and cost of natural disasters. It is difficult not to relate this trend to the progressive warming of the planet, which continued into 1998. Taking the Earth in its entirety, the 1990s have been the warmest decade of all, with 1998 the hottest year on record. In fact every single month in 1998 was the hottest ever recorded (e.g. January was the hottest January ever, February the hottest February ever, etc). There is little doubt that the planet is currently going through a period of dramatic climate change, and many attribute the prevalence of unusual and extreme weather conditions to this. With little prospect of a return to cooler conditions until at least the second half of the twenty-first century, we may have to batten down the hatches and ride out one of the most volatile episodes of our planet's recent history, at least in meteorological terms.

An additional increasing worry is that, as individual natural disasters become more and more devastating, they have the potential to destabilize the global economy, causing chaos and hardship across the world. The financial markets are now intimately linked to the global environment, and large natural catastrophes are becoming increasingly associated with panic in the markets, loss of faith in the system and a failure of the global financial infrastructures. It is no coincidence that two of the greatest stock-market crashes were associated with natural disasters: the 1987 UK wind-storms and the 1994 Kobe earthquake in Japan.

Too close for comfort

The catalogue of death and destruction presented so far, although terrifying and impressive, pales into insignificance when compared with the scale of ruination our society and our environment will have to contend with during the coming millennia. In the not-too-distant future we can expect to face one of four devastating natural mega-catastrophes, each capable of causing unprecedented disruption to our cosy, at least in the developed world, existence. Three of these titanic events are powerful enough to affect physically the whole planet or a substantial part of it, as either the oceans or the atmosphere will transmit destruction far and wide. Although the fourth will be only locally devastating, its location at the core of the global economy will result in metaphorical shock-waves that will encircle the planet, tear apart the economic and social fabric of the developed world, and bring the most powerful countries to their knees. What horror then does the future hold in store for us? We have a rather depressing choice: a volcanic super-eruption, a gigantic ocean-wide tsunami caused by a collapsing ocean island, a giant earthquake at the heart of an economic superpower or, most devastating of all, the impact of a comet or asteroid.

In the manner of the biblical Four Horsemen of the Apocalypse – Famine, War, Pestilence and Death – these events have the potential to transport twenty-first-century Earth back to the Dark Ages, and in the coming chapters, the terrifying impact of these Four Horsemen's Accomplices will be examined through dramatic accounts of a super-eruption in the western USA, the devastation of the Caribbean and eastern coast of the USA by a giant tsunami from the distant Canary Islands, the destruction of Tokyo in the inevitable great earthquake and the horrific consequences of a 1km asteroid impact off the coast of the UK.

Lessons from the past

I have already explained how the unfamiliarity of modern society with major natural catastrophes has bred general disinterest and complacency with regard to the threat we face from Nature, but what about ancient society? Is there any evidence in the surviving records of past civilizations that can tell us whether or not they had to face the sorts of natural disasters that we now know we will have to contend with? Ancient texts such as the Bible are brim full of dramatic and spectacular accounts of doom and destruction, nearly all attributed to the anger of vengeful deities, but equally explainable in terms of contemporary natural catastrophes on a grand scale. Increasingly, hard, or at least thought-provoking, scientific evidence is accumulating for catastrophic events in our ancient past, extending from Early Byzantine times all the way back to the great thaw that followed the end of the last Ice Age around 10,000 years ago. Myths and legends from Europe, China, and the American continent record events so violent that they led to the demise of entire civilizations, but just how valid are these accounts and, if true, what lessons do they hold for our future?

Even those of us who are in the know tend to forget, or at least to take for granted, the fact that one of the greatest periods of environmental change in the Earth's long history took place very recently, and not much earlier than recorded human history. When the great ice sheets started to retreat and melt in earnest barely 10,000 years ago, modern humans and their ancestors had already walked the Earth for hundreds of thousands of years. The dramatic changes to the environment that accompanied the amelioration of the planet's climate must have shocked those primitive societies that had developed within, and adapted to, a very different world. Some of the changes were catastrophic in the true sense of the word, and in particular, the flood legends common to many religions are thought by some to have their origins in a number of spectacular deluges that characterized this post-glacial period.

Not surprisingly, the melting of the ice sheets that covered nearly all of temperate Europe, Asia and the USA led to an abundance of water. Not only did sea-levels rise by 100m or so, inundating huge tracts of land that had been exposed for many thousands of years, but at times, the rate of rise appears almost impossible to imagine. Studies of the growth of coral reefs in the post-glacial period reveal that some reefs had to grow at a rate of around 10m in 150 years to keep up with the rising sea, and some scientists have proposed that, on occasion, global sea-levels may have risen by several centimetres in only a few days. The explanation for such extremely rapid rises in sea-level lies in the fact that much of the water generated from the melting ice sheets became trapped in areas of low topography to form gigantic lakes along the ice-sheet margins. Some lakes were as large as several European countries combined, dwarfing the present-day Great Lakes of North America. Such was the volume of water released by the melting ice that eventually many of these lakes could hold no more, and their contents burst through weak points along their shores to send unprecedented torrents on their way to the ocean. These lake bursts involved billions of times the volume of water that pours over the falls at Niagara and scoured and resculpted great tracts of land by their tremendous energy and erosive power.

Archaeologists and scientists have debated for many years whether or not the flood legends of religious texts can be rooted in such great post-glacial deluges. Clearly, the biblical flood could not represent a first-hand account because several thousand years had passed between the deluges and the writing of the chronicle of Noah's survival. Is it possible, however, that the tale could have been derived from an earlier source? In the case of Noah's flood this does indeed appear to have been the case, with the flood myth being twice removed from the original source. The biblical account is clearly derived from the Babylonian story of Gilgamesh (ruler of Mesopotamia in about 2600 BC), which invokes a similar biblical-style flood that wipes out all but a few. This tale in turn, however, appears to have been taken from the even earlier Sumerian account of a huge destructive flood described in the Atrahasis legend, which places the event at a time earlier than 3000 years BC.

Despite its great age, the Samarian legend is also too young to represent a first-hand account of a post-glacial deluge. Could, however, even this earliest of accounts hark back to even older times? Some scientists and archaeologists are convinced that it does. There is now considerable geological evidence supporting the idea that, until relatively recently, the Black Sea was not a sea at all, but a much smaller, freshwater lake. Sometime before 5000 BC the rapidly rising global sea-levels had filled the Mediterranean basin to such an extent that, in its northeastern part, between what is now Greece and Turkey, only a thin sliver of rock held the waters back from the lower-lying Black Sea basin to the north. With little warning, the enormous pressures of the Mediterranean water blasted through the intervening rock to send a raging torrent flooding into the basin and its freshwater lake. The equivalent of millions of Victoria Falls every day for years would have poured through the narrow rock passage that we now know as the Bosporus, until the water levels of the two basins became equalized. As the waters of the Black Sea rose by the day, the inhabitants of villages around the original lake would have been forced to pack their possessions and either seek pastures new or drown beneath the relentless salty tide. A number of scientists now believe that some of the survivors travelled southeastward, eventually finding themselves in Sumaria, where the extraordinary tale they told found its way into the local mythology.

Unprecedented catastrophic events did then happen in the very recent past, geologically speaking, and evidence for them may have been handed down to us today through myth and legend. The rising sea-levels and post-glacial deluges must certainly have led to many other great outbursts similar to that which filled the Black Sea basin, and flood legends abound in verbal and written myths from countries as far apart as Mexico, Egypt, China and New Zealand. Were these accounts also linked in some way to the dramatic redistribution of planetary water that accompanied the rapid melting of the ice sheets? Notwithstanding wholesale melting of the polar ice caps, catastrophic flooding worldwide is unlikely in the foreseeable future, but does the early history of our race provide us with evidence of any other past mega-catastrophes? The answer appears to be yes.

Over the past few decades, evidence has been accumulating for major changes in the Earth's environment coincident with the fall of many Bronze Age civilizations across the planet. Some scientists and archaeologists believe they have discovered evidence for major ecological changes during the late third millennium BC, involving climate variation, dramatically changing sea-levels, tsunami and increased levels of seismicity. Within the limits of available dating methods, these events appear to be contemporaneous, with the collapse of the first urban civilizations in Asia, Africa, and Europe occurring around 2350 BC. If this is true, what sort of catastrophe could have caused sufficient upheaval to set back civilizations as far apart as the Iberian peninsula, Greece, the Middle East, India and China?

One suggestion that is gaining ground among both archaeologists and planetary scientists is that the Earth underwent an episode of comet or asteroid bombardment at this time, leading to terror and disruption across the planet. Evidence for such an event comes from a variety of sources, including accounts in ancient texts, as well as scientific studies. Tree rings, for example, record rapid and dramatic changes of climate at the time, which is only to be expected following a significant impact event, while excavations at contemporaneous archaeological sites in Syria have revealed unusual ash-like deposits that have been interpreted as representing impact-related fallout. It seems that Bronze Age Earth, and the third millennium BC in particular, seems to have been a rather uncomfortable place to live, with our planet apparently suffering a more intense period of bombardment from space than normal.

During the very early years of urban civilization, therefore, it may be that our planet suffered from great floods and perilous impacts, the effects of which could have been global, or at least regional, and which, if they occurred today, would make it very difficult for our global economy and social fabric to survive unscathed. Coming nearer to our own time, have things really quietened down that much or are our group memories so very short that major natural catastrophes during the last 2,000 years have already been forgotten? Somewhat surprisingly, the latter does indeed seem to be the case.

Let us go back 1,500 years to the Early Byzantine period and the fifth century AD. While the legendary Arthur battled to keep Albion free of the marauding Saxons, even more dramatic events were unfolding in the eastern Mediterranean. Over the past two decades geological evidence has been accumulated that points to the period from the middle of the fourth century to the middle of the sixth century AD being a particularly shaky one for the inhabitants of this part of the world. From Syria in the east to Greece in the west, many great earthquakes appear to have thrust up to 9m skyward a gigantic block of the Earth's crust 1,500km long by 700km wide – about the size of Turkey.

This spectacular geological event, known as the *Early Byzantine Tectonic Paroxysm*, must have devastated many communities over a huge area, and accounts from surviving texts report destruction and casualties from both earthquakes and resulting tsunami. The greatest quake appears to have occurred in AD 365, at which time archaeological and geological studies find evidence for earthquake damage in Crete, Cyprus and Libya. A tsunami generated by the quake also appears to have impacted on much of the eastern Mediterranean coastline, including eastern Sicily, the Greek islands and mainland, Crete and the Nile delta in Egypt. Despite the devastation that a repeat of such circumstances would wreak upon the Mediterranean region today, and there is absolutely no reason why such a readjustment of the complex Mediterranean geology could not occur again, only a handful of scientists is aware of the threat.

Coming a little more up to date and switching continents, the North American Indians have something important to tell us about a future major tsunami threat to that part of coastal northwestern America known as Cascadia. Little in the way of large earthquakes has been recorded in the states of Oregon and Washington since the colonization of this part of the USA. Recent geological studies have revealed, however, that major offshore earthquakes have occurred in the region as recently as 300 years ago, producing tsunami on a scale sufficient to devastate the Pacific coastline of North America and with enough energy to reach Hawaii and Japan. These events were also recorded in the legends of the local Indian population, who recounted them to the explorer J. G. Swan in the middle of the last century. Some idea of the scale of the devastation that can be expected when the next Cascadia quake strikes can be gleaned from the Makah Indians who lived on Cape Flattery, the most northwesterly point on the contiguous USA. To Swan they reported a time 'not at a very remote period' when water from the Pacific made an island of Cape Flattery. They went on to talk of the water taking 4 days to ebb before returning again without any wave or breakers 'til it had submerged the Cape and in fact the whole country', and finished by saying 'many canoes came down in trees and were destroyed, and numerous lives were lost. The water was 4 days regaining its accustomed level'.

Even during the past century or so there have been major, if not global, geophysical events of which we have either been unaware or that have occurred, fortuitously, in sparsely populated parts of the planet. Many of these have involved the impact of small, 10–50m rocks with the potential to wipe out a city or a small country. In addition to the Tunguska impact in Siberia in 1908, others appear to have occurred in Brazil in 1931, again in Siberia in 1947 and in Greenland in 1997. Some have also proposed that the great fire of Chicago in 1871 was the result of an impact event.

The apocryphal account of how the fire started blames a particularly bad-tempered cow that belonged to a Mrs O'Leary. While milking the irritable animal it is said to have kicked out, knocking over a nearby kerosene lamp. The story would have been an amusing one had the fire not gone on to claim 250 lives and destroy over 17,000 buildings. There is a big problem with the validity of the story, however, principally because, on the fateful night of 8 October, great fires raged in several of the towns around Sturgeon Bay on Lake Michigan, and the one in Chicago was by no means the most destructive. The greatest death toll, in fact, occurred in the town of Peshtigo in the neighbouring state of Wisconsin, where over 1,000 lives were lost in the conflagration. Those who disputed the theory of Mrs O'Leary's cow as the firestarter blamed forest fires following an unusually dry summer, but reports from survivors point to another potential culprit.

In his book *Ragnarok*, published a few years later, the amateur astronomer Ignatius Donnelly suggested that the fires might have resulted from a comet impact or near miss. Donnelly pointed out that the fires in a number of the affected towns appear to have started simultaneously. He also talks of survivors from Peshtigo claiming to have witnessed a great, black, balloon-shaped object, which came out of the sky and exploded over the forest, while others reported great balls of fire coming down from the sky. A comet fragment colliding with the Earth remains a speculative cause for the Illinois and Wisconsin fires, and the chances are that we will never get closer to the truth. As comets are composed primarily of ice, a fragment of the order of a few tens of metres across would explode in the atmosphere, generating sufficient energy to ignite fires but leaving neither an impact crater nor any trace of itself. Like a knife carved from ice, it is a weapon for a perfect crime.

The next throw of the dice

It is now clear that our ancestors probably did not have it easy when it came to natural disasters, and there is little doubt that, on numerous occasions, they experienced geophysical events far more disruptive than any we have had to face in the past few centuries. How would our technological society with its closely interwoven global economy have fared if it had been faced with the asteroid bombardment that may have taken such a toll on Bronze Age civilizations across the world, and when can we expect the like again? We now know without question that global natural catastrophes are a normal part of our planet's history and evolution, and that our modern world has yet to experience their devastating effects. The big question then is: are we living on borrowed time? When can we expect the next Earth-shattering disaster and what, if anything, can we do about it?

Timing: return periods

The first issue we need to address in attempting to answer these crucial questions relates to the concept of a particular event being 'overdue', be it the arrival of a bus or the impact of a comet. There is, in fact, a major difference between these two types of event. Buses, although it is often hard to believe, run to timetables that we can check at the bus-stop. If a bus is due on the hour and has not arrived by 10 minutes past, then it is clearly overdue. Comet impacts, along with other hazardous natural phenomena, do not run to a strict timetable and so can never be regarded as being overdue. Although we will need to qualify the statement later, such hazardous events occur randomly in time, but with a characteristic frequency, or *return period*. As an example let us take the biggest volcanic eruptions known. These gigantic events are so explosive that they eject thousands of cubic kilometres of gas and ash into the stratosphere, drastically altering the planet's climate. Such huge volcanic blasts have occurred, on average, every 50,000 years over the last 2 million years, and the last such gargantuan explosion took place at Toba, in Indonesia, about 73,000 years ago.

This does not mean, however, that we are now 23,000 years overdue for the next one. The Earth should not be thought of as a ticking clock timed to set off giant eruptions every 50,000 years, but rather as a complicated natural system within which various processes lead to a major volcanic blast, on average, every 50,000 years. It is perfectly possible, although not very likely, that we will not see another such eruption for a million years. Similarly, it is highly unlikely, but not impossible, that two eruptions on this scale will occur next week. Having said this, the world did experience two major (although far from gigantic) eruptions in 1991, when only one is expected per century, and the 1-in-200-year windstorm that devastated the southern UK in 1987 was followed by another similar-sized storm only 3 years later.

This last example also illustrates the fact that the recent occurrence of a rare phenomenon does not provide protection from a recurrence in the short term. Notwithstanding the additional complicating factor of global warming, which appears to be encouraging an increase in the frequencies of severe wind-storms in Europe, we should certainly never entertain the idea that the UK is now safe from a major storm for another 200 years. It simply does not work like that. In a way, it is rather like the businessman who, to feel safer when flying, always took a bomb on the aircraft with him, the idea being that the chances of there being two bombs – his and a terrorist's – on the same plane was infinitesimal.

What then are the average return periods for mega-catastrophes capable of causing global devastation? One general point we can make is that the bigger the hazard the longer the return period. The reason for this is that all geophysical hazards, whether they are volcanic eruptions, asteroid impacts, earthquakes or wind-storms, follow what is called a *power-law distribution*. This ensures that the number of any size of event is proportional to the inverse of the square of their sizes. Put more simply, this means that there are many, many small eruptions, impacts, earthquakes and wind-storms, a much smaller number of medium-sized events and only a tiny number of the most destructive hazards. Given such a distribution, it should not be surprising that the small events have the shortest return periods, because there are so many of them, while the largest events have the longest return periods. This is shown in the figure below, which displays the relative frequencies of different-sized impact events and volcanic eruptions.

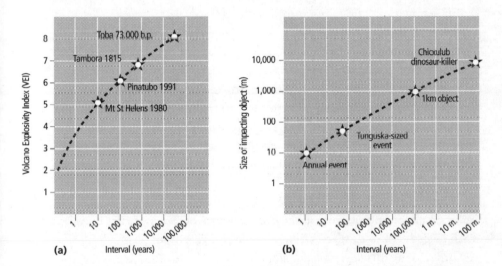

All geophysical hazards follow a power-law distribution. This means, essentially, that there are many more smaller events, e.g. impacts or volcanic eruptions, than there are larger ones. Consequently, small events occur much more frequently than their larger and more destructive counterparts. This relationship is clearly demonstrated in graphs showing the relative frequencies of: (a) different-sized volcanic eruptions and (b) different-sized impacts.

Natural catastrophes and evolution

Once we have accepted that major natural catastrophes that can affect the entire planet are possible, we have to think more carefully about the uniformity of the conditions under which our planet and the life upon it has evolved. Until the arrival on the scene of Charles Darwin, it was generally accepted that the Earth and all life upon it had arrived on the scene pretty suddenly at the whim of a deity and that any changes since then, such as Noah's flood, had taken place catastrophically. Darwin, and his Scottish geologist contemporary Charles Lyell, gradually changed this consensus scientific viewpoint from one of *catastrophism*, in which change occurred as a result of dramatic and violent events, to *uniformitarianism*, within which the evolution of life and the planet took place extremely slowly by means of the same biological and geological processes that we see acting today. This principle, which can be simply stated in terms of 'the present is the key to the past', was originally developed in the eighteenth century by another Scottish geologist, James Hutton, but it became well known only through the enthusiastic pros-elytizing of Lyell and his supporters.

In recent years the pendulum has started, to some extent at least, to swing back toward catastrophism, as we have come to see that the present is not necessarily always the key to the past. We now recognize that, generally speaking, the processes we see operating today, such as the slow crawl of the plates across the surface of the Earth or the centimetre-by-centimetre struggle for more height of the Alps and Himalayas, represent the 'normal' behaviour of the planet. We also now appreciate, however, that this *steady-state* situation is periodically inter-rupted by violent, planet-wide catastrophes that dramatically change the geological and biological situation.

The 1980 work of US physicist Luis Alvarez and his co-workers in linking a major impact event to the disappearance of the dinosaurs, together with 60 per cent of all species living 65 million years ago, went a long way toward making this idea of *punctuated equilibrium* more attractive as a work-ing model for the Earth as a combined geological and biological system. It was far from new, however, and many scientists as far back as the 1940s had considered the terrible effect that impact events might have on the planet's biosphere. Now it is suggested that many, if not all, of the major extinctions that have affected life on Earth may have resulted from asteroid or comet impacts or perhaps from other terrestrial catastrophic natural phenomena, such as gigantic lava eruptions.

Further complications

So far we have considered geophysical hazards as events that occur randomly in time and that are independent of one another. Just to com-plicate the situation there is increasing evidence that this may not always be the case. For example, recent research on the timing of explosive volcanic eruptions over the last few hundred thousand years suggests that they may be clustered in time, with more eruptions occurring at the beginning and ends of Ice Ages when global sea-levels are undergoing rapid falls and rises of 100m or more. The stresses set up in the Earth's crust and within individual volcanoes by the moving of gigantic volumes of water from the seas to the ice caps and back appear to be sufficiently great to promote the rise and explosive expulsion of magma (see Chapter 2). Impact events too may be clustered in time (see Chapter 5), with elevated levels of bombardment occurring periodically as the Earth passes through discrete clouds of rock and ice fragments. There may now also be evidence for a clustering in time of the giant tsunami that periodically devastate entire ocean basins in response to the catastrophic collapse of ocean island volcanoes (see Chapter 3).

What can be done?

As a prophet of doom of some years' standing, one of the most common questions I am asked when I expound upon cosmic or volcanic devastation is: so what can we do about it? It is a fair question and one that is not easy to answer. Plans to map the orbits of asteroids and comets that are a potential threat and to devise methods for diverting or destroying objects determined to be on collision courses with our planet are addressed in Chapter 5. The former is already ongoing, albeit slowly, and the latter is within the realms of feasibility. In contrast, actually preventing a volcanic *super-eruption* or building barriers against a 100m-high tsunami are clearly far beyond the bounds of current engineering capabilities and likely to remain so. Despite paper plans for lubricating faults in order to release accumulating strain as a number of small quakes rather than as a single, large, destructive quake, this too is likely to remain, for the foreseeable future at least, in the minds of imaginative earthquake engineers and seismologists.

When asked what we can do, therefore, I tend to focus very much on our perception and preparedness as a global society. Much remains to be done in terms of convincing national governments and international bodies that global natural catastrophes are possible and will happen. Once this message begins to get through to those in power they can begin to justify the development of contingency plans effectively to make the best of a bad situation. For example, when the currently unstable west flank of the Cumbre Vieja volcano on the Canary island of La Palma eventually collapses (see Chapter 3) and a 100m-high wave heads for the Caribbean and the eastern USA, authorities will have 7 or 8 hours to evacuate. This is clearly insufficient time to save everyone, but time enough to maximize survival rates provided that, crucially, civil-defence plans already exist that can cope with the scenario. There is little doubt that millions will die when the Earth faces its next mega-catastrophe but, as with all disasters, limiting the impact of the event, whatever form it takes, will depend more on awareness and prepared-ness than on technology.

CHAPTER 2

FIRE AND ICE:
THE VOLCANIC WINTER

A third of mankind was killed by the three plagues
of fire, smoke, and sulphur . . .

Revelation 9:18

The sky over London is a menacing iron-grey and has been so since soon after the cataclysmic super-eruption in the USA in January 2075, just 7 months earlier. *Snow lies half a metre deep in Oxford Street, and on the frozen Thames heavily clad crowds jostle at stalls to barter for scraps of unidentifiable meat to supplement their sparse state rations. Ice has stopped production of North Sea oil, and few vehicles attempt to negotiate the snow-bound avenues. Across the planet millions of people have already died from the cold, while billions starve as harvests continue to fail. A combination of the freezing conditions and civil strife has triggered the breakdown of society in many countries, and the global village has fragmented into a million isolated hamlets.*

Four deadly eruptions

Most volcanic eruptions occur on such a scale that only the local area or the country is affected. Some, however, are so energetic that their deadly effects extend far beyond their immediate environs to entire regions or, in cases of the very largest, to the entire planet. Four such eruptions, occurring within last 250 years, are described here, together with their devastating nature and widespread impacts.

Lakagigar, Iceland, 1783–85 (The 'Skaftar Fires')

On 8 June 1783, following intense earthquakes, a spectacular 27km-long system of fissures opened to the southwest of the Vatnajökull ice cap in

Iceland, spewing out highly fluid lava at a tremendous rate. Fountains of lava three times higher than the Empire State Building fed flows that poured from the fissures at a discharge rate comparable with that of the Amazon river and that travelled as much as 35km in just 4 days. Although the eruption continued into 1784, most lavas were erupted in the first 5 months, with nearly 14km³ covering an area of almost 600km². Gas and dust associated with the eruption were lofted as high as 15km, where strong winds carried them over North America and northern Europe. Nearly 100 million tonnes of sulphuric acid were formed as a result of sulphur dioxide and other sulphur gases combining with water in the atmosphere. This caused acid rain to fall in Norway and Scotland, and resulted in the formation of a dense, dry fog that blanketed much of Europe and the North Atlantic region, extending even as far as Syria. In parts of Italy the sun was so weakened by the fog that it could be viewed painlessly with the naked eye, while in southern France the setting sun disappeared into the fog layer when it was still almost 20 degrees above the horizon.

First-hand descriptions of the Lakagigar fog's effects in Europe are provided from Paris by Benjamin Franklin who, at the time, was the first diplomatic representative in France of the fledgling USA. Franklin reports how the fog led to a much cooler than usual summer and a long and cold winter season. He recounts how 'the surface was early frozen' and how 'the first snow remained on it unmelted and received continual additions' and notes that 'the winter of 1783–84 was more severe than any that had happened for many years'.

The pronounced chilling that Franklin describes resulted from the sulphurous fog stagnating in the troposphere, the lowest layer of the atmosphere, over the North Atlantic region, forming a very effective reflector that bounced solar radiation back into the upper atmosphere. As a consequence, the northern hemisphere cooled rapidly by as much as 1°C, a significant drop when it is considered that only a 5° or 6°C fall in temperature is required to plunge the planet into full Ice Age. The 1°C drop triggered by the Lakagigar eruption was sufficient to cause a bitterly cold winter in Europe and North America, with the average winter temperature for the eastern USA falling to nearly 5°C below normal. In Europe and North America, the unseasonable conditions were unpleasant. In Iceland, however, the effects of the eruption were catastrophic. A combination of acid rain and toxic fluorine from the volcanic gases led to the wholesale destruction of crops and the poisoning of 75 per cent of the island's livestock. Around 10,000 people, a quarter of the residents of Iceland, died in the resulting famine.

Tambora, Indonesia, 1815

Barely 30 years after Lakagigar, the inhabitants of Europe and North America were again to suffer the effects of a distant volcanic eruption, but this time 12,000km away in the wilds of the Indonesian island of Sumbawa. South-East Asia teems with active or potentially active volcanoes, perhaps over 500 in all, mostly confined to a narrow band that snakes its way through the Indonesian islands of Sumatra, Java and Bali before heading north into the Philippines and Japan. Indonesia itself has hosted two of the most devastating eruptions in recorded history: Krakatoa (see p. 61) and Tambora, an innocuous-looking volcano nestling quietly to the east of the islands of Java and exotic Bali.

During 1815, while the armies of Napoleon and Wellington played cat and mouse in Europe, Tambora was getting ready to blow itself apart in what may have been the greatest eruption since the glaciers retreated some 10,000 years ago. The onset of the eruption was not sudden, and today it is certain that both volcanologists and the local population would have anticipated the following events. Tambora had awakened in 1812, rumbling and grumbling on until the spring of 1815. Over this period fresh magma had been gradually accumulating within and below the volcano, ready to blast its way to the surface. This it did by means of a series of gigantic explosions that started on 5 April and lasted for 34 days, climaxing with a number of awesome detonations on 10 and 11 May.

Sir Stamford Raffles, then British Lieutenant Governor of Java, provided a graphic account of the cataclysmic phases of the eruption, reporting detonations loud enough to be heard in Sumatra 1,600km distant. He describes three columns of flame rising to immense heights and the entire surface of Tambora being covered in incandescent material extending to great distances. Rocks 'some as large as the head' fell over 10km from the volcano, while total darkness reigned, even in Java, 500km to the west. Nearer the volcano, Raffles reported utter devastation, with only 36 of around 12,000 inhabitants making it to safety, buildings crushed beneath metres of grey ash, and the sea covered with so much pumice that ships could make little headway.

The misery of the local inhabitants was not to end, however, with the demise of the eruption. So devastating was the impact of the ash-fall on the local agriculture that, with no hope of international aid, a further

80,000 of Sumbawa's inhabitants succumbed to starvation and disease as crops died and water became contaminated. Further afield, the whole world was shortly to feel the wrath of Tambora as over 200 million tonnes of sulphur-rich gases rapidly girdled the planet, combining with water in the atmosphere to form 150 million tonnes of sulphuric-acid aerosols. As at Lakagigar, these tiny liquid aerosol particles blocked out solar radiation, causing global temperatures to fall sharply (see figure below).

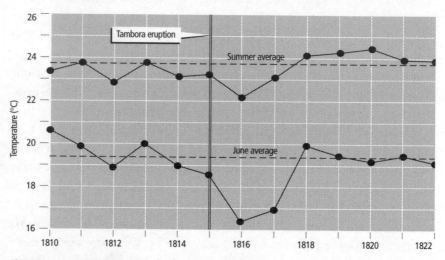

The gigantic quantities of sulphuric-acid aerosols ejected into the stratosphere by the Tambora eruption in 1815 dramatically reduced amounts of solar radiation reaching the surface of the Earth. As a result, there were sharp reductions in temperature the following summer in Europe and North America, as shown by records for the latitude of Philadelphia, Pennsylvania (upper lines of graph) and for New Haven, Connecticut (lower lines).

With the Earth's climate already going through an episode of cooling, the chilling effect of Tambora's blast was even greater than might have been expected, and it is unlikely that any other eruption before or since has had such significant and unexpected cultural effects across the planet, all consequent on its marked impact on the climate. Unseasonably heavy rains in June 1815, leading to quagmire conditions that hindered Napoleon *en route* to defeat at Waterloo, have been blamed by some on changing weather patterns associated with the Tambora eruption, although it is unlikely that its effects could have reached Europe so soon. There is little doubt, however, that the appalling European weather of the following year, 'the year without a summer', was a legacy of the eruption, which led to a global temperature fall of around 0.7°C (see figure on p. 60). Not only did the cold and wet conditions set the mood for a miserable Mary Shelley to pen the words of *Frankenstein*, but the spectacular sunsets caused by volcanic debris in the stratosphere may have provided the inspiration for artist Joseph Turner's most colourful works.

Krakatoa, Indonesia, 1883

Like many volcanoes that have slumbered for a long time, the small volcanic island of Krakatoa, located in the busy Sunda Straits between the Indonesian islands of Sumatra and Java, was largely ignored by the local populace, most of whom were probably unaware that it was even a volcano. The situation altered dramatically in 1883, however, when the gods of the sea and the underworld, Neptune and Vulcan, conspired to produce one of the largest volcanic explosions in modern times. The first rumblings took the inhabitants of the many local fishing villages by surprise at the end of May, and their curiosity increased when loud and violent explosions increasingly rocked the region throughout June and July. Although the people of Batavia (now Jakarta) and other nearby towns had expressed little concern at the growing activity, this all changed just after mid-day on 26 August, when the eruption started in earnest.

A series of titanic explosions, heard all over Java, blasted a huge, black column of ash to heights of over 25km, while pyroclastic flows – deadly mixtures of ash, gas, and molten rock – flowed down the flanks and into the sea, generating giant tsunami that pounded the shoreline fishing communities of neighbouring islands. Throughout the night hundreds of thousands of terrified people cowered in homes that shook as if caught in a heavy artillery bombardment, while being slowly buried in pumice that fell like hot, hard rain. This proved, however, to be nothing compared with the earth-shattering events they were to face as another day dawned, although the sun's rays never penetrated the utter blackness of the ash-filled atmosphere.

Since the start of the eruption 22 hours earlier, the huge explosions had evacuated much of the magma from the underlying chamber, which could no longer support the weight of the volcano above. At 10.00a.m. on 27 August, the roof of the chamber fractured and collapsed, allowing torrents of seawater to mix with the remaining magma. The resulting cataclysmic explosion was probably the loudest sound generated in recorded history, loud enough to be heard as far afield as Alice Springs in Australia, some 3,000km away, and in the Chagos

Islands of the Indian Ocean, nearly 4,000km to the west. If the explosions had been generated in the Canary Islands, they would have been heard as far away as Liverpool and Dublin.

As the sea rushed into the huge submarine void left by the collapse, it left fishing boats stranded on the shores of Java and Sumatra. It was soon to return with a vengeance, however, in the form of towering tsunami over 40m high, which scoured the neighbouring coasts of over 300 towns and villages, together with their 36,000 inhabitants. The power of the waves was almost unimaginable and was so great as to be able to carry the Dutch warship *Berouw* over a kilometre inshore, where it was left high and dry over 10m above sea-level. Total darkness continued to reign over the devastated land for another 24 hours, with a deluge of hot ash accumulating at rates of up to 15cm in only 10 minutes. The choking, ash-filled air only started to clear later on the 28 August, when the waves finally closed over the remains of Krakatoa, and the silence of the grave fell over a grey landscape of half-buried towns and their drowned inhabitants.

As in the case of Lakagigar, exactly a century earlier, the eruption of Krakatoa had an impact way beyond the immediate vicinity of the volcano. The atmospheric shock-waves generated by the climactic blasts circled the entire planet four times before dissipating, while the associated reverberations set barometer needles wavering for 9 days after the eruption. The legacy of the collapse of Krakatoa into the sea was also recorded on tide-gauges across the world; mini-versions of the giant tsunami that devastated neighbouring Java and Sumatra even registered on instruments located along the coast of the UK. The millions of tonnes of fine ash and sulphur particles ejected into the atmosphere also soon began to have an impact far and wide, lowering temperatures in the northern hemisphere by around 0.3°C. From September of that year the atmospheric debris also contributed to spectacular crimson, purple and yellow sunsets, and coloured suns and moons, including blue, across Europe and North America.

Pinatubo, Philippines, 1991

Little more than a century later, another Asian volcano was to explode spectacularly into life, this time in the Philippine islands to the east and north of Indonesia. Like many of the most devastating volcanoes, Mount Pinatubo, 100km from the teeming capital of Manila, had slumbered quietly for centuries, and no eruptions had been recorded since the islands were first settled by Europeans centuries earlier. Indeed, as at Krakatoa, many of the native Aeta peoples who inhabited the mountain and surrounding region were probably entirely unaware that it was a volcano at all. This was all to change rapidly in April 1991, however, when the mountain once again rumbled into life.

Because the volcano was unmonitored and little was known about the products of earlier activity, scientists could only guess at the nature and scale of the impending eruption. However, some very fast work by local volcanologists, together with colleagues from the USGS, permitted seismographs and other monitoring equipment to be installed in time, allowing the path of the magma toward the surface to be traced through the detection of associated earthquakes. At the same time, some very speedy geological mapping of the area around the volcano showed that earlier eruptions had been huge, and that the next one could devastate an area in which over 250,000 people now lived. As the rumblings increased, scientists for the first time made use of video demonstrations, showing the devastating power of various volcanic phenomena, to successfully persuade the majority of villagers to leave the danger zone. Sadly, the makers of the video, French volcanologist-photographers Maurice and Katja Krafft, had been killed only a few days earlier while filming on the Japanese volcano Unzen; they were never to know how many lives were saved by their sacrifice.

In June 1991, Pinatubo finally let itself go in a series of enormous explosions that culminated in a cataclysmic blast on 15 June that ejected over 7km^3 of debris over an area of over 100km^2. Terrified inhabitants cowered in pitch darkness as ash rained down like snow, and volcanologists based at the nearby US Clark Air Base debated whether they should stay and tough it out or join the general exodus. To make matters worse, the eruption coincided with the arrival of Typhoon Yunya, which dumped torrential rain onto the piles of accumulated ash, remobilizing it and rapidly turning it into rivers of mud that devastated the villages and towns surrounding the volcano. Wet falling ash collapsed the roofs of many buildings and formed heavy, sticking carapaces on the heads of anyone who ventured outside. Despite the mayhem, however, Pinatubo was very much a success story, with the timely evacuation meaning that only a few hundred lives were lost, compared with the tens of thousands who might have perished. A few days later, when the volcano had returned to its slumber, helicopter overflights revealed that the entire top of Pinatubo had been blasted off, leaving a crater 2km across, while the surrounding landscape was utterly transformed. So thick was the volcanic debris that, in places, it filled entire valleys to depths of hundreds of metres, blocking major rivers and diverting them into new paths.

Despite the 8 years that have passed since Pinatubo blasted back into life, the awful legacy of the eruption continues to affect the lives of the local inhabitants. Even today, huge quantities of loose ash remain, and these are readily converted by annual rains into rivers of glutinous mud, making life virtually unbearable by flooding towns and villages, inundating farmland, and damaging coastal fisheries. As with many volcanoes, the associated problems do not always stop when the eruption does. The continuing generation of mudflows is placing a great strain on the weak Philippine economy, and the situation is liable to persist into the next millennium. As with the great eruptions of the past two centuries, Pinatubo ejected huge quantities of sulphur gases into the stratosphere – something over 20 million tonnes in all – forming sulphuric-acid aerosols that reduced global temperatures by about 0.5°C. Within the current framework of global warming, however, this had little noticeable effect on the climate except, perhaps, by arresting the warming trend for a year or two.

Small bangs and big bangs

To most people volcanoes exist purely in the guise of the dramatic footage of spewing red lava that graces our television screens, while volcanic disasters are somehow viewed as only affecting the inhabitants of poor countries far away. So inaccurate is the general perception of the nature of volcanoes that some people think they are confined solely to hot countries, perhaps by equating hot lava with hot weather. However, the people of the Icelandic island of Heimaey, who fought a long and hard battle against the lavas produced during the eruption of 1973 might beg to differ. So too would the inhabitants of other lands of fire and ice – such as Alaska, the High Andes of South America and the Kamchatka Peninsula of Russia – where volcanoes and glaciers reside happily cheek by jowl.

In fact, volcanoes occur all over the planet and in environments as different from one another as the ocean floor and the hearts of the continents. However, as discussed in Chapter 1, the distribution of volcanoes is far from random, and the pattern they form on the surface of the planet is a reflection of the dynamic processes operating beneath and the disposition of the constantly moving plates that make up the Earth's outer layer. The pattern of active volcanoes is a respecter of neither wealth nor technology, and the developed countries of Europe and North America have their allocation, 41 and 185 respectively, together with a share of the potential devastation they can cause. Mount Rainier in the Cascade Range of the western USA, for example, continues to pose a threat to the nearby city of Seattle and surrounding settlements. In the Italian metropolis of Naples too, nearly a million people await evacuation when Vesuvius awakes from its long slumber: 54 years at the time of writing.

Generally speaking, however, the impact of volcanic eruptions in the less-developed countries of Asia and South and Central America is greater, and the incidence of volcanic disasters higher. This is partly because neither the funding nor the scientific expertise exists to support an effective volcano-monitoring programme or to put in place measures to reduce the impact of eruptions on the local inhabitants. It also reflects a coincidence of high concentrations of dangerous volcanoes and a high population density. Over 1,500 volcanoes are classified as 'active', meaning that they have erupted at least once since the end of the last Ice Age 10,000 years ago – a period known to geologists as the Holocene epoch – and this number may be even higher. Currently, 0.5 billion people live in the danger zones around these volcanoes, and the numbers of vulnerable groups are growing rapidly as populations continue to rise in less-developed countries and competition for the right to farm the fertile volcanic soils increases. The problem does not, however, end there, and by no means can the remaining 5.5 billion inhabitants of the planet sit back and relax. The biggest eruptions of all know no boundaries in terms of the havoc they can wreak, and, as we shall see, there is nowhere to run and nowhere to hide

Red volcanoes and grey volcanoes

Although there are many ways of classifying volcanoes, one of the simplest is to consider them, as some French volcanologists do, as falling into two basic types: 'red' volcanoes and 'grey' volcanoes. At red volcanoes, magma oozes out of the ground relatively quietly, forming flows of glowing red lava that creep downslope. Such volcanoes are also described as *effusive*. Grey, or *explosive*, volcanoes, on the other hand, are far more violent and consequently much more dangerous.

These volcanoes blast magma into the atmosphere in the form of explosions that break it up into fragments known as *pyroclasts*. While the larger pyroclasts, sometimes called volcanic 'bombs' because of their often distinctive torpedo-like shape, fall in the immediate vicinity of the volcano, the finer material is carried high into the atmosphere, eventually to descend again to the surface, blanketing it with grey volcanic ash. Volcanologists use the word *tephra* to describe all explosively erupted material, whether it is large blocks or fine ash, that is blasted into the atmosphere before being deposited at the surface.

In terms of the threat they pose to life and property, grey volcanoes constitute a much bigger problem than red volcanoes, and their eruptions are capable of generating an impressively varied range of destructive phenomena with the potential to devastate areas of tens of thousands of square kilometres. In order to appreciate the many ways in which volcanoes can create havoc, it is necessary to understand a little more about the principal types of volcanoes and how they work and, in particular, to recognize those factors that determine whether or not an eruption is going to be explosive.

Magma and explosivity

Magma generated in the Earth's upper mantle rises toward the surface primarily as a result of its low density relative to the rocks above and around it. Like scuba divers divested of their weights, magma ascends because of its buoyancy. Where magma resides in a reservoir beneath the surface, it may also be forced upward by the pressure of new magma entering the reservoir from below. Some volcanoes, such as Mount Etna in Sicily, have conduits connecting magma at depth with open craters, or *vents*, at the surface, thereby permitting magma to rise easily up these pre-existing routes. At other volcanoes, particularly those that have been inactive for many years, magma may have to create a way for itself as it rises by fracturing the rock above it. At open-vent volcanoes like Etna, the eruption of magma at the surface is only mildly explosive. Where the rising magma has to burst its way through, however, the eruption is typically much more violent.

The reason for the difference in what is known as the *explosivity* of an eruption lies in the behaviour of the dissolved gases – such as water vapour, sulphur dioxide, carbon dioxide and fluorine – that all magmas contain, and in particular the ease with which they can separate from the magma and escape. At open-vent volcanoes, the pressure acting on rising magma falls steadily as it approaches the surface, allowing any dissolved gases to form bubbles that rise with the magma and are free to grow and coalesce. Where there is no connection with the surface, however, the gas often remains dissolved in the magma as it enters the volcano, exerting considerable pressure on the magma itself. When the magma eventually bursts its way through the surface, the instantaneous fall in pressure causes the gases to explode out of the magma, ripping it apart with enormous violence.

The devastating consequences of this type of eruption were graphically demonstrated by the destruction of the upper part of the Mount St Helens volcano in Washington State, USA, during May 1980. Here, magma that started to enter the volcano after over a century of dormancy was unable to find an easy way to the surface. Instead, it accumulated in a large mass beneath the northern flank of the volcano, causing it to bulge outward by 100m or more. On 18 May, the destabilized northern flank finally succumbed to the increasing pressure from below and, aided by a moderate earthquake, detached itself from the rest of the volcano in the form of a gigantic landslide. As the pressurized magma beneath was exposed, the gases that were contained in it instantaneously exploded with sufficient energy to flatten mature forests up to 20km away.

The chemical make-up of the magma also has a role to play in determining how violently it will be erupted at the surface. Magmas contain virtually all the naturally occurring elements found on Earth, including aluminium, iron, magnesium, potassium, calcium and sodium. The principal component, however, is *silica*, a combination of atoms of the elements silicon and oxygen, which helps to bind the magma together. Because of this binding effect, the higher the silica content the stickier, or more viscous, the magma. High-viscosity magmas tend to erupt more explosively than their lower viscosity counterparts because the dissolved gases find it more difficult to form bubbles and to separate from the liquid part of the magma. As a result, the gases exert increasing pressure within the rising magma, and this pressure is relieved explosively when the surface is breached. Low-viscosity magmas, on the other hand, allow the gases to form bubbles, to expand freely and to escape, thus ensuring the relatively quiet extrusion of magma when it reaches the surface.

The lowest viscosity magmas form basalts and are erupted quietly, mainly at constructive plate margins. Typically, this happens beneath the oceans, whose floors consequently consist entirely of lava flows of this composition. The largest volcanic islands, Iceland and Hawaii, are also constructed from basalt, and both continue to host basaltic eruptions. On the great Hawaiian volcano of Kilauea, the Pu'u' 'O'o vent has been erupting basalt nearly continuously since the early 1980s, while, on Iceland, basaltic magma that was erupted in 1996 near the subglacial Grimsvötn volcano melted the overlying ice to generate spectacular floods called *jokulhlaups*.

Higher viscosity magmas, known as *andesites* and *dacites*, are erupted at volcanoes located in the subduction zones where one of the Earth's plates is sliding back into the planet's interior beneath another. Such magmas have fed a number of recent explosive eruptions, including Mount St Helens (dacite) in 1980, Pinatubo (dacite) in 1991, possibly the largest this century, the twin eruptions of Vulcan and Tavurvur at Rabaul on the island of New Britain, Papua New Guinea (andesite) in 1994, and the eruption of the Soufrière Hills volcano on the Caribbean island of Montserrat (andesite), which began in 1995 and, at the time of writing, is still continuing.

Volcanoes that erupt magmas with the highest silica contents, known as *rhyolites*, are the most dangerous of all. Rhyolite eruptions can be gigantic, often with hundreds, or even thousands, of cubic kilometres of debris being ejected, much of it high into the stratosphere. Typically, the evacuation of such huge volumes of magma leaves an empty chamber beneath the volcano, which then collapses into it, producing a giant volcanic crater known as a *caldera*. The calderas produced by some of the largest rhyolitic eruptions, such as that at Taupo in the North Island of New Zealand or Yellowstone in the state of Wyoming (USA), are large enough to engulf entire cities. The cataclysmic rhyolitic explosion that occurred around 73,000 years ago at Toba, Sumatra, left a caldera over 50km across and pumped enough volcanic gas and fine debris into the stratosphere to drastically alter the planet's climate.

Another factor that may be important in providing a clue to the explosivity of a future eruption is the length of time since the volcano in question was last active, known as the *repose period*. This is because, where a volcano is underlain by a large reservoir of magma, chemical changes occur in the magma over time that lead to an increase in the silica content and therefore in the viscosity. As this will often result in a more violent eruption, the general rule in these circumstances is 'the longer the wait the bigger the bang'.

Volcanoes as destroyers

Unlike other geophysical hazards, such as earthquakes, floods and wind-storms, volcanic eruptions generate a plethora of destructive phenomena (see table below) capable of the wholesale eradication of property and the inundation of huge tracts of agricultural land, and causing injury and loss of life in a variety of particularly unpleasant ways (see figure on p. 70).

Principal primary volcanic hazards and the secondary effects of eruptions.

Primary hazards	Secondary effects of eruptions
Lava flows	Famine
Tephra	Water pollution
Pyroclastic flows and surges	Disease
Lahars and floods	Disruption of the social and economic infrastructure
Landslides	
Directed blasts and atmospheric shock-waves	
Volcanic gases	
Tsunami	
Climate modification	

Lava

Although in many people's eyes the danger posed by a volcanic eruption means only one thing, lava, this is, in fact, the least threatening of all volcanic phenomena. With the exceptions of some unusually fluid lava eruptions, such as that of Nyirogongo, Zaïre, in 1971, which over-ran local inhabitants and even the odd elephant, lava flows are too slow-moving to pose a serious threat to life. Velocities may be a few kilometres an hour during the early stages of an eruption, but typically slow to as little as tens of metres an hour within days.

Lava flows are, however, particularly effective destroyers of property. As a result of temperatures that may be in excess of 1,000°C, no wooden structure is able to withstand contact with lava, and not because of the flows' enormous strength, are substantial stone or concrete buildings, which are soon flattened and buried. Lavas are also very efficient at burying agricultural land and putting it out of commission for several decades or even centuries. On Etna, for example, every point on the volcano is covered by lava, on average, every 400 years. This does not, however, deter the local farmers, and the volcano is the focus of the intense cultivation of grapes olives, and oranges. Despite the ever-present threat from lava flows, the fertile soils that result from their eventual breakdown and the prospect of up to 15 generations of uninterrupted farming have led to the flanks of the volcano attracting over 20 per cent of Sicily's population.

Volcanic ash

Although less spectacular than lava flows, volcanic ash can be far more lethal and disruptive. The columns of volcanic ash generated in large explosive eruptions can carry material over 50km into the atmosphere before depositing it far and wide. Locally, ash can settle at rates of tens of centimetres an hour and accumulate rapidly to depths of several

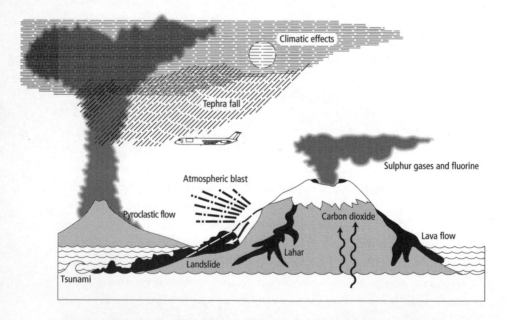

Of all geophysical hazards, volcanoes are unique in being capable of generating a range of destructive and potentially lethal phenomena. The principal volcanic hazards shown are listed in the table on p. 69 together with the secondary effects of eruptions.

metres. Poorly constructed buildings can rarely support the weight of even 30cm of ash, especially when it is wet. During the 1991 eruption of Pinatubo, for example, many of the deaths and injuries resulted either from roofs collapsing onto sheltering families or from falls by house-holders attempting to keep their roofs free of accumulating ash. Heavy ash-fall has many other disruptive effects, including hindering road, rail and air communications through reduced visibility and ash accumu-lation, bringing down telephone and power lines, damaging crops and fisheries, and contaminating water supplies. Not least, more than 80 jet aircraft have flown unwittingly into ash columns since 1980, resulting in severely damaged engines and a number of near-crashes. Volcanic ash may also have a damaging effect on human health, with the fine dust exacerbating respiratory illnesses such as asthma and lung diseases. Where silica-rich eruptions have persisted for several years, as at Montserrat in the Caribbean and Rabaul in Papua New Guinea, contin-ued daily inhalation of the fine, dust-like component may also lead to the development of the crippling illness psilicosis.

Pyroclastic flows

As well as producing clouds of volcanic ash, explosive eruptions are often also the source of those most lethal of all volcanic hazards: pyro-clastic flows. Sometimes referred to by the French term *nuées ardentes*, or 'glowing avalanches', these deadly mixtures of incandescent ash, lava blocks and superheated volcanic gases travel down the flanks of explod-ing volcanoes at hurricane velocities, destroying everything in their paths. The gases contained in the flows provide an almost frictionless layer on which the hot ash and other debris is carried, allowing them to travel at velocities in excess of 100km/hour. Due to a combination of such velocities, the mass of contained volcanic debris and the high temperatures, which may be over 800°C, few man-made structures can survive impact by a pyroclastic flow, and destruction is often complete.

Visually at least, there is little to distinguish the scale of devastation at St Pierre, the capital of the unfortunate island of Martinique (see Chapter 1), from that caused by the atomic bombs dropped on the Japanese cities of Hiroshima and Nagasaki during World War 2. Humans fare even less well than buildings, and out of a population of over 29,000, only two of the inhabitants of St Pierre survived to tell the tale of the catastrophe. In the heart of the flow, death is instantaneous and results from asphyxiation caused by the inhalation of superheated gas. Bodies are often charred beyond all recognition, and skulls are sometimes split apart as the water contained in the brain is boiled off explosively. At the very edge of the flow, which usually consists primarily of hot gases with little in the way of debris, a few metres can make the difference between surviving unscathed and sustaining mortal burns. The sharp transition from charred to untouched vegetation seen at the margins of pyroclastic flows indicates that the temperature falls off rapidly away from the surging hot gases. Therefore, in theory at least, and given judicious positioning, it should be possible to observe a pyroclastic flow from close quarters, although this course of action is not to be recommended.

Pyroclastic flows were responsible for the destruction of the bustling Roman towns of Pompeii and Herculaneum during the well-documented 79 AD eruption of Vesuvius, and for the death and incarceration of many of their inhabitants. Of the 250,000 or so deaths known to have been caused by volcanic eruptions since the beginning of the eighteenth century, some 15 per cent are due to pyroclastic flows. Recently they have claimed lives at El Chichon, Mexico, in 1982; on the Japanese volcano Unzen in 1991; at Merapi, Indonesia, in 1994; at Manam, Papua New Guinea, in 1996; and on the Caribbean island of Montserrat in 1997.

Mud and water

After the devastation of St Pierre in 1902, we had to wait over 80 years, until 1985, for the next major volcanic catastrophe. In marked contrast to the events in the Caribbean, water was the main culprit on this occasion, being responsible for over 20,000 deaths in the Colombian town of Armero and neighbouring settlements close to the Nevado del Ruiz volcano. With a summit located at over 5,000m above sea-level in the High Andes, Ruiz is capped throughout the year by a thick cover of snow and ice. Only a relatively minor eruption of pyroclastic flows was required, therefore, to melt millions of cubic metres of ice and send it hurtling down the river valleys that drained the volcano. Here, it soon picked up any available debris and become a raging torrent of mud. Repeated warnings from volcanologists had failed to persuade the authorities to authorize evacuation of Armero, and so, on the night of 13 November, with virtually no warning, the town and most of its inhabitants were incarcerated in a tomb of mud from which few were to emerge.

Mudflows generated on volcanoes have claimed almost as many lives as pyroclastic flows this century: nearly 30,000 in all. Sometimes known by the Filipino term, *lahars*, volcanic mudflows can be formed in a number of different ways: by an eruption onto snow and ice, by the overflow or breaching of a lake-filled crater, or simply as a result of heavy rain falling onto deposits of loose ash. Although it is currently 8 years since the huge eruption of Pinatubo, this last process is still generating destructive lahars. Torrential typhoon rains turn deposits of unconsolidated ash hundreds of metres thick into torrents of mud that silt up river valleys, inundate towns and villages and bury farmland. More recently, in November 1998, a persistent deluge from Hurricane Mitch, which stalled for days over the region, caused the lake-filled crater of the Casitas volcano to overflow, the waters mixing with volcanic debris to form a series of devastating mudflows that took nearly 3,000 lives

Volcanic gases

Notwithstanding rivers of lava, mud and incandescent ash, there remain many other ways in which volcanoes can take lives and devastate the surrounding landscape. As at Poás volcano in Costa Rica, noxious gases such as sulphur dioxide and hydrogen sulphide, continually emitted from open vents, can damage the health of local inhabitants and form acid rain that destroys their crops. In towns such as Furnas in the Azores, which is built inside a volcanic caldera, carbon dioxide may accumulate in basements, posing the threat of death by asphyxiation, especially to children. On a larger scale, carbon dioxide accumulating in the waters of lake-filled volcanic craters may, on occasion, spread out over the surrounding countryside, as it did twice in the mid-1980s in Cameroon, killing thousands of local inhabitants and their livestock.

The secondary consequences of volcanic eruptions can also be devastating, sometimes even more so than their direct effects. Two of the largest recorded death tolls associated with volcanic activity are, for example, associated with famine. The 1783 Lakagigar eruption in Iceland generated so much fluorine that it contaminated the feed on which the island's livestock grazed. As a result, 200,000 sheep, 28,000 horses and 11,000 cattle died, with the ensuing mass starvation reducing Iceland's population by a quarter. A few decades later, in 1815, the gigantic eruption of Tambora in Indonesia had a similar effect, with the estimated death toll of 92,000 being largely attributed to famine caused by crop and livestock destruction.

Tsunami

Some of the most devastating of all volcanic disasters have occurred where volcanoes are located on coasts or form islands. Here any significant eruption has the added potential of producing the destructive sea–waves often referred to as 'tidal waves' but more correctly known by the Japanese term *tsunami*. Most tsunami are caused by earthquakes or submarine landslides, but some of the most devastating result from the collapse of all or part of a volcano. In 1792 part of the Japanese volcano Unzen slid into the sea, generating a wave that killed over 14,000 people in the fishing villages lining the nearby coast. During the destruction of Krakatoa in 1883, waves up to 40m high devastated coastal communities on the neighbouring Indonesian islands of Java and Sumatra, taking 36,000 lives. However, these waves are insignificant when compared with the largest possible tsunami, which pose a continuing major threat to coastal communities across the planet (see Chapter 3).

Measuring the size of an eruption:
the Volcanic Explosivity Index

In the same way that seismologists use the Richter Scale to provide a value of the size, or *magnitude*, of an earthquake, volcanologists use what is known as the Volcano Explosivity Index, or VEI (see table on p. 75) to describe the scale of a volcanic eruption. Unlike seismologists, however, who use seismographs to determine the size of an earthquake, volcanologists have no single way of accurately estimating the energy generated during a volcanic eruption and, therefore, no easy way of determining its size. As a result, qualitative estimates of the size of an eruption are often wildly inaccurate. To those inhabitants of the Caribbean island of Montserrat, for example, living only a few kilometres from the summit of the Soufrière Hills volcano, the eruption that started in July 1995 must have appeared spectacularly huge. Those affected by the 1991 eruption of Pinatubo, however, would probably have regarded the Montserrat event as little more than a damp squib, with the energy released at Pinatubo being around 1,000 times greater.

In order that valid comparisons can be made between eruptions, some way is needed of making a quantitative estimate of their size. In fact, a number of parameters can be measured to provide a clue to the size of an eruption, including the volume of explosively ejected material, or tephra, and the height to which this is ejected into the atmosphere. These two measures, which are supplemented by additional descriptive information, such as how long the eruption lasts, form the basis of the VEI. Like the Richter Scale, the VEI is open-ended, although evidence for anything larger than a VEI 8 remains to be found. The index is logarithmic, so each value represents an eruption 10 times larger than the previous value. The first value on the index is VEI 0, which applies to non-explosive eruptions. Such events invariably involve the gentle effusion of low-viscosity basaltic magma, and they are particularly characteristic of the Hawaiian and Icelandic volcanoes. VEI 1 and VEI 2 are reserved for small explosive eruptions that eject up to 100,000m^3 of debris, perhaps enough to cover London with a thin dusting of ash.

Larger values designate progressively more violent explosive eruptions of stickier andesitic, dacitic and rhyolitic magmas, in which greater volumes of debris are ejected to higher levels in the atmosphere. The twin 1994 eruptions of Vulcan and Tavurvur at Rabaul in Papua New Guinea registered 4 on the index, while the Mount St Helens eruption

Volcano Explosivity Index (VEI).

Volcano Explosivity Index	Volume of tephra (m^3)	Height of eruption column (km)	Eruption rate (kg/second)	Duration of continuous blast (hours)	General description
0	<10,000	<0.1	100–1,000	<1	Non-explosive
1	10,000–1 million	0.1–1	1,000–10,000	<1	Small
2	1 million–10 million	1–5	10,000–100,000	1–6	Moderate
3	10 millon–100 million	3–15	100,000 – 1 million	1–12	Moderate to large
4	100 million–1 billion	10–25	1 million–10 million	6–12	Large
5	1 billion–10 billion	>25	10 million–100 million	>12	Very large
6	10 billion–100 billion	>25	100 million–1 billion	>12	Very large
7	100 billion–1 trillion	>25	>1 billion	>12	Very large
8	>1 trillion	>25	>1 billion	>12	Very large

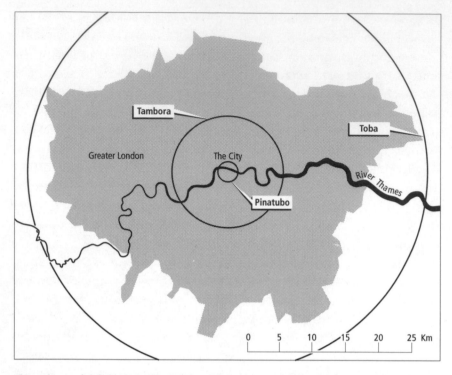

The volume of debris ejected in large volcanic eruptions is almost unimaginable. While the eruption of Pinatubo in 1991 blasted out sufficient material to bury the city of London to a depth twice that of the height of the World Trade Center in New York, the great Tambora catastrophe of 1815 ejected enough debris to cover an area 15km across to the same depth. Both events are dwarfed, however, by the Toba super-eruption of 73,000 years ago, which hurled out sufficient ash and rocks to bury the whole of Greater London to a depth of 1km.

of 18 May 1980 scored a 5. A hundred times bigger than Rabaul and ten times the size of Mount St Helens, the 1991 eruption of Pinatubo is classed as a 6, as is the 1883 eruption of Krakatoa. The only historic eruption known to merit a VEI 7 is the 1815 eruption of Tambora in Indonesia, perhaps the largest eruption since the end of the Ice Age, which blasted out over 100km³ of debris — enough to bury central London to a depth of 1km (see figure above).

As there are many more small earthquakes than there are large ones, so there are many more minor eruptions than there are volcanic cataclysms. Since the ice retreated 10,000 years ago, evidence exists for over 6,000 eruptions. All but 43 of these score 5 or less on the VEI, with only four registering a 7. No post-Ice Age eruption registers an 8, and we have to go back to the Indonesian super-eruption at the start of the last Ice Age, over 70,000 years ago, to find the most recent. This gigantic blast occurred at Toba, in Sumatra, and ejected sufficient gas and debris into the stratosphere to cause a rapid and dramatic change to the global climate, on a scale far greater than that triggered by the nineteenth-century Tambora eruption in the same country. It has been suggested by some that the severe cooling initiated by the Toba blast may have been the final straw that actually propelled our world into the grip of the ice sheets. Others have proposed that the eruption may have been caused by an already-changing climate associated with the early stages of the Ice Age. The arguments for and against these views will be examined next.

Exploding volcanoes and changing climates

It has been postulated by some that 50–100 large explosive eruptions within 100 years or so might loft sufficient quantities of sulphur dioxide and other sulphur gases into the stratosphere to cut the solar radiation reaching the Earth's surface by up to 20 per cent. This would be sufficient to lower global temperatures by as much as 3°C and have a major impact on the planet's climate. The first person to give serious thought to the climatic effect of large volcanic eruptions on the planet was H. H. Lamb who, in 1963, while working at the UK Meteorological Office, devised the *Dust Veil Index* (DVI). This recorded the amount of fine volcanic ash carried into the stratosphere from volcanic eruptions and distributed across the Earth by measuring how opaque the atmosphere was to solar radiation. Lamb determined that there was a small correlation between high DVI values and global cooling.

We now know, however, that it is the presence in the stratosphere of a fine mist of sulphuric-acid aerosols, formed from sulphur gases mixing with atmospheric water, which is most effective at reflecting solar radiation back into space, thereby cooling the Earth's surface. Similarly, we now appreciate that large explosive eruptions at volcanoes with sulphur-rich magmas are needed in order for sufficient quantities of the aerosols to be lofted into the stratosphere, within which they are transported around the planet by high-altitude winds.

Acid aerosols

The aerosols from a moderate to large explosive eruption can reside in the stratosphere for up to 2 years, forming a haze that increases the reflectiveness, or *albedo*, of the Earth. The aerosol layer can also have other effects, such as the creation of spectacularly coloured sunsets and sunrises, and unusual optical phenomena, such as blue moons and brown suns; these were observed in many parts of the world after the Tambora and Krakatoa eruptions. The aerosols can also act as nuclei for raindrops and ice particles, thereby increasing precipitation. Volcanoes release much less sulphur dioxide than industry, but they often have a much greater impact on global climate because the power of their eruptions can carry the sulphur dioxide through the *troposphere* (the lowest layer of the atmosphere, about 10km thick) and into the stratosphere, which extends upward to about 50km. Anthropogenic sulphur gases, produced, for example, from coal-burning power stations, are unable to penetrate to this altitude.

With increasing latitude, the stratosphere becomes progressively lower, which means that smaller eruptions at high latitudes may be able to pump just as much sulphur dioxide into the stratosphere as larger eruptions nearer the equator. Nevertheless, big, sulphur-rich eruptions at low latitudes are the most effective at getting sulphur dioxide distributed across the whole planet because they are best placed to form aerosols that can infiltrate the wind systems of both northern and southern hemispheres.

Although intuitively one would expect that bigger and bigger explosive eruptions would loft greater and greater numbers of sulphuric-acid aerosol particles into the atmosphere, the situation is not quite this simple. It seems that bigger eruptions produce fewer, larger aerosol particles rather than more, smaller particles. Because these are heavier they tend to settle out of the stratosphere more rapidly, which suggests that several moderate explosive eruptions would prove more effective at reducing global temperatures for longer than one very large eruption.

Just as models of the current period of global warming do not predict that everywhere on the planet is going to get hotter, so the fact that the planet as a whole is cooled down by volcanic activity does not mean that everywhere gets colder. For example, after the biggest eruptions of the last 100 years, winters appeared to be warmer over North America and Europe but cooler in Africa and the Middle East. Such variations may reflect the influence of the complex pattern of stratospheric winds. Time is also required to transport aerosols across the planet so that they can start to affect the climate in regions that are distant from the eruption site. This is reflected in the timing of cooling episodes after explosive eruptions in the tropics. At low latitudes cooling is typically encountered in the winter immediately following the eruption, while at mid- to high-latitudes the effect may not be seen until the second following winter.

Climatic signals: El Niño

There has been some speculation that sulphuric-acid aerosol particles might play a role in initiating the phenomenon known as El Niño; the second-largest climatic signal on the planet after the seasons, and one that is becoming increasingly associated with drought, increased storminess and other hazardous natural phenomena. El Niño results from a weakening of the easterly trade winds in the western Pacific, causing a pronounced warming of the ocean in the eastern Pacific. The sulphur-rich 1982 eruption of El Chichon in Mexico was immediately followed by one of the most intense El Niños of the century, and this has tentatively been attributed to sulphuric-acid aerosols heating the troposphere, leading to a weakening of the trade winds.

To avoid confusion, I should emphasize the fact that, although sulphuric-acid aerosols lead to a general cooling of the planet, they are sometimes capable of causing temporary heating of the lower atmosphere due to their absorption of the Sun's heat. Careful examination of meteorological data has revealed, however, that the 1982 El Niño had already started to form before the El Chichon eruption, so any connection must have been coincidental. Nevertheless, explosive eruptions at low altitudes do appear to be associated with an increase in sea-surface temperatures in the eastern tropical Pacific, where El Niño events start, and the complex interactions between volcanic eruptions, the atmosphere and the hydrosphere do not rule out such a causative effect. We should not, therefore, entirely discard the idea that future El Niño events may be triggered by appropriately timed, sulphur-rich, explosive eruptions.

Changes in the ozone layer

One of biggest environmental issues, and indeed talking points, of the late 1980s and 1990s focused on the rapidly growing holes in the ozone layer of the stratosphere over the Arctic and Antarctic, and their potential health impact on the populations of high-latitude countries, particularly in terms of increases in the incidences of skin cancer. Indeed, such was the degree of international concern that the levels of anthropogenic chlorofluorocarbons (CFCs), deemed to be the primary culprits, have now been dramatically reduced, reflecting a rare outbreak of global common sense on an environmental issue of concern to all. What remains only poorly appreciated by the public, environmental lobbies and many scientists, is that volcanoes are also particularly effective at depleting the levels of ozone in the stratosphere.

Ozone is a poisonous gas whose molecules consist of three atoms of oxygen rather than the more common two, and that, at high altitudes, plays a critical role in absorbing those wavelengths of ultraviolet radiation that are especially harmful to living organisms. Hydrochloric acid (HCl), released in enormous quantities in some volcanic eruptions, can cause drastic reductions in ozone levels if it is allowed to come into contact with ozone. Fortunately, most HCl produced by volcanoes appears to remain confined to the troposphere, where it is rapidly washed out by rain. Perhaps only around 3 per cent of stratospheric chlorine, derived from HCl, is volcanic in origin, compared with over 80 per cent from anthropogenic CFCs.

Although volcanic HCl plays no direct role in destroying stratospheric ozone, it may still make a significant indirect contribution to ozone depletion. This is because the volcanically derived sulphuric-acid aerosols provide numerous available surfaces on which the anthropogenic chlorine can go about its ozone-destroying business through chemical reaction. The effectiveness of this mechanism was dramatically demonstrated after the 1991 Pinatubo eruption, when ozone levels in the lower stratosphere fell by a third. The only saving grace associated with this destructive alliance of volcanic aerosols and anthropogenic chlorine lies in the fact that the effect is limited by how long the aerosol particles can remain in the stratosphere; as explained earlier, this is rarely more than a few years.

Chicken or egg?

Evidence that volcanic explosions can trigger changes in the planet's climate is clearly now overwhelming, but is the opposite ever true? Can a changing climate cause volcanoes to erupt? This is an area of speculative research that has fascinated scientists for a number of years because, if true, it means that the Earth's climate and its volcanoes are locked into a cause-and-effect feedback loop, with volcanoes triggering climate change and climate change causing volcanoes to erupt. But which comes first? Which is the chicken and which the egg?

Volume of eruptive products, sulphuric-acid production and northern hemisphere temperature falls resulting from a range of volcanic eruptions of different sizes.

Date	Eruption	Volcanic Explosivity Index	Volume of eruptive products (km³)	Eruption column height (km)	Sulphuric acid (millions of tonnes)	Northern hemisphere temperature fall (°C)
73,000 BP	Toba	8	2,800	>37	1,000–5,000	3–5
1783	Laki	4	14–15	n.a.	100	~1
1815	Tambora	7	>50	>40	200	0.4–0.7
1883	Krakatoa	6	>10	>40	55	0.3
1902	Santa Maria	6	~9	>30	25	0.4
1912	Katmai	6	15	>27	25	0.2
1980	St Helens	5	0.35	22	1.5	0–0.1
1963	Agung	4	0.3–0.6	18	20	0.3
1982	El Chichon	4	0.3–0.35	26	20	0.4–0.6

If climate change can cause volcanoes to erupt, you might expect to find the best evidence during times of the most dramatic climatic variation, in other words during the last Ice Age that held much of the planet in its chilly grip for most of the past 2 million years or so. At four times during this period dramatic and rapid temperature swings led to successive expansions and contractions of the northern and southern hemisphere ice caps. Changes in polar-ice volumes were accompanied by huge variations in global sea-levels as gigantic volumes of water were repeatedly locked up in the growing ice caps during the freezing glacial periods and then released back into the oceans during the warmer interglacials.

In high-latitude countries, such as Iceland, a clear correlation has now been established between volcanic eruptions and the alternating cold and warm episodes that characterized the Ice Age, and a convincing mechanism for the link has been proposed. During cold periods, active volcanoes on this geologically dynamic island were buried under a great load of ice, the weight of which helped to counteract the pressures generated by rising magma, thereby suppressing eruptions. During the warmer interglacials, however, the ice cover melted rapidly, reducing the confining pressure on the underlying volcanoes and permitting magma to burst through to the surface. A similar relationship between ice loading and unloading has now also been found for high-altitude volcanoes in the South American Andes and has been put forward as an explanation of the timing of Ice Age eruptions at Mount Etna in Sicily. Most of the world's active volcanoes, and there may have been 1,500 or more active during the Ice Age, are not, however, located at high latitudes or particularly high altitudes, and they did not support ice caps, even during the coldest episodes of the Ice Age. Could eruptions at these volcanoes also be triggered by the dramatic changes in global temperatures? And, if so, what could be the cause?

Increasingly, it appears likely that the answer to the first question is yes, while to the second, unlikely as it may seem, the answer is the sea. As previously mentioned, an Ice Age is characterized by the repeated locking-up and release of water from the polar ice caps. The shifting of such enormous quantities of water around the planet has for some time been presented as a trigger for the increasing numbers of volcanic eruptions during the Ice Age, and various mechanisms have been proposed to explain the link. On a planetary scale, such huge redistributions of mass over relatively small time-scales, perhaps as little as 10,000 years, may promote stress changes within the crust and mantle that encourage magma formation and eruption. Alternatively, the principal effect may be confined to the ocean basins, with the pressure release resulting from the reduction of sea-levels by 100m or more during glacial episodes permitting magma to form more easily within the upper mantle and to make its way with less difficulty to the surface.

Within this scenario, the higher sea-levels associated with the warmer interglacials would, like the ice cover on the Icelandic volcanoes, suppress volcanic activity. The effects of large changes in ocean volumes on volcanoes might be more localized, however, particularly because around 60 per cent of currently active volcanoes are either situated on coasts or form islands, and as such are in direct contact with the oceans. A further 35 per cent are located within 250km of a coast, so it is not unreasonable to propose that 95 per cent of all active volcanoes may be susceptible to variations in ocean water levels. As we have no reason to doubt that the distribution of volcanoes was pretty much the same during the Ice Age as it is today, it is fair to assume that this figure is of the same order as it was then.

How then might individual volcanoes be affected by ocean volume changes? The clue may lie in some recent research published by UK and Italian scientists working in the Mediterranean region. By comparing the ages of volcanic ash layers preserved in the sea-bed with sea-level changes over the past 100,000 years, the Anglo-Italian team discovered that the more rapidly sea-level went up or down, the more ash-producing (i.e. explosive) volcanic eruptions there were around the Mediterranean. This suggests that it is the dynamic state of *changing* sea-level that causes volcanoes to erupt rather than merely its absolute level. Using sophisticated computer models, the team showed that large, rapid variations in sea-level – and there is evidence that changes could be in excess of 10m in as little as 150 years – promoted stress changes within island and coastal volcanoes sufficient to allow the release of any stored magma. They also provided a mechanism that might specifically encourage explosive eruptions of the type needed to deposit extensive ash layers on the floor of the Mediterranean Sea.

When the northern flank of Mount St Helens collapsed in 1980 it instantaneously depressurized the magma body within the volcano, triggering a devastating blast that pumped debris over 20km into the stratosphere. The Anglo-Italian team proposed that this is a particularly likely eruption scenario at island and coastal volcanoes subjected to a significant change in sea-level. While a rapid rise may significantly erode such a volcano's flanks, a similar fall may weaken the flank by removing the weight of adjacent water. Both effects would tend increasingly to destabilize the volcano, improving the chances of flank collapse exposing an underlying magma body and generating a violent, explosive blast. Further research by a US team has recently found a similar relationship between the rate of changing sea-level during the Ice Age and explosive volcanic eruptions, this time through comparing sea-levels over the last 200,000 years or so with the ages of fine volcanic debris and aerosol layers preserved in ice cores extracted from deep within the Greenland Ice Cap. As the sources of many of these layers are likely to be volcanoes distributed across the planet, it looks as if the link proposed by the Anglo-Italian team is not merely confined to the Mediterranean region but is found over the entire Earth.

It appears that we now have reasonable explanations for how climate change can cause volcanoes to erupt and how erupting volcanoes can trigger climate change. Nevertheless, the 'chicken and egg' dilemma remains unresolved, and we still have not determined categorically whether climate change or an increasing level of volcanic activity comes first. Perhaps in the coming centuries mankind itself may play a role in the relationship. If global warming continues unabated, the ultimate consequence may be the catastrophic melting of what remains of the polar ice caps, leading to a rapid sea-level rise that may approach 70m or 80m. Such a dramatic rise may well be sufficient to cause increasing numbers of volcanoes to erupt explosively, resulting in a fiery future for our civilization as well as a wet one!

Super-eruptions: how to freeze a planet

Barring impacts by asteroids and comets, gigantic eruptions on the scale of the great Toba blast represent the most devastating of all natural catastrophes. Although we have not experienced such an event for 73,000 years, viewed on a geological time-scale they constitute a common-or-garden and relatively frequent Earth process. While VEI 7 events such as the Tambora eruption can be expected every 500 years or so, studies of the sizes of volcanic eruptions over the past 2 million years reveal that, on average, two VEI 8 eruptions occur every 100 millennia. It does not take a particularly astute brain to realize, therefore, that it would not be entirely surprising if another super-eruption occurred tomorrow, although in reality we may have to wait many thousands of years for the next Toba-sized bang. When it comes, however, it will be globally devastating.

Some idea of the scale of such an explosion can be gained from examining the details of the event that led to the formation of the giant Yellowstone caldera, in Wyoming, USA, 2 million years ago. This enormous blast pumped out 2,500km³ of debris, much of it in the form of gigantic pyroclastic flows, which covered 16 states in the present western and central USA. Another blast, almost as large, occurred here only 660,000 years ago, generating pyroclastic flows that covered over 4,000km² and leaving a caldera up to 85km across. The total volume of the pyroclastic-flow deposits amounted to around 1,000km³, sufficient to cover the entire USA to a depth of 8cm. Volcanic ash, lofted high into the stratosphere, travelled many times around the world and can be recognized within drill cores from as far away as the Gulf of Mexico. No eruptions have been recorded at Yellowstone for 70,000 years, but nevertheless the underlying magma system remains very much alive, as demonstrated by the many spectacular geysers in the area, including Old Faithful.

Although very little is known about the global impact of the Yellowstone eruptions, the more recent, and even larger, Toba explosion provides us with a natural laboratory in which to study the devastating effects that such giant blasts have had on the planet, and will have again. Both Yellowstone and Toba sit above subduction zones where one plate is sliding down into the Earth below another, although in the vicinity of Yellowstone the subduction zone is no longer active and is said to have 'locked'. At both locations, melting within the subduction zone generated huge volumes of sticky, rhyolitic magma that accumulated within the crust before bursting with unimaginable violence through the surface. At Toba more than 2,800km³ of volcanic debris were ejected. As at Yellowstone, much of the debris would have flowed over the land surface in the form of devastating pyroclastic flows, but a major part of it, along with between 1,000 million and 5,000 million tonnes of sulphuric-acid aerosols, would have penetrated into the stratosphere, where it would have rapidly spread to form a gas-and-dust veil across the planet. As relatively small eruptions, such as that of Pinatubo in 1991, can reduce the level of solar radiation reaching the Earth's surface by 0.5°C for several years, at points far distant from the eruption site, imagine the effect of an event 100 times or more larger.

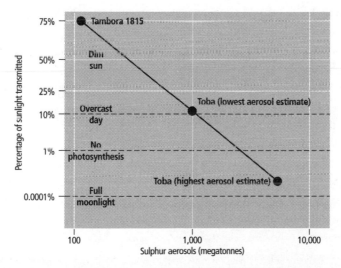

Even the most conservative estimates suggest that the Toba super-eruption would have blasted sufficient gas and ash into the stratosphere to cut the amount of sunlight reaching the surface by 90 per cent, leading to world-wide gloom. The situation may, however, have been much worse: the Sun might have been virtually blacked out for years, with widespread destruction of plant life as photosynthesis became impossible.

By comparison with the temperature-reduction effects of smaller eruptions, such as that of Tambora, Indonesia, in 1815, Mike Rampino, of New York University, and his co-workers have calculated that the Toba blast may have led to a fall in global temperatures of between 3° and 5°C. Such a drop may have been sufficient to trigger a *volcanic winter*, in the same way that the soot from burning cities would cause a nuclear winter following an all-out atomic war. Today, such a temperature fall would cause global mayhem, with bitterly cold weather across much of the planet, particularly at high latitudes, and snow half a metre deep in London's Oxford Street in August would by no means be out of the question. In addition to the lower temperatures, the gigantic amount of volcanic gas and dust in the atmosphere would also dramatically reduce the amount of sunlight reaching the surface, dimming the skies to a level seen on a bleak and cloudy winter's day (see figure on p. 85). A combination of the cold and dark would lead to failed harvests world-wide, causing mass starvation and a potential collapse in the global economy.

Searching for the next super-eruption

Given an average super-eruption return period of 50,000 years and with Toba occurring a distant 73,000 years ago, it would be understandable if we felt ourselves to be living on borrowed time. This perception would not, however, be strictly correct. Super-eruptions do not occur to order every 50,000 years. Their incidence, like that of impact events (see Chapter 1), constitute what is known in statistics as a *Poissonian process*, in which events occur randomly in time. It is perfectly possible that two super-eruptions could occur during successive years, with none then occurring for 200,000 or 300,000 years. This is not, however, likely, and it is by no means impossible that the magma to feed the next super-eruption may be accumulating at this very moment.

How would we know? What do we look for? Is it possible to pinpoint the location of the next super-eruption before it happens? Given the current technologies available to the volcanologist it appears that we can, although, sadly, there will be nothing we can do to stop it. First of all, we can narrow the area of our search quite rapidly. Super-eruption events are not randomly distributed across the planet, and like all volcanic phenomena, their locations are constrained by the pattern of the plates that make up the Earth's exterior. The sticky, rhyolitic magmas that feed these giant eruptions help us to narrow down our search even further. Such magmas, at least in volumes sufficient for a super-eruption, are produced only where plates are in collision, and more specifically where either an oceanic plate is being subducted beneath a continental plate or two continental plates are in collision. With few exceptions, these sorts of geological environment are confined to the Pacific Rim, which includes the western USA, Alaska, the Kamchatka Peninsula of Russia, Central and South America, the Philippines and Japan, to South-East Asia and the South Pacific, and to New Zealand. It is here that volcanologists must focus their attention.

Some possible candidates

There are other clues that we might use to attempt to constrain likely candidates for the next 'big one'. As at Yellowstone, there are some parts of the Earth's surface that favour the formation of giant eruptions and that have experienced several in the past. These areas can be recognized by clusters of closely spaced or overlapping giant calderas, together with associated deposits of tephra and pyroclastic-flow material that cover tens of thousands of square kilometres. In addition to Yellowstone, such caldera fields are found, among other places, in Italy, in the Bay of Naples and around Rome, on the island of New Britain in Papua New Guinea and in the North Island of New Zealand. Although they may not have erupted for many thousands of years, some of these caldera fields remain *restless*. This means that they are characterized by periodic increases in the numbers of earthquakes or by a swelling and sinking of the ground surface, or both, indicating that fresh magma is moving about below.

Despite a repose period of 70,000 years, the Yellowstone caldera field in Wyoming, USA, remains particularly lively, and the centre of the caldera rose by 75cm between 1923 and 1984. More recently, measurements from satellites have revealed that the caldera centre rose by 2cm between 1995 and 1996. Whether, however, this reflects the movement of shallow magma bodies or changes in the pressurization of the hot aquifer that feeds the geysers remains to be determined. Deformation of the ground surface is also accompanied by swarms of shallow earthquakes. Sometimes larger quakes also occur, with at least eight magnitude 6 or greater events being recorded over the last couple of centuries, and a magnitude 7.5 quake in 1959 that generated damage valued at US$11 million and took 28 lives.

Behaviour similar to that at Yellowstone caused great concern during the 1970s and 1980s in the Italian coastal town of Pozzuoli on the Bay of Naples. Pozzuoli sits in the centre of a 15km-wide caldera known as the Campi Flegrei, one of several in the area, which formed in a huge eruption around 35,000 years ago. The sea has since breached the walls of the caldera, and the southern half is now submerged. Nevertheless, magma still resides not too far down, as indicated by a relatively minor eruption in 1538. In 1970 the local population became increasingly alarmed as the numbers of earthquakes in the area began to increase dramatically, while at the same time the land surface swelled by up to 60cm; the combination of the two was termed by scientists a *bradyseismic crisis*. Understandably, there was considerable concern that the earthquakes and swelling were related to fresh magma rising once more beneath the caldera, prior to eruption. Much to everyone's relief, however, the earthquakes all but ceased the following year, accompanied by subsidence of the surface.

Unfortunately, this respite was to prove short lived, and in 1982 a new bout of ground inflation and earthquakes began. This time, the earthquakes, over 15,000 in all, and ground-swelling of over 1.5m conspired to damage many of the buildings in the oldest parts of Pozzuoli, forcing many of the inhabitants to move out. Still no eruption occurred, however, and 2 years later the situation returned to normal once again. Arguments still rage within the Italian volcanological community about whether the activity reflected fresh magma approaching the surface or whether it was simply a result of the heating and swelling of deep, subsurface water bodies. Whatever, the reason, Campi Flegrei remains restless and will undoubtedly erupt again. The important question we must ask, however, is: will the next eruption be a big one, and if so, just how big?

Campi Flegrei is by no means the only caldera to become restless in recent years, and not all have returned to their slumber without giving us a hint of the potential threat they pose. In 1983 the town of Rabaul, located on the edge of a 10km-wide, sea-filled caldera on the island of New Britain, Papua New Guinea, began to experience the same increased numbers of earthquakes and inflation of the land surface. As at Campi Flegrei, however, the situation returned to normal within 2 years, but here there was a sting in the tail. Nine years later, the local inhabitants and the scientists staffing the nearby volcano observatory were woken by near-continuous, strong earthquakes that shook the town, damaging buildings and terrifying the inhabitants. At the same time parts of the shoreline rose by as much as 10m overnight.

Only 27 hours after the earthquake started, the two volcanoes, Tavurvur and Vulcan, located on either side of the caldera, erupted simultaneously. Fortunately, remembering the training they had undergone during the previous crisis during the 1980s, most of the town's population had already self-evacuated by this time. Nevertheless, only a few days were required for this VEI 4 eruption to devastate Rabaul and its surroundings, burying it under ash and mud several metres deep. Although Vulcan returned to its slumber after 4 days, Tavurvur continues to rumble away today, covering what remains of the town in a daily dusting of ash.

At the time of writing, another restless caldera is causing concern to volcanologists, this time in the US state of California. Here the 32km-wide Long Valley caldera has, since 1980, been experiencing increased numbers of earthquakes combined with deformation of the ground surface and the release of carbon dioxide derived from fresh magma rising beneath the volcano. Activity is concentrated beneath the ski resort of Mammoth Mountain and, as at Campi Flegrei and Rabaul, both scientists and locals are wondering what they can expect next. The Long Valley caldera was formed in a gigantic eruption of rhyolitic magma 700,000 years ago, and lava-producing and explosive eruptions have taken place on and off until only a few centuries ago. In 1982 scientists of the USGS issued a Volcanic Hazard Alert, and in early 1983 more than 1,000 earth tremors in a 12-hour period caused great concern among scientists and public alike. Ground deformation and seismic activity continue in the area, and a new road has been constructed to permit more rapid evacuation of the 3,000 residents and potentially tens of thousands of skiers who visit the caldera during winter.

While Tavurvur rumbles on, and Campi Flegrei and Long Valley may erupt again soon, it is highly unlikely that any of these calderas will host the next super-eruption. The short-term swelling that contributes to the restless state of these calderas is simply not persistent enough, nor sufficiently large and extensive, to be attributable to the volume of fresh magma required to feed a super-eruption. The unfortunate truth is that the next super-eruption will probably occur at a poorly monitored or unmonitored volcano that we know little about, located in an obscure, perhaps even largely uninhabited, part of the world, or even from a site where no currently-active volcano or restless caldera field exists.

Predicting an eruption: monitoring the warning signs

As shown by the experiences of the inhabitants of Rabaul in 1994, no volcanic eruption occurs without warning signs, although, as at Campi Flegrei, the warning signs may occur without a subsequent eruption. Increased numbers of earthquakes result from the rising magma fracturing the rock ahead of itself as it forces its way upward, while the swelling of the ground surface is simply due to the accumulating magma making space for itself. As demonstrated at Rabaul, such effects are noticeable even where the volume of fresh magma is relatively small, so they should be even easier to spot for the huge volumes of magma that are required to feed Toba-sized super-eruptions.

Assuming that the magma ejected during such events represents only a proportion of the magma emplaced beneath the surface, the total volume may be of the order of tens of thousands of cubic kilometres. There is no question about our ability to recognize swelling associated with such a huge mass of accumulating magma, provided that we know where to look and have access to the area in order to undertake more detailed monitoring.

Ground swell

Probably the first sign of a new, very large volume of rhyolitic magma accumulating beneath the surface will be the large-scale swelling of an entire region, perhaps as great as tens or hundreds of thousands of square kilometres. It is perfectly likely that the updomed area will be so large and the rate of swelling so slow that the local population, should there be one, will notice nothing amiss. The enormous scale makes it probable that the overall picture will be discernible only from space using satellite-based sensors. But what should we be looking for? If uplift has been going on for a significant length of time, perhaps tens of thousands of years, its effects should be discernible in changes to the local topography. In particular, alterations in the patterns of river drainage systems may provide one of the most valuable clues. Depending on the rate of uplift, where established rivers cut across the inflating crust they may either cut down into the rising land surface, forming ever-deepening gorges, or be diverted around the bulge. Where no drainage system exists in the vicinity, one may well develop as the updomed region gets higher and forms its own watershed, with watercourses draining radially off the bulge.

Once a potential candidate has been located, satellite-based instruments can also be utilized to find out if the land surface is continuing to swell and, if so, how rapidly. This can be accomplished using an ingenious technique known as *interferometric synthetic aperture radar* (InSAR). A number of satellites now in orbit use sensors that observe the Earth's surface using radar rather than visible wavelengths. Radar has the advantage that it can see through cloud, and it is, therefore, a particularly useful medium for the surveillance of erupting volcanoes, where continuous assessment of the situation requires a reliable observation system that cannot afford to be hindered by poor weather. Satellite-based radar can also be used to detect small changes in topography, which makes it especially useful for identifying and measuring regions of uplift that might mark the position of large masses of accumulating magma.

Although the computer processing is complex, the procedure is straightforward. The satellite sensor takes a radar image of the area of interest on the Earth's surface, from which is constructed a three-dimensional image of the topography, known as a *digital terrain model* (DTM). At some future date, perhaps a year later, a second image is taken and a second DTM produced. With the benefit of some high-powered computing, the second DTM is superimposed on the first, with the difference between the two providing a measure of how much the topography has changed between the times that the two images were taken. This method is so accurate that it can detect horizontal and vertical changes of only a few centimetres, and it has already been used successfully to measure deformation of the crust caused by the 1992 Landers earthquake in California and deflation of Mount Etna following the major eruption that ended in 1993. Once InSAR has located a large, actively uplifting region above a subduction zone that might pose the threat of a future super-eruption, the full array of standard monitoring techniques available to the volcanologist can be brought to bear in order to determine whether or not an eruption is likely in the near to medium-term future.

Volcanic tremors

Since shortly after the construction of the first volcano observatory was ordered in 1841 by Ferdinand II, King of the Two Sicilies, earthquake monitoring has formed the backbone of eruption-forecasting methods. This is because, as mentioned earlier, no volcano erupts without at least some associated earthquake activity. Sometimes, this is of such low magnitude as to be detectable only with the use of sensitive seismographs designed to detect the smallest tremor. On other occasions, however, as at Campi Flegrei, Montserrat and Rabaul, the quakes can be intense enough to be felt and to cause severe damage to buildings.

Two different types of earthquakes are generated during the ascent of magma toward the surface. Each time the magma fractures the rock ahead of itself it generates a sharp seismic shock-wave distinctive of a brittle material being cracked. This type of shock, known as a *tectonic* earthquake, has a characteristic appearance on a seismograph, namely a strong signal that starts abruptly and becomes weaker rapidly. Many such signals beneath a volcano are usually the result of a mass of rising magma making room for itself. High levels of such earthquakes are recorded before each eruptive episode of the Pu'u' 'O'o centre of the Kilauea volcano on Hawaii and also during growth spurts of the active Soufrière Hills lava dome on Montserrat.

Once magma has opened up a route for itself, the character of the earthquakes that it generates changes. Magma travelling through an open fracture, or conduit, causes the walls of the conduit to vibrate or tremble, rather like a house on a busy road when a heavy truck passes. On a seismograph this generates a signal that does not start as abruptly, but that lasts for longer. The appearance of such earthquakes, known as *volcanic tremors*, following a period dominated by tectonic quakes is often a sign that magma is on its way, unhindered, to the surface, and that an eruption is imminent. At Pu'u' 'O'o such tremors start hours before an eruption and continue during the eruption itself as the magma continues to power its way upward to the eruption site.

In order to make a reasonable forecast of the timing of an impending eruption, it is useful to be able to pinpoint the positions of earthquakes beneath the surface. In this way the rate of ascent of magma toward the surface can be determined and the likely eruption site constrained. One seismograph is simply not sufficient to locate an earthquake, and at least three instruments are needed, preferably more. As it is both expensive and labour intensive to maintain an array of many seismographs on a potentially active volcano, most have only a single instrument in place for much of the time. Should this, however, record increasing numbers of earthquakes, additional seismographs are brought in to provide a more detailed picture of the earthquake distribution beneath the volcano, and to look for any migration of the quakes, and therefore the magma, toward the surface. It may not always be necessary to look in detail at the characteristics of volcano-related earthquakes in order to recognize that an eruption is imminent. Just tracking the total energy released by all earthquakes can provide a clue to the timing of a future eruption, with the rising numbers of earthquakes as magma approaches the surface being reflected in an accompanying increase in the total amount of seismic energy released. This method, known as *real-time seismic amplitude measurement*, or RSAM, was utilized by the USGS and the Philippine Institute of Volcanology and Seismology to monitor the build-up to the 1991 eruption of Pinatubo and has more recently been used to track explosive events during the eruption on Montserrat.

Surface deformation

As well as triggering earthquakes, it is normal for magma to cause the land surface above it to rise prior to an eruption, and identifying such a phenomenon (see p. 90) is probably the only way volcanologists are going to be able to pinpoint the site for the next super-eruption. Once the updomed region has been located, however, and some idea of its rate of uplift gleaned from the use of satellite-based InSAR, only ground-based instruments can provide a more detailed picture of the deformation. A range of high-tech methods (see figure on p. 94) is now available to enable volcanologists to observe tiny changes of less than a centimetre in the ground surface of an active volcano.

Most methods of monitoring movements of the ground surface are based upon establishing a network of survey benchmarks, normally metal disks firmly fixed to rocks or metal rods buried deeply in ash. The behaviour of these benchmarks as the volcano swells can be easily visualized by imagining a partially inflated balloon on which a pattern of small dots has been marked. As the balloon is blown up further, the dots will increase in height relative to the balloon nozzle, and they will also move apart relative to one another. This is exactly what happens to the benchmarks when a volcano inflates prior to eruption. After the eruption, most volcanoes behave like deflating balloons, causing the survey benchmarks to fall in height and move closer together.

The earliest ways of monitoring surface deformation at volcanoes were developed in the first few decades of this century by Japanese volcanologists, who used the technique of *levelling* to record height changes between fixed survey points strategically placed on the Sakurajima volcano. By comparing the height changes with a stable benchmark, the Japanese scientists were able to obtain an estimate of the amount of

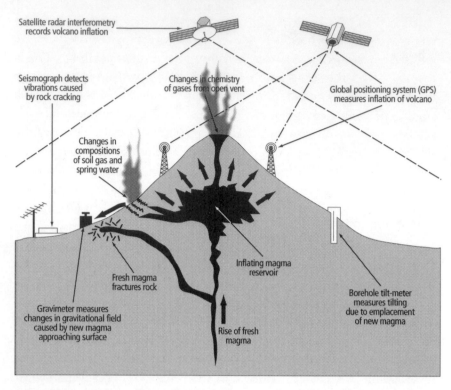

Satellite radar interferometry
records volcano inflation

Seismograph detects
vibrations caused
by rock cracking

Changes in chemistry
of gases from open vent

Global positioning system (GPS)
measures inflation of volcano

Changes in
compositions
of soil gas and
spring water

Fresh magma
fractures rock

Inflating magma
reservoir

Borehole tilt-meter
measures tilting
due to emplacement
of new magma

Gravimeter measures
changes in gravitational field
caused by new magma
approaching surface

Rise of fresh
magma

Volcanologists now have an impressive armoury of techniques at their disposal with which to monitor activity and forecast eruptions. In particular, seismographs record the earthquakes associated with the ascent of fresh magma, while satellite instruments are becoming increasingly important for detecting the swelling of magma reservoirs prior to eruption.

uplift associated with the emplacement of fresh magma below. Furthermore, by contouring the changes, they could obtain a picture of the ground–deformation pattern that might provide a clue as to the precise location of the impending eruption. Similarly, they were able to record a deflation of the surface after magma had been evacuated during an eruption.

At about the same time, researchers at the Hawaii Volcano Observatory introduced and operated an alternative method for monitoring deformation of Kilauea. This involved a triangular arrangement of three 'pots' connected by water–filled tubes resting on the surface. As the volcano's flanks swelled, so the arrangement was tilted, with the amount and direction of tilt being determined from the distribution of water in the pots.

More recently, this 'wet-tilt' method has been superseded by electronic *tilt-meters*, which are located in boreholes for protection, to ensure stability and to insulate them from surface temperature changes that can affect the sensitive electronics. These instruments are able to provide a continuous record of the tilt of a volcano's flanks as fresh magma rises from below. When this happens, the instrument records a tilt away from the summit or main crater of the volcano, a condition sometimes referred to as *crater-up*. Following an eruption, it is common for the volcano to subside once more, resulting in a tilt toward the summit, a situation known as *crater-down*.

As well as recording height changes or ground tilt, volcanologists also use methods for measuring horizontal movements associated with the swelling of a volcano prior to eruption. *Electronic distance measurement* (EDM) was first used in volcanology in the early 1970s to determine the degree to which survey benchmarks on the flanks of Mount Etna in Sicily moved apart before eruption. With this method, an electronic distance-meter is mounted on a tripod precisely located over a benchmark, while a reflector is set up on a second tripod on another benchmark. Depending on the type of instrument, a beam of infrared, laser or microwave radiation is generated by the instrument and bounced back from the reflector. Using a calculation involving counting the number of radiation wavelengths of known length in the return beam, and taking into account factors such as atmospheric temperature and pressure, which can affect the beam, the distance between the two benchmarks can be determined to within a centimetre or two. EDM does suffer from a number of drawbacks, the main one being that line-of-sight is required between benchmarks, thereby constraining the pattern of the network, but it has been and continues to be successfully used to monitor deforming volcanoes around the world.

During the past few years, the measurement of volcano deformation has been revolutionized by the appearance of the *global positioning system* (GPS). This satellite-based means of location has already penetrated the consumer market in the developed countries, with handheld-GPS receivers in regularly use by walkers, and car-based receivers providing drivers with their position at all times. Such systems, however, allow users to position themselves on the Earth's surface to within only 10m or so at best, which is of little use to volcanologists trying to detect vertical and horizontal movements of a centimetre or so. The GPS consists of a *constellation* of 24 satellites in orbit that are constantly beaming radio signals earthward. Because the orbits of each satellite are very precisely known, locking on to at least four of these satellites using a GPS receiver can give the precise position of that receiver on the Earth's surface. Using a network of survey benchmarks of the type used for EDM, volcanologists use tripod-mounted GPS receivers that are locatable above the benchmarks.

Rather than measuring the distances between benchmark pairs, however, *differential GPS* is used to locate the position of every benchmark to within as little as a centimetre in both horizontal and vertical dimensions. Of course, once this has been accomplished, distances between benchmark pairs can be determined. Differential GPS involves the use of two tripod-mounted receivers, one of which is established over a benchmark, the position of which is already known very precisely. A second receiver, known as the *rover*, is then set up, perhaps for 15 minutes or so at a time, on all the other benchmarks in turn, providing their positions relative to the known benchmark. GPS has a number of advantages over EDM, the principal ones being that radio-waves are not affected by meteorological conditions and that line-of-sight is not necessary between benchmarks. This means that, provided there is enough sky visible to detect at least four satellites at any one time, the survey benchmarks can be established where they will give the best picture of the surface deformation pattern.

Although it is beyond the scope of this book to address them in any detail, an impressive battery of other surveillance methods to support seismic and deformation monitoring is now at the disposal of volcanologists. These include techniques to detect changes in the rates of emitted volcanic gases, such as sulphur dioxide and carbon dioxide, which might indicate the approach of magma to the surface, and others that measure variations in the gravitational, magnetic, and electrical fields associated with the ascent of fresh magma.

★ ★ ★

I have suggested that the next super-eruption is most likely to occur at a volcano we know little about, or even somewhere new, where no volcano currently exists. It remains possible, however, that the next great blast may take place from a volcano or caldera field with which we are familiar and are already monitoring in some detail. What, for example, would happen if the next super-eruption occurred in the heart of the USA? Let us find out by taking a look at the build-up to a hypothetical twenty–first century super-eruption in the Yellowstone National Park, a region that has already experienced three great volcanic explosions, and examine the devastating consequences such an event could have for the USA and the world.

The Yellowstone super-eruption, AD 2075

• *Scientists monitoring the Yellowstone volcanic field in Wyoming, USA, are becoming increasingly concerned that a major eruption is now both inevitable and imminent.* *It became apparent more than 50 years ago that the swelling of the region, which started toward the end of the twentieth century, was not a short-term event but the start of a persistent and ominous trend. Almost 80 years of uplift have now led to nearly 4,000km^2 of the crust in the vicinity of Yellowstone Lake rising by up to 40m in places, with new geysers bursting through increasing numbers of open fractures.*

Earthquakes strong enough to feel are now a daily occurrence, telling the worried scientists that huge masses of magma are moving closer to the surface. Both the rate of ground deformation and the numbers of earthquakes are accelerating to such an extent that volcanologists expect a major explosive eruption within the next 12 months. Although the precise scale of the eruption remains impossible to forecast, many involved in the US Geological Survey (USGS) monitoring programme believe it could be the greatest eruption since a gigantic blast in Indonesia over 70,000 years ago – what volcanologists call a VEI 8 event. Evacuation plans are in place for the state of Wyoming and neighbouring areas of eastern Idaho and southern Montana, which are expected to be devastated when Yellowstone finally blows. Meanwhile, the rest of the country and the world are bracing themselves for what could be the greatest natural catastrophe to hit modern society.

BBC World Service *News on the Net*, 16 May 2074.

To experience a major volcanic eruption in VIRTUATACTILE access VEI 8 brainmesh.link through BBCyborg.net (available to GenMod. H. Sapiens Types II and III only).

Countdown to disaster

For the last 17 million years the North American Plate has been creeping south-westward at a few centimetres a year across the Yellowstone 'hot-spot', a zone where hot and buoyant mantle material rises until it is stopped in its tracks by the base of the lithosphere, the brittle layer of crust and uppermost mantle that makes up the Earth's rigid plates. Periodically, runny basaltic magma from the

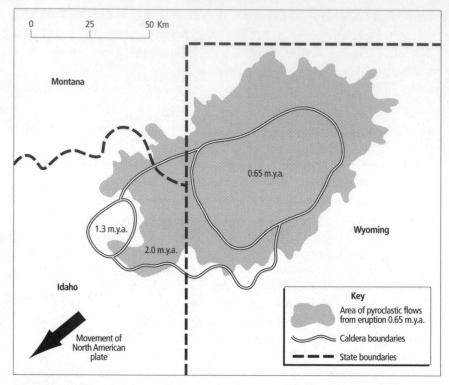

Three gigantic super-eruptions have occurred in the Yellowstone region of the USA during the past 2 million years, leaving behind huge calderas, tens of kilometres across. The last great blast occurred around 660,000 years ago, ejecting devastating pyroclastic flows that travelled up to 50km from the eruption site and dumping ash as far away as Los Angeles.

hot mantle has burst through to the surface, forming huge outpourings of lava that have buried an area equivalent to the size of the UK to a depth of 1km or more. Unable to penetrate all the way to the surface, some of the hot basalt ponded at the base of the crust, causing the rock to melt and generating gigantic volumes of sticky, rhyolitic magma, some of which periodically blasted its way upward and outward in a series of cataclysmic explosive eruptions.

Every time this happened, the emptying of the underlying magma reservoir in the crust caused its roof to collapse, thereby forming a giant caldera. These calderas are now stretched out across the northwestern USA like a string of beads, as the North American Plate continues to move southwestward across the stationary hot-spot (see figure above). At Yellowstone alone, there have been caldera-forming eruptions three times over the past 2 million years, the last great blast occurring around 660,000 years ago. Hurricane-force pyroclastic flows of superheated volcanic gases, hot ash and pumice left nothing alive within an area of over 4,000km^2, while ash fell across the USA, and sulphur aerosols in the stratosphere played havoc with the global climate. Now it looks as if the next volcanic cataclysm might be just around the corner.

Rather like the slow breathing of a sleeping dragon, the giant Yellowstone caldera has swelled and subsided three times since the end of the last Ice Age around 10,000 years ago, with each 'breath' involving a change of about 20m in the height of the overlying land surface. Between the early 1920s and the mid-1980s the centre of the caldera crept up by as much as 1m, after which time it began to sink once again. In 1995, however, things started to change dramatically. Satellite radar measurements, together with ground-based levelling surveys, revealed that the caldera was on its way up once again, initially at a rate of about 2cm/year. By 1998 some areas, such as Mount Washburn, just to the north of the caldera rim, were rising even more rapidly, at a rate of up to 3cm/year. Accustomed to much longer cycles of swelling and subsidence, the monitoring scientists were surprised by the rapidity with which the sinking of the 1980s had been replaced by renewed uplift. It was not until the early decades of the twenty-first century, however, that the situation began to give some cause for concern.

Warning signs

In 2004 a major earthquake registering 7.9 on the Richter Scale occurred near the town of Madison on the northern rim of the Yellowstone caldera, causing several hundred deaths and severe damage in northwestern Wyoming, eastern Idaho and southern Montana. Shortly after the quake, acceleration was observed in the rate of uplift, with the central area of the caldera rising by close to 1m during the following 12 months. Sensitive monitoring instruments were no longer needed to spot the changes in topography as the shores around Yellowstone Lake rose and the lake area shrank noticeably. Following a further increase in uplift rates in 2006, a concerned USGS opened a volcano observatory at West Yellowstone in Idaho and increased monitoring levels to try unravel what was going on deep beneath the surface.

In 2007 an international workshop, organized jointly by the USGS and the International Association for Volcanology and the Chemistry of the Earth's Interior, was held at Madison, focusing on the increased restlessness of the caldera and its possible causes. Opinion was split over whether the continued uplift was the result of increased pressure within subsurface reservoirs of the hot water that fed the spectacular geysers of the region or to the rise of fresh magma from deeper within the crust. Later that year the USGS introduced a

Volcanic Alert Levels at Yellowstone caldera.

Alert level	Activity	Interpretation and forecast
No alert	Background levels of deformation and seismic activity	No eruption in the foreseeable future
1	Elevated levels of deformation and seismic unrest	Magmatic or hydrothermal disturbance: no eruption imminent
2	Moderate level of deformation and seismic unrest with positive evidence of magma involvement	Emplacement of fresh magma: outcome could be an eruption
3	High and increasing level of deformation and seismic activity; gas emissions and increased thermal activity	Continued increase in trend of unrest could lead to an eruption within 2 weeks
4	Intense unrest; accelerating deformation and numbers of magmatic earthquakes	Eruption possible within 24 hours
5	Eruption in progress	Eruption in progress

system of Volcanic Alert Levels similar to that adopted for other active volcanic regions in the USA (see table above), in order to provide a means of informing the local population of the condition of the caldera and the expectation of a future eruptive event. At the time of its introduction, the alert level was set at 1, corresponding to low-level deformation and seismic unrest.

Following a slowing of the uplift rate over the next several years, the caldera began to subside again in the autumn of 2014, leading to sighs of relief all round. The respite was, however, to prove a short one, and after only 18 months, two magnitude 6 earthquakes, one near Norris and the other further north on the Hebgen Lake fault zone that extends into the northwestern part of the caldera, triggered renewed swelling. A detailed seismic survey involving dozens of seismographs was undertaken by the USGS in the summer of 2019. This was designed to examine the behaviour of the seismic waves generated by the increasing numbers of earthquakes in the Yellowstone region as they passed through the crust, in order to construct a detailed picture of the Earth's interior beneath the caldera. After collecting data for over a year, seismologists discovered what they were hoping not to find. The long delays as seismic waves passed beneath the Yellowstone region and other characteristic changes in the seismic signals revealed that a huge body of magma was accumulating beneath the northern part of the caldera at a depth of about 10km. This conclusion was soon confirmed by another geophysical campaign that monitored very small changes in gravity at the Earth's surface, and that revealed the existence beneath Yellowstone of a large mass of low-density, rhyolitic magma that had been undetected 30 years earlier.

In response to the renewed activity and the new evidence for the emplacement of fresh magma at shallow depths beneath Yellowstone, the USGS raised the alert level to 2. Much of the caldera had now risen by 6m or so over the three decades and an eruption was a clear possibility. The state government had taken an interest in the situation for some years, and news of the potential crisis had now caught the attention of the White House. In late 2023 a panel of experts, put together at the national government's behest by the National Science Foundation, debated the likelihood of a future eruption and its timing. In their technical report, *The Continuing Bradyseismic Crisis at Yellowstone Caldera*, the panel concluded that an eruption was a likely, but not imminent, eventual outcome of the current activity at the caldera. The panel recognized the possibility that the eruption, if and when it came, could be on a scale unprecedented in the modern world and strongly encouraged contingency planning at both regional and national levels to cope with its potential devastating impact.

Although surface uplift continued over the next 20 years, the rate barely accelerated. By now, both the scientists, some of whom had now been monitoring the caldera for their entire working lives, and the local population had become completely familiar with the situation. As ever in such circumstances, familiarity had bred contempt, and the possibility of an eruption was now far from most people's minds as they went about their daily business. Once again Nature had a shock in store, and the great earthquake swarm of Thanksgiving Day 2047 brought fear into the hearts of many who had been lulled well and truly into a false sense of security. Close to midnight on 25 November, the entire Yellowstone region was jolted by a magnitude 6.5 earthquake; not great enough to cause major damage but sufficient to bring down poorly built structures, crack walls and cause underground pipe breakages. The problem with this quake was that it was followed by another, almost as large, 10 minutes later and by yet another a few minutes after that.

From Mammoth in the north to the southern margins of the park, the terrified families of park officials and other locals, together with the few hardy campers braving the November snows, grabbed what possessions they could and took the nearest route out of the park area. For 6 hours the ground shook nearly continuously, bringing down landslides that trapped many of those attempting to leave. Emerging shell-shocked and bewildered in the freezing dawn, those who remained were greeted by new ground fractures and by an unfamiliar shoreline around much of Yellowstone Lake. The Earth had shaken itself out of the malaise of the previous 30 years and the entire central part of the caldera had heaved itself skyward by 3m overnight.

Tremors continued to hit the area over the next several days and concern increased when teams of scientists, combing the region for other effects of the earthquake swarm, reported new geyser activity, extensive fissuring and numerous dead animals and birds, which had succumbed to releases of deadly carbon dioxide gas from the accumulating magma below. After a meeting with local people, officials and representatives of the state government, at which tempers became frayed to say the least, the USGS monitoring team finally convinced sceptical bureaucrats and businessmen of the need to raise the Volcanic Alert Level from 2 to 3. An eruption was now possible within a few weeks. However, even while detailed plans were being drawn up to evacuate the park and its surroundings, a pronounced reduction in both the number and intensity of earth tremors and a fall in the deformation rate over the succeeding week soon resulted in the alert level being reduced once again to 2.

The next 15 years saw a slow but very gradual increase in the rate of uplift, and by midsummer 2062 the caldera had swelled by a further 10m. Yellowstone Park remained, however, a mecca for the hiker and naturalist, and the spectacular increase in geyser activity attracted even more visitors to the park than before. The numerous signs that warned the visitors not to linger in hollows or areas of low topography because of the danger from noxious volcanic gases and to camp only on the new sites located on higher ground failed to deter the more adventurous, and the park was packed to bursting in late summer 2063 when all hell broke loose.

On a hot, sultry dawn, with thunder in the air, a low rumbling woke campers with a start, but this was no electrical discharge in the skies. This rumbling came from below. The reverberation was rapidly followed by a series of sharp cracks like rifle shots, each corresponding to a great jolt that picked up tents and their inhabitants bodily from the ground and hurled them across the camp sites. South of Madison a fearsome ripping sound accompanied a series of growing tears in the Earth's surface as the caldera to the south pulled itself skyward along a 14km-long crack, forming a north-facing cliff up to 4m high. At the same time, the southern shores of Yellowstone Lake sank beneath the pounding waves generated by the quake as the entire caldera tilted southward. Smaller quakes rumbled on for months afterward as the northern part of the caldera continued to rise, and there was now little doubt that a serious eruption was in the offing.

The alert level was set at 3 – an eruption possible within 2 weeks – for over a month before being reduced once again to 2. Few, however, expected it to stay at this level for long. For the remainder of the decade park infrastructures were gradually run down, and those living within the confines of Yellowstone were moved to safer locations. USGS scientists fought on two fronts: firstly to persuade remaining local people and businesses that an eruption was now virtually certain, and secondly to convince the national government that, when it came, the eruption could affect a third of the land area of the country and devastate its economy. Another overnight tilting of the caldera in 2069, this time with the northern rim rising a further 6m, convinced the last locals to leave the area, but the bureaucrats on the eastern coast still lacked the imagination to accept the picture of national devastation painted by the scientists.

Eruption!

Over the past 250,000 years more than 6,000km^3 of magma had been erupted from the Yellowstone volcanic field, during three distinct cycles of activity. Each cycle started with the eruption of two different types of magma – runny basalt and sticky, explosive rhyolite – and ended with the extremely rapid and devastatingly violent expulsion of rhyolitic magma accompanied by major caldera collapse. After the last great collapse 660,000 years ago, a 400,000-year hiatus ensued before the voluminous eruption of rhyolitic lavas marked the renewed insurgence of magma into the caldera system and the start of a fourth cycle. Lavas continued to be erupted from great circular fractures coincident with the rim of the caldera, filling it entirely and overflowing to cover much of the surrounding land. Between 150,000 and 70,000 years ago more than 1,000m^3 of lava was erupted. Since then, however, activity had been confined simply to periodic deformation of the caldera – until the current crisis.

A few days after New Year 2075, a new sound was heard across Yellowstone, not the sharp, cracking sounds of rock breaking, but a constant rumbling tremor of the ground that went on and on, rather like the continuous passage of a convoy of heavy trucks. Monitoring scientists instantly recognized the signals as magmatic earthquakes – the tremors caused by magma travelling through open cracks in the rock en route to the surface. A level 3 alert had been in place for a week in response to elevated levels of uplift, and this was instantly increased, for the first time, to a 4: eruption expected within 24 hours. Only 2 days earlier the USGS had held a meeting to review new geophysical data gathered over the previous 12 months. Detailed analysis of the deformation pattern, undertaken using the latest TERRANET positioning satellites, revealed that the eruption, when it came, would probably start on the northern rim of the caldera somewhere between Madison and Norris. Recent seismic and microgravity data, supported by magnetic and electrical potential studies, provided evidence for a body of magma beneath this part of the caldera in excess of 3,000km^3, the upper part of which now resided within 4km of the surface. At 3.56a.m. local time on 5 January 2075, following a magnitude 7 earthquake, the confined magma was finally freed from its prison – and the world would never be quite the same again.

Although the evacuation of everyone within 200km of the caldera rim was well under way when the eruption started, a number of stubborn residents in West Yellowstone were either burned to a crisp or torn apart in their beds as a burning hurricane first levelled the town and then buried it under deposits of hot ash tens of metres thick. Four USGS volcanologists packing up monitoring equipment in preparation for a rapid getaway also left it too late. Before being mangled by the power of the blast, seismographs and GPS receivers in the field confirmed to USGS scientists at their headquarters in Vancouver, Washington State, what they already suspected. Magma had finally found its way along the numerous fractures that had developed along the northwestern margin of the caldera during the past few decades. Released from the enormous pressures exerted at several kilometres depth, the sticky, gas-rich, rhyolitic magma had torn itself apart with a violence that sent shock-waves across the USA and registered on barometers as far away as Hawaii, the UK and New Zealand. No one could get anywhere near the eruption site, but the times at which USGS seismographs and GPS receivers stopped operating provided evidence of the devastating pyroclastic flows that now hurled themselves outward from the new eruption site, devouring all in their paths.

In anticipation of inaccessibility during the forthcoming eruption, USGS scientists had also laid out a grid of tiny sensor-transmitters, designed to stop working at a temperature of 300°C, so that a picture of the extent and progress of the eruption could be built up from a remote location. The rate at which sensors were knocked out revealed that the pyroclastic flows travelled radially outward from the eruption site in all directions, ignoring variations in topography and rolling over hills and other obstructions. Within 10 minutes, Madison and West Yellowstone ceased to exist, while an hour later no signals were being received from sensors at Indian Creek and Mammoth in the north, at Mack's Inn to the east, and at the southern entrance to the park. No dawn greeted the inhabitants of Cody, 150km east of the eruption site – only utter blackness, continual shaking of the ground and a rain of hot ash and pumice that, by

8.00a.m., was already 20cm thick. A persistent downpour helped to load surfaces with wet, heavy ash, and within a few hours roofs were beginning to collapse across the town, trapping terrified families inside.

By mid-morning, reconnaissance flights, keeping a safe distance, recorded a towering column of ash 10km across and rising to at least 40km, where stratospheric winds deformed it into a gigantic black mushroom, its leading edge being progressively pushed south and east. Heavy ash was now falling across much of Wyoming, and strong northwesterly winds were driving the ash-cloud rapidly toward Denver. Over the next 24 hours much of Wyoming, Idaho and Montana continued to shake as more and more magma was blasted out of a series of great curving fractures along the northern rim of the Yellowstone caldera with the unimaginable force of 1,000 Hiroshima bombs every second.

Three days later the eruption still showed no signs of slowing and 10 states, stretching as far as Illinois in the east and Texas in the south, were under ash. Entire cities were at a standstill as ash brought down buildings and power and communication lines, made driving near impossible and caused severe respiratory problems. Over 10cm of ash had already fallen 1,000km from Yellowstone, and Denver in Colorado, Rapid City and Sioux Falls in South Dakota, and Lincoln in Nebraska were all badly affected. Curfews were in place in thousands of towns and cities, although few needed to be persuaded to stay indoors, while the National Guard patrolled empty streets and fought pitched battles with bands of opportunistic looters. On the fifth day the wind direction changed, and while Nebraska and South Dakota received a respite from the ash, Salt Lake City in Utah, Tucson and Phoenix in Arizona, and Los Angeles now came under attack. As filming ceased on the ash-covered sets of Hollywood and the inhabitants of the City of Angels thanked God for their anti-smog masks, scientists and government wondered how much longer the eruption could last.

Aftermath

Near dawn on 13 January, 8 days after the start of the eruption, seismographs at USGS headquarters went mad. At the same time, a series of gigantic shocks rocked the continent, from the Yukon in the north to Louisiana in the south, coinciding with deafening reports heard across Wyoming, Montana, Idaho and parts of Utah, South Dakota, and Nebraska. As the Earth's surface shook violently over a quarter of the USA, buildings in many ash-affected towns and cities, already weakened by the thick cover of volcanic debris, crumbled and collapsed. Although they would need to wait for several more days before their suspicions could be confirmed, monitoring scientists correctly surmised that the quakes were the result of a caldera-forming event. Eight days of eruption had left a gigantic cavity in the crust beneath Yellowstone, and with nothing to support it, the roof had collapsed to form the next in the string of great volcanic craters that march across eastern Idaho and into Wyoming. Within a few days, activity had reduced markedly, and the first aerial reconnaissance flights since the first day of the eruption were underway. A veil of fine ash still hung across much of the USA, stretching as far as the Gulf of Mexico and northern Mexico, but conditions were clearing sufficiently rapidly to permit the Yellowstone area to be approached within a few weeks.

On 6 February volcanologists aboard a USGS plane from Spokane in Washington State became the first people to view the unimaginable devastation of a VEI 8 volcanic eruption. Still finding it difficult to believe what they were seeing, the team leader reported back to USGS headquarters:

• *'. . . flying over Ennis now, approaching from the north. Still a bit hazy but not enough ash around up here to cause us any real problems. Doesn't seem to be any eruption column but there is a huge steam cloud – really difficult to get any idea of scale from here but it could be several kilometres across. God, it looks as if we are over PF [pyroclastic flow] deposits already and the GPS shows we are still 80km from the eruption site. Seems like they have been channelled down the river valley here. Deposits look a bit muddy, perhaps the ash-flows have been reworked by water action – either what's left of the river or heavy rains.*

It's started drizzling again now and the deposits are kicking up a hell of lot of steam – certainly still damned hot! Shit! – just got a glimpse ahead through the clouds, the topography ahead is utterly flat – all the valleys completely filled by PF deposits. Jesus, must be half a kilometre thick in places! No sign of the – no, there it is. We can see the crater – it's gigantic – definitely a caldera. Looks like the eruption site was on the north margin of the old caldera – just as we thought, and the collapse is centred on that. It's difficult to get a decent view through the steam but – God, the thing must be 50km across. The entire northern half of the original caldera has been taken out, and it looks as if everything has gone down as far as West Yellowstone. Visibility's getting really bad – it's really bucketing down now and we can't see a damn thing. Heading back – let's see if things have cleared up a bit tomorrow. Out!'

As the steam cleared and the coarser ash particles began to settle out, the true scale of the devastation became more apparent. Northwestern Wyoming was a flat and featureless volcanic desert, a plain of baking pyroclastic-flow deposits already being dissected and gullied by heavy rains. Around the periphery of the steaming plain, great chunks of pyroclastic-flow material collapsed periodically, like polar ice sheets calving into the ocean, generating torrents of mud in the remnants of river valleys draining the Yellowstone area. Such collapses released pressurized gases trapped in the deposits, triggering explosive blasts that sent columns of hot ash to heights of several kilometres, reminiscent in some ways of the great geysers now buried many hundreds of metres below. At the centre of the steaming plain was a gigantic caldera, 50km long and 20km across, bordered by crumbling cliffs 2km high. In the crater a new lake was already forming, while to the east the old Yellowstone Lake was now filled to its banks with ash and mud.

Further afield, as far south as Los Angeles and El Paso, and east to Des Moines and Kansas City, thousands of towns and cities across 16 states began the enormous task of ridding their houses and streets of the ubiquitous ash. Even 1,500km away from Yellowstone, at Wichita and Oklahoma City, the compacted ash was 20cm thick, and over much of Wyoming, South Dakota, Colorado, and Nebraska roads and buildings were under nearly a metre of the stuff. Despite the appalling conditions during the eruptions, millions had taken to the roads and headed south and east to get out of the ash. Thousands of towns were virtually uninhabited except for looters and feral dogs, and the highways were littered with abandoned vehicles. As the National Guard attempted to move back into these essentially no-go areas they came face to face with heavily armed vigilante and survivalist groups. The eruption provided just the opportunity they had been waiting for: a collapse in law and order, and a chance to get back at the national government and establish their own rule. By March 2075 tens of thousands of National Guardsmen were bogged down in guerrilla warfare with their own countrymen, as everyone who had harboured a grudge against Washington took the opportunity to hit back. Problems with aid distribution compounded the situation, and looting became a necessity for starving families in the most badly affected and inaccessible states.

At the same time, the US economy collapsed almost overnight. Even before the eruption had ceased, stocks and shares had crashed as investors lost any confidence in the country's ability to handle the sheer scale of the catastrophe. Where the US led, others quickly followed, and the markets and economies of Europe and the Far East rapidly descended into chaos and collapse. Soon rioting was rife throughout the major cities of the eastern coast and California, Texas and Florida, as frightened savers demanded payment that the banks simply could not make. By the time the fires from within the Earth were dying, new ones were bursting into life throughout Washington DC, Boston, New York,

Baltimore, New Orleans, Atlanta and Los Angeles. Once-great industrial giants shed their work forces and closed their doors, swelling the growing tens of millions of people with no money, no work and very little food. Throughout the sweltering and soaking summer months of 2075, civil strife spread far and wide, and the country appeared to be on the edge of anarchy.

By September, there was little doubt. The hot and humid August was wiped away within a few days by an unprecedented freezing blast that swept down from the Arctic as far as southern California, Louisiana and Florida. The few crops that had not been buried in ash or rotted in the summer downpours succumbed to the severe frosts and unseasonal blizzards that swept across the continent, and stored supplies were simply not sufficient to feed a population in excess of 300 million. As the volcanic winter began to tighten its grip, the lights began to go out all over the USA, and only the howls of starving dogs and the screams of hungry children drowned the incessant hiss of laser fire.

CHAPTER 3

WAVE GOODBYE:
DEATH BY WATER

The second angel sounded his trumpet,
and something like a huge mountain, all ablaze,
was thrown into the sea.

Revelation 8:8

It is a hot, steamy day in southern Florida, and the highway heading west out of Miami is packed solid with tens of thousands of stationary cars, brought to a halt by a big shunt up ahead. A deafening cacophony of horns blares across the pools and mangroves of the Everglades on either side of the road, while drivers and passengers fight and scream at one another in frustration. Some grab what possessions they can carry, drop off the road and continue their journey westward on foot through the lush vegetation. A terrified cry cuts through the clamour like a knife, and for a few moments silence reigns. Then a murmur begins to spread through the throng as a thin silver line appears on the horizon, growing thicker at an alarming rate. Screams punctuate the renewed bedlam as the silver strand resolves itself into a gigantic wave. The sea has arrived at last. A 60m-high wall of water crashes onto the packed highway with the force of an atomic bomb and the speed of a jet fighter, scouring it of both cars and all human life before continuing to speed west across the state.

Waves of destruction

Tsunami are no ordinary waves. Unlike a breaker crashing onto a beach, a tsunami hitting land will just keep on coming, perhaps for half an hour or so. This is because a tsunami wavelength is typically 300–400km long compared with a few tens of metres for normal waves. Furthermore, all the water that surges onto land as the tsunami hits has to pour off it again, carrying with it a mixture of debris, the dead and the living. Often bodies are carried so far out to sea that they are either never found or turn up bloated and rotting months later, hundreds or even thousands of kilometres away. As the following accounts of some of this century's worst tsunami will show, few survive the impact of these devastating waves, and eyewitness accounts are rare.

Southern Chile, 1960

On 22 May 1960 the Earth off the coast of southern Chile suffered a more violent earthquake than has ever been recorded before or since. Under enormous strain for many years, the so-called Nazca Plate beneath the eastern Pacific thrust itself under the South American Plate in a series of violent jerks. The earthquake registered magnitude 8.6 on the Richter Scale and released as much energy as 500 Hiroshima bombs; it was followed by a number of major aftershocks, all with magnitudes in excess of 7.8. In Chile itself poorly constructed buildings in towns across the south succumbed rapidly to the devastating shocks, crumbling instantly to bury those unlucky enough to be inside. Because of the widespread impact of the quake and the numerous isolated towns and villages affected, the final death toll will never be known, but some put it as high as 5,000.

As the sea-bed buckled under the impact of the quake, a series of enormous waves fanned out across the Pacific Ocean in all directions. Terrified by the violence of the earthquake, the still dazed and injured inhabitants of the Chilean fishing communities on Isla de Chiloé took to their boats and headed out to sea, seeking safety from the powerful aftershocks. This was to prove a great mistake and the last they would ever make. Less than 15 minutes after the quake ended, a distant white line on the horizon quickly formed itself into a giant, churning breaker that devoured the tiny boats and everyone who had sought safety within them. Two hundred lives were taken in the seconds before the wave crashed onto the fishermen's houses, taking any further souls who had remained on land. Similar acts of violent death were being played out all along the coasts of Chile and Peru, as perhaps as many as 2,000 lives were lost to waves up to 25m high.

This was not the end of the tsunami threat, however, and the deadly waves continued to speed west at over 200m/second – in excess of 700km/hour. Right in the way were the islands of Hawaii and their unsuspecting inhabitants. Sitting not so pretty, right in the middle of the Pacific, Hawaii has always been under threat from tsunami generated by earthquakes anywhere around the Pacific Ocean's churning Ring of Fire. As far back as 1868 the islands suffered severe damage as a result of a huge earthquake off the coast of Peru that took 25,000 lives, while in 1946 tsunami almost 10m high, generated by a quake off Alaska, crashed onshore, taking nearly 150 lives.

Because of Hawaii's somewhat precarious position, a tsunami warning system was in place by 1960 and, 4 hours before the arrival of the waves, sirens sounded at 8.30a.m. to warn inhabitants in the town of Hilo of the impending threat. Memories are short, however, and lessons that should have been learned as a result of the destruction caused only 14 years earlier appear to have been rapidly forgotten. Although the inhabitants of the town evacuated at the sound of the sirens, some impatient individuals, suspecting a false alarm, returned to their homes. They did so just in time to face a series of devastating waves up to 11m high. More than 60 of the returnees were drowned or battered to death against their own houses, over 500 of which were destroyed. So great was the impact of the waves that parking-meters were bent flat by the force, and only buildings constructed from reinforced concrete and steel remained standing.

It had taken the tsunami nearly 15 hours to travel the 10,000km to Hilo, but the waves had retained an enormous amount of energy and lost little of their lethal capacity. Still, however, they raced on, heading for the western Pacific. Over 20 hours after Chile had been so badly shaken, the tsunami reached Japan, the waves growing in size as they entered shallow water, so that the largest towered 9m over Hokkaido and Tohoku. Despite travelling across the greatest extent of water on the planet, a distance of over 16,000km, the waves still retained sufficient power to pound the eastern coast of Japan and take a further 180 lives. Tsunami continued to head across the Pacific for a total of 18 hours, causing damage to property as far away as New Guinea, New Zealand and the Philippines.

Alaska, USA, 1964

By the spring of 1964, in Alaska, so much strain had accumulated between the North American Plate and the Pacific Plate that plunged beneath it that something had to give. On the evening of 27 March – Good Friday – it did so, in the form of the greatest earthquake in North American history, at least since the colonial settlement of the continent, and the second largest ever recorded. The quake's source was located off the southern coast of Alaska, less than 20km beneath northern Prince William Sound, about 80km west of the town of Valdez and 120km east of Anchorage. As the Pacific Plate thrust itself further beneath North America in two separate and sudden jolts, the enormous amount of energy released was sufficient to generate a quake that registered a magnitude of between 8.4 and 8.6 on the Richter Scale, only slightly less powerful than that which had caused so much devastation in Chile 4 years earlier.

The quake caused the entire planet to ring like a bell, setting the water in the Great Lakes, 5,000km away, sloshing back and forth, and making water levels in wells as far away as South Africa oscillate. The ground shook violently for nearly 5 minutes, triggering numerous landslides and starting avalanches on the snow-covered peaks. Each thrust of the Pacific Plate involved about 5m of movement, causing the ground to buckle over a huge area. In places the land surface rose instantaneously by 10m, while elsewhere it sank by over 2m. At some points along the coast, barnacles, limpets and other sea creatures were immediately stranded far above sea-level. Despite the enormous power of the quake and the fact that there was significant damage over an area almost half the size of South Carolina, the death toll due to building collapse was small – only nine – and largely confined to downtown Anchorage, primarily because many of the buildings were of wooden construction.

That was not the end of the story, however, and a whole series of great sea-waves generated by the quake took the lives of more than 10 times as many in the worst tsunami disaster ever to hit the western coast of the USA and Canada. The main tsunami resulted from the sudden vertical uplift of thousands of square kilometres of sea-bed, which displaced a huge volume of water above it, sending it out in a series of waves not only onto the coast of North America but right across the Pacific. The height of the largest wave that poured into Valdez Bay was a colossal 67m. Minutes after the Earth stopped shaking, the giant waves began to spread outward, causing death and destruction all down the western coast of Canada and the USA. Along the southern coast of Alaska in particular, the waves overwhelmed coastal installations with enormous violence, taking 106 lives and causing damage estimated at US$100 million. Here the tsunami triggered by the vertical movement of the sea-bed were accompanied by local waves, formed as landslides crashed into the sea because of the severe ground-shaking. In the

Alaskan town of Seward, for example, a huge section of the waterfront slid into the sea, creating a tsunami that smashed into oil installations, killing workers and leaving a film of flaming oil across the waters of Resurrection Bay. The inhabitants had only 20 minutes respite before the main tsunami hammered into the shell-shocked town, taking further lives and causing more destruction.

As the tsunami travelled down the western coast of North America, the height of the waves and the violence of their impact became strongly dependent on the precise form of the coastline. In places the waves were small and had very little effect. At certain bays and estuaries, however, the waves became strongly focused, growing in height and power so as to devastate coastal communities as far away as Oregon and California. In Oregon, four deaths and most of the damage were caused by rivers overflowing as the focused tsunami poured into estuaries. Outside Alaska, the highest level of destruction was experienced thousands of kilometres away at Crescent City in California, which had already suffered from the impact of tsunami formed during the Chilean quake 4 years earlier. Here, the first wave that pounded into the seafront was some 4m above low tide-level, and they were followed by three further waves that became progressively smaller. As inquisitive townsfolk, believing the waves had ceased, approached the front, they were hit by a fifth wave, over 6m high, which destroyed most of the waterfront buildings and flooded over 30 city blocks. A dozen of the curious locals lost their lives as the waves smashed them bodily into the nearest buildings. Several hours later, the tsunami hit first Hawaii and, eventually, Japan, causing damage but, fortunately, having lost sufficient energy to be no longer lethal.

Hawaii, USA, 1975

Even with a tsunami warning system in place, loss of life can be unavoidable. This was tragically demonstrated in late November 1975, once again on Hawaii, when a magnitude 7.2 earthquake occurred beneath the island. Holiday-makers camping at the beach resort of Halape were suddenly woken by a violent shaking of the Earth and the sounds of dislodged rocks and boulders tumbling from the high cliff, at the base of which the resort was located. Understandably concerned about the stability of the cliff, some of the campers moved nearer to the sea. The rest had started to flee seaward when a strong aftershock began to bring down larger blocks from the cliff. At the same time the beach dropped vertically by over 3m, causing those who had fled earlier to run back terrified toward the falling rocks. Seconds later, a 1.5m wave, generated by the displacement along the coast, flooded into the mass of confused campers, to be swiftly followed by a huge wave, nearly 8m high, which crashed into the resort and battered the unfortunate holiday-makers into the base of the cliff. When the wave eventually withdrew, it left behind two dead and nearly 20 injured; only 11 surviving the incident unscathed. In fact, the campers were lucky. If the waves had been 14m high, like those that pounded the coast elsewhere on the island, it is unlikely that any would have survived the onslaught of the sea.

Aitape, Papua New Guinea, 1998

Hot sun, blue sky and fluffy white clouds. Another fine morning in paradise as the inhabitants of Sissano and neighbouring villages on the northern coast of Papua New Guinea went about their daily business of fishing and tending their gardens. Scattered along a narrow strip of land between the Bismarck Sea and a palm-fringed lagoon, the villagers' houses rang with the sound of hundreds of playing children, released from school for the National Day holiday. As the hours passed and dusk began to fall, preparations were made for the evening meal and for a celebratory *sing-sing* – a sort of outdoor cabaret. At around 6.30p.m., however, hell came to paradise.

An almighty bang out to sea froze the villagers in their tracks, although they soon came to life again as the ground shook and cracks burst open along the beach. As they examined the cracks they became aware of a rumbling sound, described by many as resembling the sound of a jet taking off. Looking up just in time to see the first of three giant waves bearing down on them, many tried to run but were overtaken, picked up and dashed into palm trees and mangroves with a force sufficient to tear bodies limb from limb. The force of the wave was so great that it completely sheared off the tops of trees 7m above ground level, providing evidence of the height of this first wave. Two even bigger waves followed, towering 17m above the land, scouring clean the narrow strip of land that was home to the villages of Sissano, Arop, Warapu and Malol, and carrying debris, bodies and survivors into the lagoon.

As the waters retreated, more victims were claimed as the injured, struggling to keep their heads above water, were battered and crushed among floating tree trunks and the remains of their homes. Although the final death toll will probably never be known exactly, as many as one in three of the local population may have succumbed to the killer waves, many being carried far and wide by the retreating waters, their bodies never to be found. Out of a population of around 10,000 for the four villages, over 3,000, many woman and children, would never again awake to the warmth and blue sky of another day.

As the bang and shaking ground that preceded the waves testifies, the tsunami were generated by an undersea earthquake less than 100km offshore. As the Pacific Plate lurched southward beneath the Australian Plate on which Papua New Guinea sits, the sea-bed dropped vertically and instantaneously by 2m along a 40km-long segment of the sub-duction zone. The sudden movement displaced the water above into three great waves that took less than 30 minutes to reach and devastate the northern coast of the island. In retrospect, and as for many recent disasters, a close scrutiny of the past history of the region would have revealed the perilous nature of this part of Papua New Guinea. As recently as 1907 and 1934 the area was buckled by quakes, the later one generating a disastrous tsunami in the same area; in fact Sissano Lagoon itself was formed during the 1907 quake as a new depression formed and filled with water.

What are tsunami?

The term 'tsunami' comes from the Japanese *tsu*, meaning 'harbour' and *nami*, meaning 'wave', and there is a good reason for this. Although tsunami are barely detectable in deep water and can sneak under the keels of ships at sea as little more than a minor swell, when the waves reach shallow water and approach a coastline, they build to great heights and become focused according to the local topography. Consequently, a tsunami unnoticed far from land may become a terrifying 30m high wall of water as it approaches a harbour.

How are tsunami formed?

As mentioned in Chapter 1, there are a number of ways in which tsunami can be formed. The most common is as a result of a submarine earthquake, and over 90 per cent of all tsunami are generated in this way. There is also a predictable relationship between the height of a tsunami and the size of the earthquake that generated it (see p. 118 and figure on p. 116). Sometimes, however, the wave is larger than expected for the size of the quake as, for example, at Papua New Guinea in 1998,

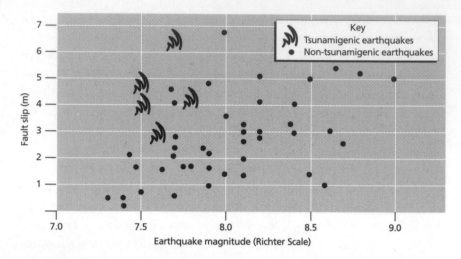

Less than 90 per cent of all submarine earthquakes generate tsunami. Generally speaking, tsunamigenic quakes are strong (at least magnitude 6.5 on the Richter Scale), shallow and involve the significant vertical movement of the sea-bed due to slip along the fault where the quake originated. A graph of fault slip plotted against quake magnitude shows that the amount of slip is more important than the magnitude of the quake in terms of generating tsunami.

and this often happens because the sudden movement of the sea-bed triggers a submarine landslide that enhances the efficiency of tsunami formation.

Submarine landslides can also cause tsunami in their own right, and major submarine landslides have in the past produced some of the largest waves known. Tsunami may also have a volcanic origin and can be generated by submarine eruptions, from the entry into the sea of a volcanic landslide or a pyroclastic flow, or as a result of caldera collapse following a major eruption. Indeed, perhaps the most destructive tsunami of the last 300 years were formed as a result of the cataclysmic explosion, followed by collapse, of the Krakatoa volcano in 1883, while the greatest tsunami of terrestrial origin are produced by the collapse of gigantic volumes of material from ocean island volcanoes.

It is often difficult to appreciate how relatively localized events can cause giant waves that can travel half way around the planet and cause death and destruction even 10,000km away. Let us, therefore, take a closer look at the formation of tsunami. Although most tsunami are associated with submarine earthquakes, very few of these events are actually *tsunamigenic*, or 'tsunami-producing'. For example, between the mid-nineteenth century and the end of World War 2, it is estimated that there were over 15,000 significant submarine earthquakes, of which only just over 100 generated tsunami. Similarly, along the western coast of South America, one of the most tsunami-prone regions on the planet, the last 1,000 or so offshore earthquakes produced only 20 tsunami. It is indeed fortunate that submarine earthquakes are so inefficient at producing giant sea-waves, otherwise many coastal areas around the Pacific Rim and in other seismically active regions would be uninhabitable.

In fact, many more submarine earthquakes probably do generate tsunami, but in most cases they are too small to be noticed, except on tide-gauges and other sensitive instrumentation for measuring sea-level changes. This can pose a problem in terms of tsunami forecasting, which, despite considerable research over the last several decades, remains, to some extent at least, an inexact science. For example, on a number of occasions after a quake somewhere around the Pacific Rim, the Pacific Tsunami Warning System has issued tsunami warnings for Hawaii, only to discover, when the waves reached the islands, that they were just a few centimetres high. Understandably, this caused consternation and irritation among citizens required to leave their homes, who regarded the warnings as 'false alarms' rather than accurate forecasts that overestimated the wave height. The danger with such a situation, if it is repeated too often, is that those living in zones of high tsunami risk will become inured to the threat and fail to respond to future tsunami warnings. This example of the 'cry wolf' syndrome is increasingly becoming the bane of both scientists and civil authorities involved in trying to reduce the impact of geophysical hazards.

The reason why over 90 per cent of all submarine earthquakes do not generate tsunami is that they need to have just the right characteristics. Firstly, they should be sufficiently powerful to impart a decent jolt to the sea-bed. This, in most instances, requires a quake with a magnitude in excess of 6.5 on the Richter Scale. Secondly, they need to be shallow, usually less than 30km deep, so that much of the energy released is not absorbed by the overlying rock but penetrates upward into the water. Thirdly, and most importantly, the quake should involve the vertical movement of part of the sea-bed, thereby providing a direct impulse that displaces the sea above the region of the quake.

In the most efficient tsunamigenic quakes, tens of thousands of square kilometres of sea-bed, equivalent to the size of a small European country or a US state, are jolted up or down by several metres within a few seconds. The critical element in tsunami production, whether caused by a submarine earthquake or landslide, or as a result of volcanic activity, is that a large amount of energy must be transferred near-instantaneously, or *impulsively*, into a body of water over a large area. It is this factor that differentiates tsunami from large waves generated by hurricanes and severe storms. Although sea-waves generated by wind have been observed to reach heights in excess of 30m, they do not share the other characteristics of tsunami that make the latter so destructive, namely their persistence over great distances, their tremendous velocities and their enormous wavelengths.

Water depth is also an important factor in determining the scale of a tsunami generated by an earthquake, and tsunami produced in shallow water by an earthquake close to shore will not, in general, be as large as those formed by a quake further out to sea. A potentially dangerous exception to this rule, however, may apply where an earthquake occurs along the coastline itself, generating a tsunami within an area of partially enclosed sea, such as a harbour, bay or estuary. In such circumstances, the waves may resonate back and forth, getting bigger and more destructive before they eventually lose energy and dissipate.

After considerable study, the Japanese have devised a scale for tsunami that relates them to both earthquake magnitude and run-up (wave) height. As the table on p. 119 shows, an earthquake of magnitude 7 on the Richter Scale will generate a tsunami of magnitude 0 with a run-up of 1–1.5m. At the top of the scale, a magnitude 8.75 quake will trigger a magnitude 5 tsunami and a run-up height in excess of 32m.

As mentioned earlier, the tsunami-generating potential of a submarine earthquake may be increased if the severe shaking associated with it triggers one or more landslides. This is not uncommon, particularly if the quake is located in a subduction zone, such as anywhere around the Pacific Rim or in South-East Asia, where deep, steep-sided and unstable trenches mark the positions where one plate is sliding beneath another back into the Earth's interior. Like the quake itself, the collapse of a substantial volume of debris down the flanks of such a trench would impart a further blast of energy into the body of water above. Submarine landslides may also occur without the aid of initiating earthquakes, particularly where piles of unstable sediment have accumulated along the edges of subduction-zone trenches. They have also been recorded along the margins of the relatively shallow continental

The relationship between earthquake magnitude, tsunami magnitude and run-up heights devised for Japan.

Earthquake magnitude (Richter Scale)	Tsunami magnitude	Maximum run-up (metres)
6	-2	<0.3
6.5	-1	0.5–0.75
7	0	1–1.5
7.5	1	2–3
8	2	4–6
8.25	3	8–12
8.5	4	16–24
8.75	5	>32

shelves that surround much of the Atlantic shoreline of North America and Europe.

One of the most damaging aspects of tsunami lies in the fact that they rarely occur in isolation. The processes that result in their formation favour the generation of a number of waves, known as a *wave train*, that follow one after the other, often with little respite. Sometimes, such a wave train can consist of dozens of waves spread out over a period of 5 or 6 hours, within which the biggest and most destructive wave may be either one of the first to reach shore or hidden away well back in the wave sequence. Tsunami wave trains formed as a result of volcanic activity are less predictable than those formed by discrete events, such as single earthquakes or submarine landslides. This is because the caldera-collapse process, which involves the foundering beneath the sea of a volcanic island such as Krakatoa following a major eruption, can be a complex and drawn-out process, involving several tsunami-generating events taking place over a number of hours or days. Similarly, the characteristics of tsunami trains caused by volcanic landslides depend very much on the nature of the slide and whether, for example, it takes the form of a gigantic chunk of rock that slides into the sea without breaking up or an avalanche of pulverized and disaggregated rock.

Where do tsunami occur?

Because tsunami are particularly closely linked to earthquakes and volcanoes, they tend to be formed at plate boundaries, especially where one plate is being subducted beneath another or where two plates are scraping past one another. Most tsunami are produced around the margins of the Pacific Ocean, where various oceanic plates are being consumed beneath North and South America and Asia (see figure below). During the past 100 years alone, the lives of over 50,000 coastal residents in the circum-Pacific region have been lost to almost 400 tsunami. Most deaths, however, have resulted from localized tsunami, and only 20 or so tsunami have been sufficiently large to cause significant damage and loss of life at any great distance from their source.

The part of the Pacific most at risk from tsunami lies along the western margin of the ocean, from the Indonesian islands, up through the Philippines, Taiwan, and Japan, and into the Kamchatka Peninsula of easternmost Russia. Here, something like a quarter of all tsunami over the past century have been generated, the largest spreading out to batter

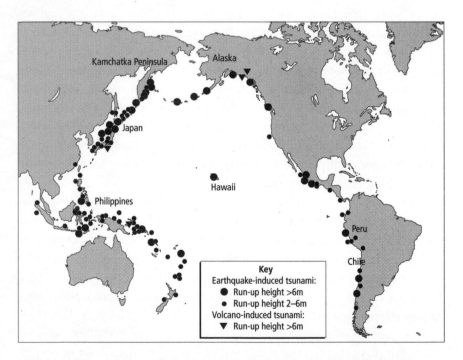

Most tsunami are generated by earthquakes around the Pacific rim. Here over 400 tsunami have taken over 50,000 lives during the twentieth century alone. (Source: Bryant, 1993)

much of the Pacific Rim. The most wide-ranging tsunami are produced either between Japan and Kamchatka, along the chain of islands known as the Aleutians, which trail off the end of Alaska, or along the coasts of southern Alaska and South America.

In terms of where tsunami hit rather than where they form, Japan and Hawaii are the two most vulnerable areas in the world, both being hit by about 20 per cent of all tsunami observed. The Hawaiian Islands are situated right in the middle of the Pacific and are battered not only by locally triggered tsunami but also by 85 per cent of all the tsunami generated in the Pacific basin. Japan is somewhat less exposed but is badly affected by locally generated tsunami. Over the last 1,200 years, more than 70 tsunami have been recorded in Japan, taking the lives of well over 100,000 people. Indeed, there is a possibility that this number of casualties may have been exceeded in 1703 alone by the arrival of a single devastating tsunami originating somewhere in the eastern Pacific. Honshu, the largest of the Japanese islands, is particularly vulnerable, and on average a 10m-high tsunami hits somewhere on the eastern coast of the island every decade.

In 1933 a huge magnitude 8.5 submarine earthquake off the north-eastern coast of Honshu produced a 25m wave, which pounded coastal communities along the Sanriku coast of eastern Honshu, the most tsunami-prone coastline in the world, killing over 3,000 people and destroying 5,000 homes. A little less than 40 years earlier, a tsunami triggered by a similar local quake killed nearly 30,000. One of the most terrifying Japanese tsunami was generated in 1792, when part of the flank of the Unzen volcano on Kyushu island collapsed into the sea without warning. Waves possibly up to 100m high devastated fishing villages along the nearby coast, claiming over 15,000 lives.

Chile and Peru are also particularly vulnerable to tsunami, most of which are generated by the many local, and often large, earthquakes that are an almost daily occurrence. The western coast of South America is also the source of many of the wide-ranging tsunami that affect the entire Pacific basin, and events such as the great Chilean quake of 1960 occur on average every quarter of a century, sending waves across the entire ocean to reach Japan a mere 22 hours later.

Compared with the Pacific, the Atlantic Ocean is virtually tsunami free, with only 2 per cent of all recorded tsunami occurring in the Atlantic basin. There are, however, two Atlantic tsunami worthy of note: one generated by the Lisbon quake in 1755 and another off the coast of Newfoundland, Canada, in 1929. Although also probably caused by an earthquake, the 1929 tsunami owed its existence primarily to a submarine landslide off the continental shelf, which also cut trans-Atlantic communication links on the sea-bed. While few destructive Atlantic tsunami are known from historic times, there is increasing evidence for gigantic waves having been generated during prehistory, and the next tsunami in the Atlantic basin may well be the most devastating ever experienced by modern society.

Because of its long history of civilization, the most complete record of tsunami relates to the eastern Mediterranean. Here, over 250 earthquakes since 450 BC have generated 80 or so tsunami, about 20 of which have been destructive, and areas of Greece in particular continue to be regularly damaged by tsunami generated by local earthquakes.

Movement and destructive power of tsunami

One of the most lethal characteristics of tsunami is the speed at which they travel. When a body of water is displaced by a sudden earthquake shock or by the rapid removal of part of the sea-bed, individual particles of water do not move much at all; they simply rise a metre or two vertically and then fall back again under the influence of gravity. This vertical motion is, however, rapidly taken up by adjacent particles, which form horizontally propagating waves that, in deep water, can travel at speeds in excess of 800km/hour. As a wave propagates, each individual water particle follows an elliptical path within a restricted volume of water, so a wave does not actually involve the transfer of water over large distances but only the transfer of energy.

The manner in which a wave or wave train moves in water can best be visualized by imagining two children holding between them a long skipping rope. If one child gives the rope a sharp flick, a wave will be generated that will travel rapidly to the other end. Individual molecules of the rope are not, however, moving from one end to the other, but are simply moving up and down in turn. Only the energy provided by the child's hand movement is being transferred.

Normal water-waves generated by the tides, currents or winds have a distance from crest to crest, known as the *wavelength*, that is usually less than 100m. Tsunami wavelengths, however, are often of the order of several hundred kilometres. Another parameter of a wave, which is useful in determining the threat they pose, is known as the *wave period*: the time taken for a single wavelength to pass a fixed point. Once again, tsunami periods are much greater than those that characterize normal waves: typically 30 minutes or more compared to only a few seconds.

For all types of wave, including water, there is a simple relationship between wavelength and wave period, and the speed of the wave. Thus, by knowing two of the parameters, the third can be calculated. This relationship can be expressed by the formula:

$$\text{wavelength} = \text{wave period} \times \text{wave speed}$$

Using this formula, it can be determined that a tsunami with a speed of 800km/hour, and a period of 0.5 hours will have a wavelength of 800 x 0.5, or 400km. Similarly, by adapting the formula a little, it can be determined that a tsunami with a wavelength of 200km and a period of 0.5 hours will travel at a speed of 200 ÷ 0.5, or 400km/hour.

As well as from its speed, much of the destructive power of a tsunami comes from its height, and taller waves are many times more destructive than their lower counterparts. Doubling the height of a tsunami will actually increase the energy available for destruction four-fold, while tripling it will increase the tsunami's energy nine times. The 15m waves that pounded the shores of Sumatra and Java during the 1883 explosion of Krakatoa would, therefore, have had four times the destructive power, all other things being equal, of the waves that hammered into the Hawaiian beach resort of Halape in 1975.

As well as wave height, wavelength is important in determining the destructiveness of a tsunami, and the energy of a tsunami can be calculated as follows:

$$\text{energy} = \text{wavelength} \times \text{wave height}^2$$

If the parameters of a normal wave and a tsunami wave are compared using this relationship then the enormous energy carried by the latter can be appreciated. A normal storm-wave with a wavelength of 100m and a height of 5m gives an energy value of 2,5000 (100 x 5^2). In contrast, a tsunami with a wavelength of 200,000m and a height of 10m results in an energy value of 2,00,000 (200,000 x 10^2). This means that the tsunami has 8,000 times more energy available for destruction than a wave generated on a stormy day at the seaside.

It should be pointed out, however, that factors other than wave height and wavelength also affect the destructiveness of a tsunami (see figure on p. 124). In particular, the width of the wave controls the length of coastline impacted by the wave, while the depth of the water and the precise form of the coastline are also crucial. Tsunami are particularly efficient at preserving the energy they contain as they travel further from their source. This energy is eventually dissipated as it is spread out over an increasingly larger area of ocean. As a tsunami approaches a coastline, however, its energy may become more concentrated once again, particularly where it is focused into bays, estuaries and harbours. As the wave becomes increasingly constrained by the coastal topography, and more and more water is crammed into a smaller and smaller space, so the wave will compensate by increasing in height.

The shallowing of the sea-bed as a tsunami approaches a coastline is also critical in determining its height and destructiveness when it finally hits land. Because water-waves travel faster in deep water than they do in shallow water, as a tsunami approaches land the leading part of the wave slows down before the rest, and the more rapidly moving part, which is still out in deeper water, begins to pile up on top of the slower wavefront. This results in a higher wave with a smaller wavelength. In the deep ocean, a tsunami may only be a metre or so high. It is also likely, however, to have a wavelength of 400km or thereabouts, and perhaps

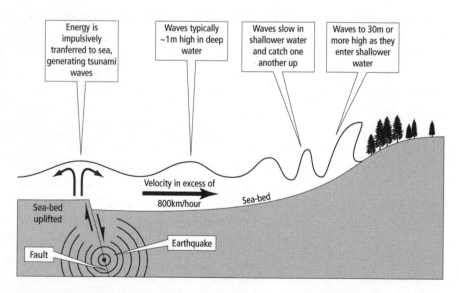

During a tsunamigenic earthquake, a large area of the sea-bed suddenly drops down or is uplifted, transmitting an enormous amount of energy to the water above. The tsunami formed are initially only a metre or two in height and travel through deep water at velocities in excess of 800km/hour. When they reach shallower water, however, the waves start to increase in height dramatically, sometimes reaching 30m or more on landfall.

a speed of 800km/hour, or 220m/second. Imagine what happens to the height of such a wave when it approaches the shallow water adjacent to a coastline. If the speed of the wave is reduced 10-fold to only 22m/second, then, as the faster-moving part of the wave from behind begins to pile up, the wavelength will shrink to little more than 30km while the height of the wave will increase to a terrifying 12m or so.

Most people who have never seen or experienced a tsunami have completely the wrong impression of the nature of the wave as it reaches land, mainly because they are familiar only with the ever-present breakers constantly crashing onto beaches around the world. Because a tsunami has such a long wavelength, it often hits the shore without 'breaking' at all and pours across the coastline as a wall of water that continues to flood in for tens of minutes or longer. Such behaviour characterized a lethal tsunami that devastated El Transito in Nicaragua, after an offshore earthquake in 1992. A series of tsunami up to 10m high struck at night, killing over 100, including many sleeping children, and leaving over 10,000 homeless. The death toll would have been much higher, however, had the water poured in as a violent, crashing breaker rather than as a great, slow-moving swell. Many people were washed hundreds of metres inland by the wave but managed to pull themselves up onto dry land or floating debris. The reason for this rather gentle wave-approach may have been that the tsunami-wave trough reached land first.

The withdrawal of the sea before the arrival of the tsunami crest itself can be spectacular, with the sea disappearing as far as the horizon, as if someone had pulled a plug in the ocean. Depending upon how well educated the population, such a phenomenon can prove either a godsend or a disaster. Populations trained to understand tsunami and the devastation they can cause will immediately recognize the withdrawal as a precursor to the imminent arrival of a tsunami and will take refuge away from the coast. In contrast, uninformed populations are much more likely to wander curiously out onto the exposed sea-bed, there to be wiped out by the returning sea.

Even gentle, trough-first tsunami arrivals are extremely destructive, and the enormous energy carried in the waves is sufficient to bulldoze all but the most sturdy of structures. The huge drag forces generated by tsunami literally pull buildings apart, while anything not securely fixed simply floats off. Strong currents within the waves can rapidly erode foundations, causing bridges and sea defences to collapse, while floating cars, boats and bits of buildings become battering rams that reinforce the direct destructive effects of the waves themselves. Following a magnitude 8 earthquake off the Pacific coast of Mexico in 1995, the currents associated with a 5m-high tsunami were powerful enough to erode away a large part of a concrete breakwater and to bring two old sunken ships to the surface. Each ship weighted around 200 tonnes and had lain buried 25m deep in sand for 10 years. Even more amazingly, the tsunami caused by a huge earthquake off southern Peru in 1868 carried the US warship *Wateree* 3km inland, where it was dumped unceremoniously at the base of the coastal mountain range. Too far from the sea to be refloated, the 235-man crew was picked up 3 weeks later by another US vessel. After being sold at auction, the ship became first a hotel, then a hospital and finally a warehouse, before being destroyed in the Peru-Chile war. Although drowning is, unsurprisingly, a common form of death resulting from a tsunami impact, much loss of life and injury results from victims being battered and crushed by floating debris.

Waves from the past

After these dramatic accounts of the devastation and terror instigated by a number of post-war tsunami – what of the past? Tsunami have always been with us and, being such memorable events, are often recorded, either accurately and scientifically, in the form of reliable written accounts, or in a vague or embellished manner in myth and legend.

As discussed in Chapter 1, the biblical story of Noah and the flood has been related by some to the catastrophic filling of the Black Sea by an overflowing Mediterranean some time after the end of the last Ice Age. Another Old Testament story involving water might also be rooted in fact, but this time in tsunami rather than flood. Around 1626 BC, the island of Thera, now known as Santorini, blew itself to pieces in one of the most violent volcanic explosions in the Mediterranean region. Although there is still much debate about how exactly it came about, it is suggested by some that the huge volcanic blast ultimately led to the demise of the rich and cultured Bronze Age Minoan civilization that prospered in the eastern Mediterranean at the time. Up to 20m of tephra and pyroclastic flows devastated Minoan settlements on Thera itself, while the main centre of Minoan culture on Crete appears to have been pounded by some of the biggest tsunami ever seen in the Mediterranean.

The quality of life of the Minoans was quite extraordinary for a people that walked the Earth over 1,500 years before Christ. Excavations near the village of Akrotiri, on Santorini, have exposed three- and four-storey houses with running water, toilets and wonderfully executed frescoes. Some aspects of the building construction even suggest that the Minoans were aware of earthquakes and how to build in order to minimize their impact. The absence of human remains in the Akrotiri excavations suggests that the population must have evacuated the island before the eruption became too serious, probably moving to Crete, which was only a day's journey by boat to the south.

When the great explosion came, however, Crete, a mere 100km distant, was to prove to be right in the firing line. The death throes of Santorini would have rumbled on like distant thunder for weeks, but the final earth-shattering explosion would have been heard all over Crete and, indeed, as far as 3,000km away. Reconstructions of what happened next suggest that the sea withdrew from the northern coast of Crete for as far as the eye could see, before returning, less than half an hour later, in a series of devastating waves that may have been up to 90m high. Unimaginable as such waves might sound, pumice blocks stranded up to 250m above current sea-levels may have been carried into place by waves two and a half times higher, which were focused by local coastal topography.

There is no question that such waves would have wiped out all coastal settlements – a terrible blow to a seafaring civilization such as the Minoans. Although Minoan maritime commerce continued after the cataclysm, it was never to dominate the eastern Mediterranean as it had before, and in only a few generations, Crete was invaded from the Greek mainland and the Mycenaeans quickly took the place of the failing Minoan civilization.

Like most mythologies, that of Greece also contains a flood story, which may be rooted in the destruction of Santorini and the devastation of the entire eastern Mediterranean coastline by giant tsunami. The Santorini cataclysm is also probably the source of the Atlantis legend recounted by Plato in his *Critias*, in which he describes a fabulous city that foundered and sank between the waves, never to be seen again.

An appealing link has also been proposed by some between the Santorini blast and the plagues of Egypt described in that part of the biblical Old Testament known as Exodus, particularly as current ideas suggest that the timing is just about right. The discovery of volcanic ash from the Santorini eruption in soils from the Nile delta has led some scholars and scientists to suggest that accounts in Exodus of 3 days of darkness in Egypt may, in fact, be describing heavy ash-fall over the countryside. Similarly the 'river of blood' referred to in the same book has been attributed to the presence of pink pumice from the eruption. Of all the descriptions in Exodus, however, the parting of the Red Sea is the most intriguing, and some have suggested that the phenomenon described could be explained in terms of a tsunami related to Santorini. Despite the fact that the Red Sea is not connected to the Mediterranean, the shock-wave generated by the Santorini blast may have caused the waters to oscillate back and forth – a phenomenon known as *seiching*. Such oscillations are often triggered by earthquakes, and the Krakatoa blast also appears to have set up the rhythmic sloshing back and forth of water bodies many thousands of kilometres away. It is not unreasonable to suggest that the Israelites may have made a crossing of the marshes at the narrow, northern end of the Red Sea at a time when seiching had caused the waters to withdraw southward. Later, when the water oscillated back again, the pursuing Egyptian troops were caught and swamped.

Written accounts, a little more up to date but still referring to the Mediterranean region, provide more incontrovertible evidence of devastating tsunami. In 479 BC, for example, the defenders of the Greek town of Potidea cheered as the attacking Persian army was inundated by an earthquake-generated tsunami that killed thousands. Over 800 years later, a great earthquake produced tsunami that appear to have struck the entire coastline of the Mediterranean, although little is known about the scale of destruction. Over 1,000 years later, in 1509, what is now Turkey bore the brunt of another earthquake-triggered tsunami that overtopped the city walls of Constinople and Galata.

Not quite 200 years after the drenching of Constantinople, the wrath of the sea was transferred half-way across the globe to the Caribbean. In June 1692 an earthquake struck Port Royal in Jamaica, causing much of the city, which was constructed on soft sediment, to slide into the sea. The mayhem was amplified by a tsunami that swept through the devastated town with such force that ships from the town's harbour were hurled bodily over two-storey buildings.

Only 8 years later, it was the turn of the northwestern coast of what is now North America, where a great earthquake generated a series of tsunami that still live on in the legends of the native American population (see

Chapter 4). Buried in peat layers along the coasts of British Columbia in Canada, and in Oregon and Washington in the USA, sheets of sand testify to a major tsunami that is thought to have been triggered by an earthquake of magnitude 8 or more in the Cascadia Subduction Zone not far offshore. It is estimated that, within 15 minutes of the quake, this entire coastline was inundated by tsunami 5m high, which are likely to have been focused in the many fjords to heights in excess of 15m. On the basis of accounts of the arrival of the tsunami in Japan 10 hours later, it is known that the last great Cascadia quake occurred on 27 January 1700. The next is awaited with considerable trepidation.

Little more than half a century later, the prosperous city of Lisbon in Portugal was to be shaken to the ground by one of the greatest earthquakes ever recorded in Europe, before being pounded by Atlantic tsunami that resulted in a substantial part of the ruined city being submerged. Lisbon was not the only place to suffer, and the southern Spanish port of Cadiz was also hit by waves up to 15m high. Tsunami of a similar height were also recorded on the island of Madeira in the northeastern Atlantic, and even by the time they reached the West Indies, the waves were 3–4m high. The tsunami were also recorded on tide-gauges around the coast of the UK, as the North Sea oscillated back and forth for a time in response to the great shock.

The great explosion of Krakatoa has already been discussed in terms of both the eruption itself and the devastating tsunami it generated (see p. 116 and figure on p. 130). The tsunami were so far ranging, however, that it is well worth saying a little more about them. The lives of the 36,000 victims of the waves generated when the volcano blew itself to bits on 27 August 1883 were taken within an hour of the blast. The tsunami did not stop there, however, but set course for more distant climes.

To the west, the waves crossed the Indian Ocean and rounded the Cape of Good Hope before heading north to the English Channel, which they reached 37 hours later, albeit so much reduced in height that they were detectable only by tide-gauges. The waves heading east crossed the Pacific and were detected off the coast of Central America and in San Francisco Bay. One of the most extraordinary features of the volcanic blast is that it generated waves in water masses that were not connected to one another, including bodies of inland water. Lake Taupo in the North Island of New Zealand, for example, was seen to oscillate by as much as 50cm or so in response to the atmospheric shock-wave generated by the climactic explosion.

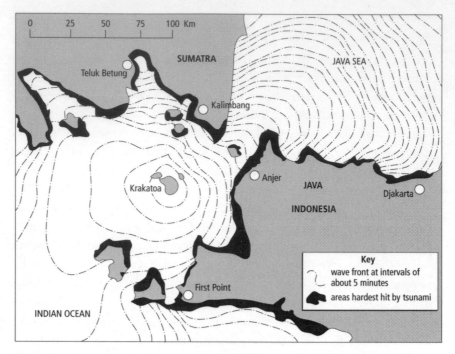

The destruction of the Krakatoa volcano in 1883 produced a series of tsunami up to 40m high, which devastated the neighbouring coasts of Sumatra and Java, killing 36,000 people. (Zebrowski, 1977)

Monitoring tsunami and minimizing their effects

Although three destructive tsunami occur every year on average, taking over 10,000 lives this century alone, there is no reason for them to lethal. Preventing destruction to property is difficult, if not impossible, particularly for large tsunami, but an efficient warning system combined with effective education of populations in tsunami-prone regions should minimize loss of life and injury. Because tsunami are constantly washing back and forth across the Pacific basin, it was here that the first tsunami warning system was established in 1948. Over 30 seismic-monitoring stations located around the Pacific Rim relay information on earth-quakes to a main warning centre at Honolulu in Hawaii. When an earthquake in excess of magnitude 7 occurs, tide-monitoring stations in the vicinity of the quake watch for anomalous wave activity that might point to the formation of a tsunami. If this is detected, a tsunami warning is issued. Unless there are unforeseen problems, all coastal communities thought to be at risk should receive the warning within an hour of the quake. This is perfectly adequate for threatened communities distant from the source to make plans for evacuation. For example, tsunami generated during a quake on the western coast of South America can take over 20 hours to reach the Japan on the other side of the ocean, while waves from a Japanese quake would take 10 hours or so to reach the western coast of the USA.

What, however, about those living close to a tsunami-triggering earthquake? As in the cases of the 1960 quake in Chile and the 1998 Aitape disaster in Papua New Guinea, communities close to the source can be devastated by tsunami within 10 or 15 minutes. To combat this problem, a number of regional tsunami warning systems, serving the most tsunami-prone areas, have also been established in the Pacific region. A regional warning system aims to issue a tsunami alert within minutes of a large earthquake to communities within 750km of the source. One of the most effective regional warning systems is that established by the Japanese Meteorological Agency in 1952. The Japanese service seeks to issue a tsunami warning less than 20 minutes after a tsunami-generating earthquake within 600km of the Japanese coast. The effectiveness of the service is supported by the large reduction in loss of life due to tsunami. In the 60 years before its launch, more than 4,000 Japanese had lost their lives to tsunami hitting the eastern coast. Since then, only a few hundred lives have been taken.

Despite such initiatives, however, many tsunami-prone areas in developing countries remain unprotected, especially from local earthquakes. In order to improve the situation, a satellite-based warning system is now undergoing test at Valparaiso on the coast of Chile, which can be hit by tsunami within a few minutes if a quake occurs in the subduction zone not far offshore. The Project Thrust (Tsunami Hazards Reduction Utilizing Systems Technology) system is triggered automatically by sensors that detect earthquake-induced ground-shaking and changes in sea-level in the region that might presage a tsunami. A warning is sent via the Geostationary Operational Environmental Satellite West (GOES) to the tsunami warning centre in Valparaiso within 3 minutes of a potentially threatening quake, triggering evacuation procedures that have already been set in place. Local earthquakes remain the big threat in terms of serious loss of life from tsunami, and until the Thrust system becomes generally available, earthquakes close to shore will continue to wreak havoc, particularly in the many island archipelagos scattered throughout the western Pacific.

In order to minimize as much as possible the impact of tsunami in such areas, education of the local population is critical. Simply instilling a reflex that links ground-shaking with the need to move away from the shore could save many lives. It remains difficult, however, to persuade people not to gather on the coast when the sea withdraws unexpectedly to the horizon. Following the 1964 Alaska earthquake, for example, over 10,000 people crowded the beaches of California to watch the anticipated tsunami, completely oblivious to the danger. Encouragement or incentives for people not to build too close to the sea would also help to reduce both damage to property and loss of life in the event of a tsunami. Unfortunately, trying to persuade communities who have relied for generations on the sea for their livelihood to move further inland will always prove very difficult.

In addition to warning and education, the Japanese have added a third string to their bow when it comes to minimizing the tsunami threat. Along the particularly tsunami-prone Sanriku coast of Honshu, giant concrete walls up to 16m high have been constructed to protect coastal cities from future major tsunami, such as that which took nearly 3,000 lives in 1933. Their effectiveness, together with that of the offshore breakwaters designed to disrupt tsunami before they reach land, has yet to be tested. Although the threat of everyday tsunami is now, at least to some extent, being tackled, nothing we do could prepare us for the gigantic waves that were generated during prehistoric times, nor for the great tsunami that await us in the future. Let us look at these in a little more detail.

Mega-tsunami, landslides and collapsing volcanoes

In 1958 a huge chunk of ice, broken off by a nearby earthquake, fell from a glacier into Lituya Bay in Alaska. The water displaced by the ice fall sent across the bay a huge tsunami that surged up the opposite side to a height of 490m – substantially higher than the World Trade Centre buildings in New York. However, although the height of the wave was impressive, it was too restricted in extent to have any effect outside the area. Imagine a wave on this sort of scale pouring into the English Channel or overwhelming the eastern coast of the USA and you will have some idea of how huge and potentially devastating really big tsunami can be. These *mega-tsunami* have three possible sources: a giant submarine landslide, the collapse into the sea of the flank of an island volcano or an asteroid or comet impact into an ocean (see Chapter 5). Let us concentrate on how giant landslides can trigger tsunami.

The Storegga Landslide

Around 10,000 years ago, as the Earth was warming up once again after over 60,000 years of ice, snow and bitter cold, sea-levels were rising at an incredibly rapid rate as fresh water from the melting ice sheets poured into the oceans. Around the margins of the continents, where sediment brought down by rivers accumulates on the edge of the steep continental slope leading down into the depths of the deep ocean, rising sea-levels were beginning to cause a problem. The weight of the added water, together with increased numbers of earthquakes caused by stresses resulting from the redistribution of gigantic volumes of water around the planet, was beginning to make the edge of the continental slopes around the Atlantic margin increasingly unstable. Inevitably, something had to give, and it did so off the coast of southern Norway about 7,000 years ago. Here a great chunk of the flat, shallow continental shelf collapsed, sending over 1,700km^3 of debris down the continental slope and into the depths of the North Atlantic.

The effect of this huge collapse, known as the *Storegga Landslide*, was to generate a tsunami wave train that headed west and south. It would have taken only a few hours at the most for the waves to reach northeastern Scotland 700km away, pouring over the region now occupied by the city of Aberdeen, the heart of the UK North Sea oil industry. Although it is not known exactly how large the waves were, they have left behind an impressive legacy in the form of a thick layer of marine sand within the peat bogs of northeastern Scotland. The sand body now rests 4m above sea-level, but this does not provide an accurate measure of the tsunami run-up because Scotland has been uplifted substantially since its load of ice was removed 10,000 years ago, and sea-levels now are also substantially higher than when the waves flooded inland. Little is known either about the extent of the tsunami generated by the Storegga collapse, although it would be surprising, given its scale, if its impact were restricted to northeastern Scotland. Northern England, and perhaps Denmark and the Netherlands, might also have been expected to feel the force of the waves.

Certainly, there can be little doubt that a similar event today would devastate oil production in the North Sea and perhaps also in the increasingly important area west of Shetland. Not only would coastal installations be affected, but pipelines could be severely damaged by sediments flowing along the sea-bed, causing a major environmental catastrophe. Although production and exploration platforms in deeper water might not even notice the passage of the tsunami, those located closer to shore might be severely affected or even destroyed.

Volcanic landslides of the Hawaiian Islands

If the Storegga Landslide makes you think about the tsunami threat, then the scale of the tsunami formed by the collapse of volcanic ocean islands might make you cower under the bedclothes. There are numerous chains of island volcanoes scattered across the face of the Earth, many of which remain active today. The Hawaiian island volcanoes in the Pacific basin are the biggest on the planet, and Mauna Kea, rising over 10,000m from the sea-bed, is the tallest mountain on the planet – over 1,000m higher than Everest. In the Atlantic, large active volcanic islands are concentrated in the east, where they cluster together to form the Canary, Azores and Cape Verde archipelagos.

Because volcanoes are such dynamic structures, they are constantly changing their form over time. As new lava flows are erupted, and fresh magma squeezes up from below and solidifies within, they tend to grow larger and larger. At the same time they become more and more unstable, because either their flanks become too steep to support them or the volcanoes become so heavy that gravity starts to make them sink and, at the same time, spread outward. In either case the end result is the same. The volcanoes begin to shed huge volumes of rock in the form of gigantic landslides, which may have volumes in excess of 1,000km³ and which can travel thousands of kilometres across the sea-bed.

Over the last few decades, both manned and unmanned submersibles have travelled back and forth through the sea that surrounds the Hawaiian Islands, using sonar and related techniques to slowly build up a detailed picture of the ocean floor. What has been revealed is quite extraordinary. The entire chain of islands sits among a great apron of debris that has been periodically divested by its constituent volcanoes over the past several tens of millions of years (see figure on p. 195) Although much of the debris is sediment eroded from the islands by rivers or wave action, a substantial portion goes to make up around 70 huge landslides, so large that some individual blocks within them are over 1km across.

Because the Hawaiian volcanoes are so large, they deform under their own weight, rather like a strawberry jelly when it is removed from

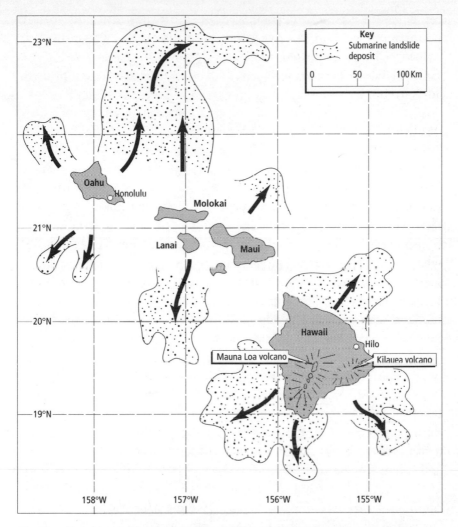

The Hawaiian volcanic islands are surrounded by submarine deposits, sometimes in excess of 1,000km³ in volume, formed from giant landslides. The last great collapse, which occurred around 100,000 years ago from the Mauna Loa volcano, generated a tsunami that may have approached 400m in height locally and remained destructive even on reaching Australia 7,000km away.

its mould. A Hawaiian volcano is so heavy that it causes the underlying oceanic crust to bend downward, so that each volcano is actually resting in a saucer-shaped depression. At the same time, the soft sediments toward the edge of the saucer on which each Hawaiian volcano sits are squeezed outward and upward by the weight of the volcano. The outer flanks of the volcano are destabilized by this 'spreading' beneath, and in response, large chunks periodically break off the main body of the volcano and slide up and over the rim of the saucer. This process is enhanced by the repeated emplacement of fresh magma within the volcano, which helps to push the destabilized flanks seaward prior to collapse.

At present there is not enough information to determine how frequently giant landslides are produced by the Hawaiian volcanoes, but most researchers believe that such an event occurs, on average, once every 25,000–100,000 years. The last well-documented collapse occurred just over 100,000 years ago, when up to 2,000km³ of rock slid into the sea from the southern flank of the Mauna Loa volcano; this should make us feel distinctly uncomfortable, considering the estimated return periods, The wave train generated by the entry into the sea of what is known as the *Alika Slide* was gigantic. On the island of Lanai, over 100km distant, coral-reef debris stranded far up on the coastal cliffs suggests that the wave run-up was 375m. Tsunami deposits identified on the southern coast of New South Wales in Australia indicate that, even here, after a journey of 7,000km, the waves had a run-up of 15m.

It takes little effort to imagine the mayhem that such a tsunami would cause should it occur today. With most of urban Hawaii concentrated on the coasts, the islands would almost certainly be devastated in less than an hour and, despite the Pacific Tsunami Warning System, with great loss of life. Four hours after the collapse the waves would hammer into California and the rest of the western coast of the USA, and barely 3 hours later the eastern coast of Japan would take the brunt of the huge wall of water. At a conservative estimate, loss of life would run into many millions, while damage running into trillions of US dollars would plunge the global economy into chaos.

Although we cannot make an accurate forecast about when the next great collapse will occur in the Hawaiian Islands, there is growing evidence that volcanic island collapses in general may be clustered in time. Like the numbers of large explosive eruptions, such events appear to correlate with times of rapidly changing sea-level. The two may in fact be connected, with collapses actually triggering eruptions by exposing the pressurized magma beneath. If we are not sure when the next great collapse in Hawaii will occur, we can, however, make a good guess as to where. On the southern coast of the Big Island of Hawaii, a great block of the very active Kilauea volcano is on the move. The block is now separated from the rest of the volcano by a series of faults and open fissures, along which the partially detached block slides periodically. This behaviour itself is a threat to the population of the island, and movement along one of the faults in 1975 caused the magnitude 7.2 earthquake that triggered the tsunami that rolled over the Halape beach resort (see p. 113).

Volcano collapses in the Canary Islands

It seems then that the Pacific is not the ideal place to open a beach hotel or even a Punch and Judy show. But what about the other major ocean basins? Have these experienced major tsunami due to volcanic landslides, and can we expect more to come? New research suggests that the answer to both questions is a resounding yes! Following the discovery of the Hawaiian landslides, similar undersea surveys were undertaken around the Canary Islands, off the coast of northwestern Africa, where enormous onshore rock amphitheatres, together with distinctly shaped coastlines, suggested that major landslides had taken place in prehistoric times. The Canary Island volcanoes are an order of magnitude smaller than their Hawaiian counterparts and, as a result of different styles of eruptive activity and the different chemistry of the magma, have much steeper flanks. There is little evidence that these volcanoes are heavy enough to bend the oceanic crust beneath them nor that they are becoming unstable due to spreading outward on layers of soft oceanic sediment. Instead, instability and eventual collapse are related to flanks that become too steep to support themselves and so slide off into the sea, in response to either an earthquake or an input of fresh magma.

Evidence for the unstable nature of the Canary Island volcanoes is everywhere. On the western island of La Palma, much of the great Taburiente volcano, which was active in the north of the island some 500,000 years ago, has now disappeared into the sea, leaving a spectacular cliff-bounded amphitheatre 10km across. Further south a new volcano has grown rapidly over the past 125,000 years, the western flank of which appears to be ready to collapse at any time. The form of the neighbouring island of El Hierro has been sculpted by three giant collapses, which have formed three great concave gulfs. El Golfo, on the northern side of the island, is a huge depression, over 20km across and surrounded on the landward side by towering cliffs up to 1km high. Imagery of the ocean floor to the northwest of El Golfo reveals a gigantic landslide, extending 80km from the island and containing blocks of rock 1km across. Although the age of the collapse is as yet not well constrained, it probably occurred sometime between 90,000 and 130,000 years ago. The volume of the landslide was probably something of the order of 100km^3, by no means as big as the Alika Slide on Hawaii but large enough to generate a highly destructive tsunami.

In fact, despite not being as large, the Canary Island landslides may be more efficient at producing large tsunami than their Hawaiian counterparts because of the way in which they enter the water. Although we have obviously never seen such a collapse in action, evidence for the behaviour of the Canary Island landslides is provided by a failed landslide on the eastern coast of El Hierro, which has recently been studied by Simon Day of University College London and Juan Carlos Carracedo of the Volcano Station of the Canaries. Here, a gigantic block of rock slid seaward for 300m along a fault known as the San Andres before grinding to a halt – what is known as an *aborted collapse*. Why the huge chunk of rock stopped before it hit the sea remains undetermined, although it could have been because the rock was too dry. Water is an excellent lubricant and makes landslides slide more easily. The San Andres fault, however, looks as if it contained little if any water and as if temperatures generated during the slide were so high that the rock actually melted along the fault surface. The aborted San Andres collapse is very important because it tells us that the Canary Island landslides move as great coherent blocks of rock. If they enter the sea in this way, they will prove far more effective at generating large tsunami than if they broke up as they moved and crashed into the ocean in the form of a disaggregated mass.

There is plenty of evidence for ancient collapses of the Canary Island volcanoes, but what about the mega-tsunami they would be expected to generate? Do we see evidence for these great waves? The answer once again is yes, both within the Canary Island archipelago and, most ominously, on the other side of the Atlantic. Very recently Simon Day and Juan Carlos Carracedo have successfully scoured the islands looking for ancient tsunami deposits. On both Gran Canaria and Fuerteventura they have come across deposits of wave-rounded pebbles together with seashells. These are just the sort of things you might expect to be lying about on a beach, but these are resting up to 100m above current sea-level. As there is no evidence that these islands have been uplifted, the deposits can have been emplaced only by giant tsunami. In fact, the run-ups of these waves might have been even greater. The shells contained within the deposits appear to reflect colder water conditions than those that currently exist around the Canary Islands, suggesting that they were emplaced during the Ice Age, when sea-levels were even lower. The tsunami that surged up the flanks of Gran Canaria and Fuerteventura were generated by collapses somewhere in the Canary archipelago, although so far there is insufficient evidence to link their formation to any particular collapses. Nevertheless, the deposits do provide a useful guide to the scale of the tsunami produced by past giant landslides in the Canaries.

Clearly waves of this size would not be confined to the archipelago but would spread further afield, potentially threatening both sides of the Atlantic. Only recently, evidence has come to light that gigantic waves coming from the east have smashed into the Bahamas. On the Bahamian island of Eleuthera, boulders of coral limestone as big as houses and weighing thousands of tonnes have been stranded 20m above sea-level and up to 500m inland. The only way they could have got there is by being physically catapulted onto the island by a great wave, or waves, bigger than any storm-waves that we see today. Right across the Bahamas archipelago, the same waves were responsible for piling up sand into gigantic wedges several kilometres long and up to 25m high.

Although it has been proposed that unprecedented storm-waves, generated when the climate was deteriorating around 120,000 years ago, were responsible for the sand wedges and the boulders, another cause is possible. We may be seeing here the first evidence on the western side of the Atlantic for giant tsunami formed when one of the Canary Island volcanoes collapsed into the sea. In fact, the estimated ages of Bahamian features match quite well the probable timing of the El Golfo collapse on the island of El Hierro, when around 100km³ of rock piled into the sea in minutes. The tsunami wave train produced by the collapse would have hurtled across the Atlantic to smash into the Bahamas around 8 hours later and into the Florida coastline barely 20 minutes after that.

★ ★ ★

Imagine the devastation that such an event would cause today, not only in the Caribbean but also along the entire eastern coast of the USA. Well, perhaps imagination will not be required for long, because the western flank of the Cumbre Vieja volcano on the Canary Island of La Palma started to slide seaward a mere 50 years ago. Let us look at what might happen when it finally crashes into the sea.

The great Atlantic tsunami, AD 2011

• *The inhabitants of the western Canary Island of La Palma woke with a shock this morning when two strong earthquakes rocked the island during the early hours.* Registering 5.3 and 5.6 on the Richter Scale, the quakes caused slight damage to buildings in El Paso, Fuencaliente, and some villages in the south of the island, but no casualties are reported. One of the tele-scopes at the island's international astronomical observatory has developed alignment problems as a result of the ground shaking, but otherwise it is business as usual for the astronomers.

Seismologists estimate the depths of the quakes, which were separated by 35 minutes, at around 10km and locate them directly beneath the active Cumbre Vieja volcano. Following eruptions in 1949 and 1971, the volcano has been quiet, although deep earthquake swarms in 2004 and 2009 have been interpreted by some scientists as reflecting the rise of fresh magma beneath the volcano.

The mayor of Santa Cruz, the largest town on the island, has asked citizens not to panic and has moved to quash rumours that the earthquakes might trigger an eruption of the volcano. Staff at the La Palma Volcano Observatory, based at Santa Cruz, are continuing to monitor the situation, but confirm that at present there is absolutely no evidence for an impending eruption.

Translated from *El Pais*, 3 September 2011.

The Canary Island volcano

The Cumbre Vieja volcano on the island of La Palma first popped its head above the waves around 125,000 years ago. Since then it has grown rapidly to form a 20km-long, ridge-shaped volcano, the summit of which now towers 2km above sea-level and an impressive 6km above the sea-bed. This makes it almost three-quarters of the height of Mount Everest. As the exposed part of the volcano is not much more than 15km across at its widest, it is not difficult to work out that it must be very steep sided, and the flanks slope at over 30 degrees in places. As we know from the common occurrence of landslides all over the world, steep slopes often do not last long, but quickly succumb to gravity and collapse. Steep slopes on volcanoes are, in fact, even more unstable than their counterparts elsewhere, for example along man-made road cuttings or the steep sides of river valleys. This is because gravity is not the only force conspiring to reduce the angles of such slopes.

Fresh magma pushing up into a volcano can also cause its flanks to bulge outward, making them more liable to collapse, while earthquakes accompanying the rise of magma can shake the ground with sufficient force to cause it to break away and slide downslope; this is exactly what triggered the Mount St Helens eruption in 1980. Fresh molten magma may also cause a steep slope to collapse by heating up any water contained within voids and cavities in the rock, causing it to expand and put pressure on its surroundings. If the slope is sufficiently unstable, this extra pressure could be just sufficient to start it to slide. The tendency for steep-sided volcanoes to collapse is also increased by their structure, which often consists of strong lava flows separated by softer and weaker layers of volcanic ash. When stresses are applied to the slope, by either an influx of new magma or gravity, the weaker ash layers can provide ready-made surfaces along which a landslide can form.

The Cumbre Vieja has been one of the fastest growing volcanoes on the planet over the last 10,000 years, and it remains very active. Although sleeping at the moment, it has already erupted twice this century, in 1949 and 1971, and renewed activity can be expected at any time. The last time magma reached the surface, it produced some spectacular lava fountains and flows in the extreme south of the island, but posed little threat to all but a few of the local inhabitants and none to the long-term stability of the volcano. The 1949 eruption was, however, a different matter. In February of that year, the island was shaken by a series of earth tremors that continued into March, when a strong earthquake in the south of the Island damaged the local lighthouse. More quakes followed in the middle of June, related to rising magma that eventually blasted its way to the surface at the end of the month. Ash and blocks continued to be hurled into the sky for the next week or so, before strong earthquakes returned, accompanied by the tearing open of the ground surface near the summit.

When the Spanish seismologist Bonelli Rubio visited the eruption site on 6 July 1949, he was amazed to find that the western flank of the volcano had dropped seaward by as much as 4m along a 3km-long system of gaping fractures. Although the volcano continued to erupt lava and ash until the end of July, the fractures that opened at the beginning of the month did not appear to have grown in size. In retrospect, this is just as well, because scientists now think that the appearanceof the fractures marked the first sign that the entire western flank was beginning to collapse. The western flank of the Cumbre Vieja volcano is now recognized as the newest giant volcanic landslide in the world. A 200km³ chunk of rock, the size of Greater London, is poised precariously above the Atlantic Ocean. In 1949 it slid 4m, although, during the 1971 eruption, it remained ominously static. Next time molten magma bursts to the surface of this sleepy and picturesque island, the whole world may have to sit up and take notice.

Build-up to eruption

The earthquakes that shocked the residents of La Palma during the early hours of 3 September 2011 also had the scientists at the La Palma Volcano Observatory (LPVO) privately worried. The pattern of earthquakes was beginning to look suspiciously similar to that which preceded the last but one eruption of the Cumbre Vieja in 1949, and although they were sure that an eruption was not 'imminent' in the true sense of the word, if the quakes were related to magma breaking through the crust deep down, something unpleasant could certainly happen within a few months. They were not entirely surprised; after all, eruptions of the volcano did tend to occur in clusters, and there had been four eruptions between 1585 and 1712. Therefore another one soon – what would be the third in 60 years or so – would not be unexpected.

Apart from the quakes, however, no other signs of activity had been detected, although it must be said that the volcano was not the most comprehensively monitored on the planet. The surveillance situation was, however, a considerable improvement on the late 1990s, when the continued movement of the western flank landslide was confirmed and the regional and national governments began to sit up and take notice. Then there had been no seismic monitoring at all, just a once-a-year global positioning system (GPS) survey to look for swelling associated with the rise of fresh magma into the volcano or an acceleration in the rate of sliding of the western flank. Now the LPVO scientists had five seismographs, not the highest of high-tech but sufficient to record any quakes and to pinpoint them with some degree of accuracy. Furthermore, a new network of six continuously recording GPS receivers allowed them to monitor in real time even the tiny movements of the ground surface that might foretell of a new body of rising magma. They were not too worried about the unstable western flank at the moment, because this had been sliding slowly and consistently seaward by about a centimetre a year ever since observations began in 1994, and it seemed that, without the impetus of fresh magma, it was liable to continue this slow creep downslope. The question was: what would it do in a few months if new magma did burst to the surface?

By the end of October, the civil authorities and the local population had largely put the quakes of the previous months out of their minds, particularly with the terrible weather to talk about. Normally in October, La Palma basked in warm, dry sunshine, perhaps with the very occasional rainy day thrown in, just to keep the vines happy and the island green. This year, however, the island had been battered almost continuously by gales piling in from the Atlantic. Over 40cm of rain had fallen in the past 12 days, and a continuous, brooding layer of thick stratus cloud had kept both astronomers and volcanologists inside, beavering away at their writing and catching up on their journals. Flash floods had caused considerable damage to a number of small villages at the mouths of valleys, including Tazacorte on the western coast, whose seafront restaurants had also suffered badly, with two being carried off into the raging Atlantic by crashing breakers. On the dull, drizzly evening of 1 November, All Saints Day, the churches of the island were packed with worshippers when the ground was wrenched from beneath them; many struggled to stand and run for the exits but the shaking stopped almost as quickly as it had begun. A few minutes later, however, the ground shook again, less violently this time, and continued to do so periodically until the early hours of the next morning.

At the LPVO the first shock registered with a magnitude of just over 5 on the Richter Scale, while the rest were between 2.5 and 4. The scientists were deeply worried; this was clearly a seismic swarm and, at around 5km depth, it was considerably shallower than the two discrete quakes of the previous month. It was impossible to keep the facts from the local population any longer, and the scientists and civil authorities acted swiftly to quash rumours and prevent panic. A level 1 alert was called, indicating to the islanders that increased levels of seismic unrest were being recorded, as if they did not already know. Barely a week later, scientists' worries were confirmed as two of the continuously recording GPS receivers began to pick up the first signs of deformation of the ground surface over the central ridge of the Cumbre Vieja. The receiver near the village of Jedey on the western flank had moved over a centimetre with respect to another located on the eastern side of the island. What exactly did this mean? Was it a result of the swelling of the volcano as new magma rose within, or did it mean that finally the giant landslide on the western flank was about to crash into the sea? Without further data it was impossible to say. By the second week of November, the situation was clearer. Instruments in the north and south of the island were also recording changes, which showed that all the GPS receivers were moving away from one another, like dots marked with a pen on an inflating balloon. The volcano was swelling with magma and it looked as if another eruption was on its way, perhaps within weeks, but almost certainly within months. The western flank remained static, but what it would do when the eruption started was quite another matter.

The new GPS results led to the alert level being raised to 2, indicating a moderate level of deformation and seismic activity caused by the rise of fresh magma. Earthquake swarms continued to strike the island throughout the month, most at depths of only 4 or 5km, within the volcano itself. At the same time, the rate of deformation recorded by the GPS receivers accelerated, showing that the volcano had expanded by around 10cm in an east–west direction and risen by around 6cm. By late November, forest workers, who were still allowed into the summit region, reported increasing numbers of dead birds, indicating that carbon dioxide and other noxious gases were beginning to work their way through to the surface in increasing amounts, a sure sign that magma would not be far behind.

On 1 December, concerned representatives of the Canary Island and national governments held a meeting in the island's capital, Santa Cruz, with the volcanologists from Spain and the UK who were most involved in the monitoring effort. Also present were the island's civil authorities and representatives from those towns most likely to be affected. Because of the potential threat to its eastern coast, should the forthcoming eruption cause the western flank of the Cumbre Vieja to crash into the sea, the US government had also sent representatives, in the form of scientific experts on landslides and tsunami generation. The meeting was a disaster. Although the scientists were able to convince the Spanish authorities that an eruption was likely, probably within the next few weeks, the authorities refused point blank to accept the possibility that the western half of the island could vanish beneath the waves as a result. With elections coming up, the island's authorities in particular were keen not to ruffle any feathers, refusing even to consider an evacuation plan for coastal areas should an eruption start.

Although few of the local population had been alive during the 1949 eruption, several remembered queuing up to watch the 'fireworks' near the southern town of Fuencaliente 40 years earlier and failed to see how such a spectacular but essentially harmless display could result in their wonderful island falling into the sea. In contrast, the US scientists were rightly worried, returning to Washington to report their concerns to the President's scientific advisor. Despite warning of the dire consequences for the USA of an eruption triggering the instantaneous entry into the North Atlantic of 200km³ of rock, their words fell on deaf ears. The start, early the following month, of the House of Representatives inquiry into the Space Station *Alpha* disaster had concentrated the minds of the presidential advisor and his team wonderfully – but sadly not on a rumbling Spanish volcano on the other side of 'the pond'.

The first half of November saw the return of the storms, with the northern and western coasts of La Palma taking a battering once again from winds of over 100km/hour and the island being drenched in deluge after deluge. Mudflows poured down several of the steep-sided valleys, locally known as *barrancos*, which drained the Cumbre Vieja. Still the volcano continued to swell like a huge bubble, while the cracking of rock caused by the rising magma jiggled the traces on the observatory's seismographs every few hours. As a soggy Christmas Eve dawned, a series of moderate earthquakes began to shake the southern part of the island, from Fuencaliente in the south to Los Llanos in the north. This time, however, they did not stop, but rumbled on and off for over 15 minutes. This is what the LPVO staff had been waiting for. On their seismographs the quakes looked different: they did not show the sharply defined trace of the tectonic earthquake associated with magma breaking rock as it forced its way upward. The traces produced by these quakes lasted much longer and were more akin to the signals that might be caused at a roadside café by a passing truck. There was no doubt that the seismographs were detecting volcanic tremors caused by magma surging its way through an open fracture. Within hours it would reach the surface. On the advice of the LPVO, the authorities issue a level 4 alert: eruption expected within 24 hours.

Eruption

As the volcanic tremors started, so all the GPS receivers showed a change in the deformation pattern. As the magma was released from its reservoir deep down, the volcano started to collapse like a deflating balloon, bringing all the GPS stations closer together. High on the slopes of the Cumbre Vieja, however, tilt-meters buried in the ground showed that the summit ridge was beginning to expand near its highest point, close to the crater Hoyo Negro. As the skies darkened and the citizens of Los Llanos began to light Christmas candles in their windows, a much brighter glow flared above the silhouette of the Cumbre Vieja ridge as a new fissure spewed forth a rain of ash and chunks of rock over 1m across. The ground shook as the new magma blasted a path for itself through the solidified lava of older eruptions, before bursting through to form a 1km-high fountain of red molten rock.

• *And now over to Greg on that new volcano that's spouting forth on that little island out there in the eastern Atlantic – what's it called again? Las Palmas? La Palma – that's the one. What's the latest then Greg? Looks like a pretty spectacular firework display we can see over your left shoulder there.*

Sure Jim – it's just like the fourth of July here at the moment – apart from the fact that it's early January. The volcano has been going hard at it now for about 3 weeks, and there are six new active craters strung out all along the ridge you can see behind me. The eruption looks pretty spectacular but it is little more than a firecracker compared to the big eruption of Vesuvius

8 years ago. If you remember, that dumped tonnes of ash on Naples and over 1,000 lives were lost in the chaos of the evacuation. Most of the debris being hurled out here is confined to the upper part of the volcano, although some ash has fallen on nearby towns. Just over a week ago lava began to issue from one of the craters and head eastward toward the airport, but it looks as if it has stopped flowing now. In fact, things do seem to be calming down a little, and there is certainly not as much activity as there was only a few days ago.

What's this stuff we hear about the side of the volcano collapsing into the sea and sending a tidal wave headed our way? Is there anything in this?

Well yes, Jim, there is. In 1949 the whole western side of the volcano, an area bigger than Staten Island, started to slide toward the Atlantic but then stopped. Scientists at the volcano observatory here are very concerned that this eruption might send the whole caboodle into the sea. According to the observatory staff, the way this might happen is if the molten magma heats up the subsurface water, and there is certainly plenty of that here after an extremely wet autumn. The expansion of the water, if and when this happens, might just provide the extra shove needed to get this gigantic chunk of rock moving. And believe me, if it starts it is difficult to see anything stopping it.

Sounds pretty scary. So what are the authorities doing about it Greg?

As far as I know, surprisingly little. Since it was recognized in the mid-1990s that the western flank of the volcano was unstable, they have pretty much ignored warnings from the scientists. Since then they have even built a 2,000-bed tourist complex and a golf course on it.

They clearly don't seem too concerned then Greg, but what about over here on this side of the pond. Should we start to pack our bags and head for the hills?

Well, some scientists, including some pretty eminent US guys I should point out, think perhaps that we should. Apparently these giant volcanic landslides are pretty common on a geological time-scale and this one seems to be ready to go. Mind you, as I said earlier, things do seem to be quieting down now, so perhaps we have got away with it this time.

OK Greg, that's all we have time for now. Thanks for getting us up to speed on the situation over there and let's hope viewers that we don't get our feet wet tonight.

Transcript from a CNN evening news bulletin, 13 January 2012.

As well as keeping an eye on the activity over the previous 3 weeks, Spanish and UK scientists had also been regularly sampling the material ejected at the active craters, and they were not pleased by what they found. Although the spectacular red fountains of lava captured all the attention of the television cameras, most of the ejecta consisted of fine ash of a particular type. This *phreatic* ash was a characteristic result of magma bursting through wet soil and rock, and it told the scientists that, after the deluges of the previous few months, the volcano was in a pretty soggy state. They crossed their fingers and hoped that the water pressures generated by magmatic heating would not be sufficient to set the western flank moving again.

By 18 January, activity at the new craters had stopped and crowds of locals were already strolling up the Ruta de los Volcanes to have a closer look. Things were clearly not over yet, however, and now that the tremors associated with the eruption had stopped shaking the seismographs and GPS receivers, it was possible to get a clearer picture of what else was going on beneath the surface. The LPVO scientists were shocked by what they saw. A couple of kilometres down, beneath the western flank of the volcano, dozens of small earthquakes were spread over a huge area, from the tip of the island in the south to beyond Los Llanos in the north. At mid-morning the next day, the biggest quakes yet shook the south, bringing down buildings, cracking roads and walls and fracturing gas mains. Two older inhabitants of the village of Jedey were killed in their beds by falling masonry, and a third died of heart seizure.

More importantly, a helicopter flyover by LPVO scientists revealed that new gaping fractures had opened up along the summit ridge, stretching for 6km and linking up with those formed in 1949. The western flank was on the move again, a fact confirmed by the GPS receivers, which showed that the strong quakes were associated with the entire side of the volcano dropping by 2m and jolting 40cm toward the Atlantic. Furthermore, the movement was continuing, with the receivers to the west of the newly opened fractures creeping away from those to the east by 1cm/hour. A brief helicopter visit to the fractures revealed fresh water bubbling upward at several locations, indicating that the water in the rock was under such enormous pressures that it was being forced to the surface. It was clear now that this same water pressure was also levering the western flank away from the rest of the volcano like a huge wedge.

The situation was now desperate, and the whole side of the volcano could collapse within hours. The LPVO issued an urgent e-mail warning to the local authorities, the Canary Island and national governments, and the presidential office in Washington. The message stressed the reactivation of the western flank landslide and the possibility of imminent failure of the slope and the formation of major tsunami throughout the Atlantic basin. It fell largely on deaf ears. By mid-afternoon, the seaward movement of the western flank was beginning to accelerate, first to 3cm/hour, then to 10cm/hour. A second desperate plea from the scientists at 4.30p.m. elicited a response from the island's government, who issued radio advice suggesting that those living on the western side of the island should head north and east. A general warning advised all islanders to make for high ground, preferably above 500m. The response of the population was slow, because many were at work in the open and out of range of a radio, but by 7.00p.m. there was a steady, if leisurely, exodus to safer areas. By the time the bureaucratic machinations on the other islands had resulted in an appropriate response to the crisis it was after 11.00p.m., and the warnings to head for higher ground were not issued until after midnight. On the Spanish mainland and in Washington there was no response until 1.00a.m. on the following day – too late – while the populations of North Africa and the Caribbean remained blissfully unaware of the threat.

Collapse

At just after 1.00a.m. the western flank of the Cumbre Vieja volcano decided enough was enough and headed for the sea. With a sound like tearing cloth, the fractures along the summit ridge began to snake north and south five times faster than the quickest sprinter. At the same time, the land surface to the west of the fractures began to subside, scraping against the rock making up the rest of the volcano. The terrible screeching as the two rock masses tore past one another was like a billion fingers scraping across a similar number of blackboards, and all over the island terrified men, women, and children froze with fear or buried their heads beneath their pillows to ward off the infernal noise.

Within minutes the fractures along the summit ridge had merged to form a gigantic line of cliffs 15km in length. As the western flank continued to sink, the cliffs grew taller and taller – 10m, 50m, 100m – and more. Great chunks of soil and rock, together with thousands of fully grown trees, tumbled down the growing escarpment and thundered onward down the moving flank, as if trying to race it to the ocean. The juddering passage of the gigantic block of rock shook the surface this way and that, levelling every building within minutes and chopping the roads into a million separate pieces.

Opposite: **Sketches of the Cumbre Vieja volcano (a) as it is now and (b) after a future collapse. The removal of around 200km³ of rock will leave a concave depression some 20km across surrounded by cliffs up to 2km high.** (Source: Simon Day, University College London)

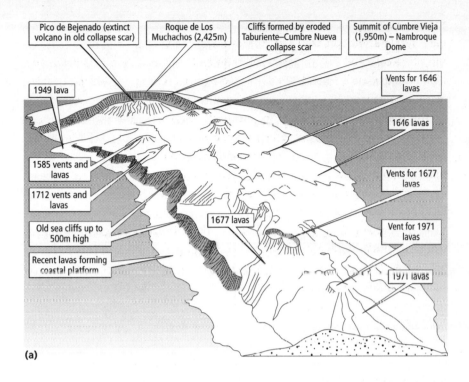

Pico de Bejenado (extinct volcano in old collapse scar)

Roque de Los Muchachos (2,425m)

Cliffs formed by eroded Taburiente–Cumbre Nueva collapse scar

Summit of Cumbre Vieja (1,950m) – Nambroque Dome

Vents for 1646 lavas

1646 lavas

1949 lava

1585 vents and lavas

1712 vents and lavas

Old sea cliffs up to 500m high

Recent lavas forming coastal platform

1677 lavas

Vents for 1677 lavas

Vent for 1971 lavas

1971 lavas

(a)

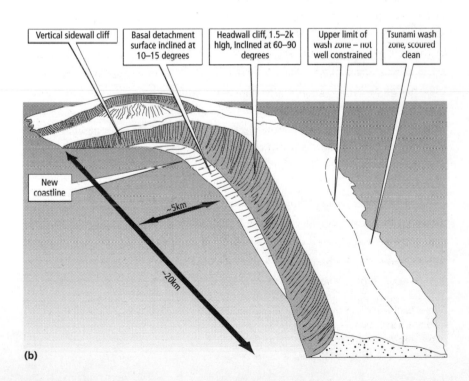

Vertical sidewall cliff

Basal detachment surface inclined at 10–15 degrees

Headwall cliff, 1.5–2k high, inclined at 60–90 degrees

Upper limit of wash zone – not well constrained

Tsunami wash zone, scoured clean

New coastline

~5km

~20km

(b)

Any who had remained in their homes were crushed and buried instantly, with no hope of escape or rescue, while those still heading north were battered to the ground – condemned to slide beneath the waves with their beloved neighbourhood. At the foot of the great sliding block, the sea surged and boiled, smashing boats like matchwood and drowning the many little beach restaurants. Two minutes after the collapse started, a third of the western side of the volcano had disappeared beneath the tumbling waves, hurling the sea back and leaving behind a wall of rock 700m high and over 15km long. In places the rock face glowed bright red where the friction caused by the rock masses scraping against one another had turned it to magma. Great blasts of steam exploded from the cliffs where groundwater and hot rock came into contact, while clouds of dust from hundreds of landslides increasingly obscured the view.

Suddenly a report like the loudest and longest gunshot ever heard echoed across the island as the gigantic moving slab split in two along its length. Another huge cliff formed, parallel to the first but 0.5km beneath it, and more terrible screeching ensued as the lower block accelerated seaward and smashed into the ocean within barely 30 seconds. As the Atlantic tried to wash into the newly formed bay, the upper block crashed into the boiling surf, sending the waters out again. Finally the western flank of the Cumbre Vieja was gone. The great blocks of rock continued to tumble down the side of the island beneath the waves, breaking up as they went and hammering into the sea-bed, 6km down, barely 15 minutes after the break-up of the volcano started. The waters could now at last pour into the great curving bay, surging 500m up the newly formed 2km-high cliffs before hurtling out to sea again: eastward to North America and the Caribbean, north and south around the island toward the rest of the archipelago, and on to southern Europe and North Africa. On La Palma thousands had died within minutes in the great collapse and its accompanying earthquakes, but the worst horrors were yet to come.

Wipe-out

As though a giant had hurled a massive rock into the sea just off the coast of the island, huge tsunami radiated out in all directions. Heading north and south, waves 100m high scoured the entire western coast of all signs of human habitation before colliding on the opposite side of the island to devastate Santa Cruz. Southward to El Hierro and eastward to La Gomera, Tenerife and beyond, the deadly waves caught thousands of refugees on their way to higher ground. In the vast coastal tourist ghettos of Tenerife and Gran Canaria, bemused and intoxicated British and German visitors were crushed and battered in the ruins of the many bars and clubs whose owners refused to heed the call to close.

Barely 1½ hours later, the tsunami, travelling as fast as a jumbo jet, trashed the Moroccan cities of Casablanca and Rabat and sped northward to the Iberian Peninsula. Just 2½ hours after the collapse, the waves were focused in the Strait of Gibraltar to form towering columns of water almost 100m high, devastating Tangier and surging around the base of the Rock in a boiling maelstrom of wreckage and human remains. The harbour area of Cadiz went the same way minutes later, while further north, a 60m-high tsunami attempted to emulate the destruction wrought in Lisbon by the great quake-generated tsunami of 1755.

Meanwhile, the bulk of the energy produced by the collapse of the Cumbre Vieja volcano headed westward in the form of a dozen huge tsunami. In the deep water of the North Atlantic they rocketed westward unimpeded and detectable only as a slight swell. The nuclear submarine USS *Colin Powell*, heading home from the Mediterranean 1,000km north of the Canary Islands, picked up the sound of the landslide on its sonar, but the tsunami passed by unnoticed. By 1.45a.m., news of the collapse had reached Washington and the US government realized it had a catastrophe on its hands. The first waves would hit the coast of New England in barely 6½ hours – simply not enough time to mount any effective evacuation. A heated argument about whether it would be better not to warn the public at all, the idea being that more people might be killed in the ensuing panic than by the tsunami, was quickly squashed by the President, who announced that a warning must go out – and now.

Within 15 minutes, all radio and television stations along the eastern coast continually broadcast the simple message: 'Move as far as possible from the coast and head for high ground if possible. If this is not feasible seek shelter in high-rise buildings at least 10km from the sea.' Although most of the inhabitants of the east-coast towns and cities were deep in slumber, most were awakened within the hour by National Guardsmen with loud-hailers. As expected, panic ensued within minutes as desperate people grabbed what they could, piled into their cars and headed inland. By 3.00a.m. the roads of every major city on the eastern seaboard were gridlocked as tens of millions of terrified Americans fought tooth and nail to find safety. By 4.30a.m. the situation was little changed, and the streets were packed with millions trudging on foot away from the menace of the sea. Many of the inhabitants of high-rise condominiums had barricaded themselves inside, prepared to defend their homes and families to the death against desperate outsiders seeking safety from the coming waves.

In the heart of the North Atlantic the Azores had already taken a battering, and by 7.30a.m. the waves crashed with incredible force on the rich-man's retreat of Bermuda. The capital, Hamilton, was devastated as marinas and expensive waterfront villas were obliterated and debris was hurled across the islands by waves up to 50m high. A few minutes later, Barbados got the same treatment, rapidly followed by the string of exotic islands known as the Lesser Antilles and then Puerto Rico. Warnings from Spain and the USA had led to some evacuation of coastal areas, but tens of thousands, who either missed or ignored the warnings, drowned within minutes as wave after wave swamped the coastlines and headed inland for several kilometres. In the thousands of low-lying islands that made up the Bahamas archipelago, terror reigned. There was no high ground to escape to, and by 8.00a.m. the sea-level around the islands had already starting to drop as the waters poured eastward. As the sea shallowed dramatically over the plateau of limestone on which the Bahamas were built, the eastward-pouring waters fed huge waves that began to flood across the southern and easternmost islands by 8.30a.m. With nowhere to hide, there were few survivors, and many islands, some only a few metres above sea-level, were scoured of all human life.

Tsunami experts, dragged from their beds in the middle of the night, informed the US President that the waves might be big enough to start to break hundreds of kilometres off the eastern coast, where the deep ocean shallowed to only 100m or so, thereby losing much of their energy and destructive power. However, this forecast was to prove far too optimistic, and most of the waves sped across the edge of the continental shelf with little impediment. It was rush-hour in the coastal cities of the eastern USA, but today nobody was going anywhere, not in an automobile that is. Since 7.00a.m. the sea had been retreating all along the coastline, exposing vast expanses of sand and mud all the way to the horizon. Those in the highest buildings in Portland, Maine, had a tremendous view of a waterless North Atlantic and the thin silvery streak along the horizon that marked the end of their city. The silver strand grew rapidly, soon making itself known as the first of the dozen devastating tsunami. The first wave, 30m high, blasted across the seafront with the force of an explosion, instantaneously reducing all buildings to rubble, before pouring into the city centre to catch those unfortunates still trying to reach safety. Over the next 90 minutes another 11 waves pounded into the city, leaving little more than a gigantic mess of debris and bodies when the sea returned to normality.

All down the coast the same thing was happening, and millions caught in the open or watching from vantage points in tall buildings, screamed with utter terror as the raging torrents poured inland, obliterating everything in their paths. New York was particularly badly hit as wave after wave was focused into the confined bays and narrows. The Empire State building survived – battered but proud – but little remained of the UN, while much of Wall Street was a wreck. In the aftermath, fires raged across Staten Island after refineries succumbed to the irresistible battering of the waves. Washington, Baltimore and Philadelphia fared somewhat better, with the tsunami breaking at the mouths of their respective rivers and flooding up in the form of gigantic bores, hugely destructive in their own right but without the devastating wave energy that pulverized Portland or New York.

Further south, the waves took a massive toll on the US Navy and its Atlantic Fleet. When the tsunami struck the naval base in Norfolk, at around 9.00a.m., some ships had already made it out to the safety of deeper water, but the great carriers simply did not have time to escape the wrath of the sea. The nuclear-powered carrier USS *Ronald Reagan* was 1km from its dock and side on to the waves when they hit, the first three smashing the deck and pushing the ship closer to the shore. Three gigantic waves toward the end of the tsunami train hurled the 100,000-tonne monster onto its own dock, cracking the ship open like a nut and smashing the reactor into fragments. Later waves carried the plutonium far and wide, irradiating an area of hundreds of square kilometres.

At Charleston in South Carolina and at Groton in Connecticut, nuclear submarines of the Atlantic Fleet also took a hammering, with four ships completely destroyed, several damaged and two reactor cores exposed. One of the worst catastrophes on a day of a million disastrous incidents occurred at Savannah in Georgia, where a pre-loaded US Army munitions ship, allocated to the North Atlantic Treaty Organization (NATO) Rapid Reaction Force, blew itself to bits in the greatest non-nuclear explosion ever known. So titanic was the blast that, even 5km from the ship, buildings that had survived the tsunami were devastated. A billion slivers of glass and metal, travelling at half the speed of sound, ripped to shreds those who had ventured outside to look at the aftermath of the waves; moreover, the explosion produced its own wave that hurled ships both large and small inland. The thousands of tonnes of shrapnel and masonry blasted into the air then rained down on the town, while a great mushroom-shaped cloud of dust panicked the survivors into thinking that the explosion had been nuclear. Apart from Bermuda and the totally vulnerable islands of the Caribbean, Miami and the coastline of Florida were the most severely affected by the giant waves. To this flat land of swamps and mangroves the Atlantic Ocean gave no quarter, and it would be many years before any more *Venture Star* flights would blast into space from Cape Canaveral.

Although the exact death toll will never be known, it is estimated that over 12 million people died within a similar number of hours on that dreadful day in January 2011. The fact that fewer than 10,000 were killed on the source of all the trouble, the island of La Palma itself, brought home to many in power the stark realization that their countries remained wide open to Nature's wrath, even if that wrath was expressed half a world away. Slowly it dawned on the movers and shakers that the oceans and the atmosphere were common to everyone, and through these media Nature could transmit her fury far and wide.

The legacy of the 'great tide', as it rapidly became known, was a collapse of the global economy that took many years to rebuild. In Spain the government in power was overthrown by popular outrage, and in the USA the President was drummed out of power, close on the heals of his scientific advisor. It was a long time before anyone set up home on the now uninhabited ghost islands of the Bahamas, and never again did the rich sun themselves and sip chilled champagne on the verandas of their Bermudan villas. On the plus side, however, an Atlantic Tsunami Monitoring Network was quickly established, although many said 'too little too late', and a Global Catastrophe Alert Web was instituted. Never again would the world be caught on the hop by a seemingly minor hiccup on an inconsequential volcano far, far away.

CHAPTER 4

SHAKE, RATTLE, AND ROLL:
THE GREAT QUAKE TO COME

*No earthquake like it has ever occurred since Man has been on Earth,
so tremendous was the quake. The great city split into three parts,
and the cities of the nations collapsed.*

Revelation 16:18–19

**It had been an appalling few days at the new agency and Helen had been work-
ing non-stop for the last 12 hours.** The furore following the mid-air collision
between the US Jumbo and the Japanese Airbus 3 days ago at last looked as if
it was beginning to die down a little now that everyone was accounted for and
the investigators were on-site.

A hot shower, a cosy meal and now Peter's lips on hers again. She dug her
fingers hard into his shoulders, massaging the muscles that had knotted during the 24 hours shoehorned into the cramped and noisy C35 transport. Peter
had used what little influence he had in the Pentagon to cajole a 4-day pass
and squeeze himself among a cargo of munitions heading east. It was their first
wedding anniversary and no way was he going to miss it.

Peter swept Helen off the sofa, carried her into the tiny bedroom and
dumped her unceremoniously on the bed. She laughed as it swayed, threatening to collapse, and kissed him as he leaned over her, his muscular arms
outstretched on either side of her mane of red hair. They were still now, but
the bed continued to shake. 'Quake!' she yelled and after a split second, 'Under
the bed!' But it was too late.

A terrific wrench of the Earth brought the heavy red-tiled roof of the old
Tokyo Inn crashing down onto the bed and smashing it through the floor into
the room below. Battered into instant unconsciousness, the couple neither saw
nor felt the collapsing walls that first buried and then slowly suffocated the life
out of them.

Three great earthquakes

Anyone who has experienced even a minor earthquake will tell you that it is a terrifying and unsettling experience. The feeling of an absence of control over one's own body and one's surroundings is total, the brain is numbed, and the will confused. In a major quake the violence of the ground-shaking can be so great as to hurl adults bodily across rooms and through windows, leaving their broken bodies stunned and helpless before entombing them seconds later in crushing piles of rubble. There is often no possibility of taking avoiding action and little time for constructive thought. The following three accounts shed some light on the utter devastation wrought by three of the great earthquakes of historic times, revealing that earthquakes are not simply about a violently shaking Earth but also about giant sea-waves and enormous conflagrations that, together, have levelled some of the grandest cities on the planet.

Lisbon, Portugal, 1755

Lisbon in the middle of the eighteenth century was one of the great cities of the world: a bustling metropolis and port of nearly 300,000 people located on a bay near the mouth of the Tagus river, and the heart of a seafaring nation busy building for itself an empire in distant parts of the planet. On a sunny morning in late autumn 1755 everything was to change, however, as Lisbon was effectively wiped off the face of the Earth in one of the most destructive earthquakes ever recorded. Shortly after 9.30a.m. on 1 November, churches and cathedrals across the city were crammed full of worshippers celebrating the feast of All Saints' Day. On that day, however, they were praying to a God who was not listening.

Heralded by the sound of a crashing thunderstorm, the Earth began to shake with the violence of a housemaid shaking dust from a carpet. Observers reported three separate seismic waves that lifted buildings bodily and threw them from side to side. Constructed by unsuspecting architects who were unfamiliar with earthquakes and the devastation they could wreak, the great stone churches of the city collapsed into heaps of rubble within seconds, burying a puzzled faithful even before they could understand what was happening to them. Although many quakes are over in seconds, the Lisbon quake went on and on for more than 3 minutes, not ceasing until virtually every building, large and small, was reduced to a pile of dust and debris containing the entombed dead and a very few, terrified, screaming survivors.

Even then the Earth had not finished with the city, and as many survivors flocked to the open spaces of the seafront, a second awful sight greeted them. Shortly after the ground stopped shaking the river level fell and its waters retreated from the city's great harbour. Little more than an hour later, however, they returned with a vengeance as three titanic tsunami headed up the estuary and hammered into the seafront, scouring it of human life and any buildings that had survived the quake. Again, reports of the incident are sketchy, but it appears likely that the largest of the waves was over 10m in height, not far off that of a four-storey house. By now, the few remaining survivors might have thought that Nature had surely finished with them and would allow them to lick their wounds, bury their dead and start on the long task of rebuilding. Not so, however, and even as the final waters were draining back through the empty and broken streets, the first wisps of smoke were beginning to drift across the ruins of the city.

Although Lisbon was famous for its great stone buildings, many of the smaller structures were made of wood, a feast for the fires that were started and fed by overturned stoves and smashed oil lamps. Strong winds whipped the flames into a firestorm that raged for over 4 days, burning alive those still trapped in the rubble and leaving the few who still survived to a winter with no supplies. As with many natural catastrophes, the aftermath was only a little less of an ordeal than the event itself. Looters and criminals haunted the streets, helping themselves at the expense of the weak, while the military attempted to uphold martial law and bring something approaching normality back to the situation. It was, however, many years before any of the survivors could feel at home in the city again, and many spent years under canvas on the hills that surrounded Lisbon. With time, new buildings rose from the ruins, although nothing could replace the wealth of culture that perished in the quake, including some of the great libraries and map collections of Europe, and masterpieces by many painters such as Rubens and Titian.

There were no seismographs in existence to measure the strength of the Lisbon earthquake, but its extent and the damage it caused suggest that it may have been one of the most violent earthquakes of recent centuries, possibly registering a magnitude of 8.75 on the Richter Scale. The event was felt throughout the rest of Portugal, across Spain and as far away as northern Africa, France and even Italy. Smaller versions of the devastating tsunami were detected in southern Ireland and southwestern England, and across the Atlantic in the Caribbean. It is impossible to estimate the death toll with any accuracy, but many who have studied the quake suggest a figure of 30,000, perhaps with another 20,000 lives being lost to starvation, disease and civil strife in the aftermath.

Messina, Italy, 1908

Head directly north from smoking Mount Etna on the eastern coast of the beautiful Mediterranean island of Sicily and you will come to the bustling port city of Messina, guardian of the Strait of Messina and gateway to mainland Italy. On a sunny day in the late twentieth century, with the clear blue sea lapping against the hulls of brightly painted fishing boats, it is almost impossible to imagine the utter devastation wrought barely a century earlier as the shaking Earth took the lives of over half the population of the city. Toward the end of the eighteenth century the city had been flattened by a quake that killed almost 30,000 of the inhabitants, and more quakes followed in the last decade of the nineteenth century and again in 1905. The people of Messina and the surrounding region should not then have been entirely surprised by the great roar that woke them in the cold, grey dawn just 3 days after Christmas and that heralded the deadliest of European earthquakes.

With a history stretching back to the time of Ancient Greece, Messina was an impressive sight: great stone municipal buildings and ornate churches, and houses built from granite and lava blocks from the nearby volcano. According to that mantra of earthquake engineers, 'It is buildings not earthquakes that kill people,' and the buildings of early twentieth-century Messina could not have been better designed for the task. As the great Messina Fault that parallels the coast of northeastern Sicily snapped and slid 8km beneath the arm of sea that separates Sicily from mainland Italy, the city shook as if a giant was pounding the Earth's surface with his fist. Buildings toppled one after the other like delicately constructed houses of cards, and in little over 30 seconds the surviving inhabitants' hopes and wishes for the coming New Year lay, like the city itself, in ruins.

Within half a minute the living population of Messina, its neighbouring city of Reggio Calabria across the Strait, and dozens of surrounding towns and villages were cut by half as over 120,000 men, women, and children were crushed and broken by the very same stone walls and roofs that gave the city such splendour. The reason for the desperately high death rate lay in the manner in which the buildings were put together. Heavy red-tiled roofs were supported on little more than wooden timbers that were, in turn, poorly connected to massive stone walls. The ground-shaking associated with the magnitude 7.5 quake proved particularly effective at loosening the timbers, bringing down first the roofs and then the unsupported walls on the unsuspecting inhabitants.

Although the survivors may not have thought so at the time, Messina was lucky to be spared much of the post-quake devastation wrought upon Lisbon. Perhaps recalling the thousands of deaths caused by tsunami during the 1783 earthquake, the remaining inhabitants must have looked nervously out to sea. As much of the local coastline sank by a metre or two, tsunami were generated, the first as high as 12m, but these, fortuitously, did not make a major impact on the remains of the city. As for fire, this was practically non-existent, partly because few stoves or lamps would have been lit during the early morning, but mainly because, in this great stone city, there was very little wood to burn.

The Great Kanto Earthquake – Tokyo-Yokohama, Japan, 1923

The great metropolis of Tokyo on the Japanese island of Honshu is a city waiting to die. It has already been severely wounded once this century when, together with the neighbouring city of Yokohama, it succumbed to one of the most destructive earthquakes of the twentieth century: the Great Kanto Earthquake of 1923. What happened on that autumn morning almost 80 years ago provides some idea of the terror awaiting the inhabitants of the city, perhaps well into the next century – but perhaps tomorrow.

Shortly before noon on 1 September 1923, Tokyo was settling down to lunch. In homes meals were being prepared on cooking stoves and charcoal-burners, while the cafés, tea-rooms and beer-halls began to fill with hungry office workers. The quake struck at exactly 2 minutes to mid-day, preceded by a sound described by some as an explosion. Within seconds the crowded cafés became flattened wrecks, entombing within them both the dead and the living. The shaking was sufficient to hurl people downstairs and into fissures that snapped open across the crowded streets. Many of those who escaped being crushed in their homes or in the cafés and bars clung to life for only a few more seconds before being battered into oblivion by debris falling from the outsides of the violently shaking buildings.

The quake originated on a fault beneath Sagami Bay to the south and reached Yokohama first, before crashing into Tokyo a little over 40 seconds later. Even before the ground had stopped moving, columns of black smoke heralded the true horror of the Great Kanto Earthquake: fire. Fed by overturned cooking stoves, all over the city flames began licking at the rubble and at both the dead and living incarcerated within. The dry timbers from which many buildings were constructed ignited easily, and within minutes millions of small fires began to merge, first into local infernos and then into unimaginable walls of fire that marched across the ruins of the city. Faced with firestorms on every side, the city's firefighters soon found themselves helpless, while others, seeing the deadly fires consuming everything in their paths, fled to the rivers or to open spaces where they felt safer.

This proved to be a deadly mistake for many and led to one of the great tragedies of this or any other earthquake. As the firestorms merged into conflagrations that threatened more and more parts of the city, thousands began to gather in a vacant plot of open land in the district of Honjo. Terrified survivors surged into the space, and by mid-afternoon nearly 40,000 people were crammed into an area the size of a football field. By nightfall the great mass of humanity was completely surrounded by a wall of fire, and the majority must have suspected what was going to come next. A vacuum created by the flames above the crowd created tornado-force winds that sucked the fires together, forming an incinerating blast that roasted alive all but a few hundred appallingly injured survivors. Elsewhere, thousands were immolated by burning oil released from broken tanks into the sea, while others were boiled to death in the very rivers that they hoped would provide refuge.

Having exhausted the available fuel, the firestorms began to diminish and, after nearly 2 days and nights, eventually burned themselves out. Dazed survivors emerged from the rivers and the few buildings spared by the holocaust to gaze upon a scene of utter devastation, comparable to the destruction that a few decades later would be visited by atomic bombs on the cities of Hiroshima and Nagasaki. In all, as many as 200,000 of the inhabitants of Tokyo and Yokohama may have perished in the magnitude 8.3 quake and its fiery legacy – the worst natural catastrophe in Japanese history. At today's prices the cost of the devastation totalled over US$50 billion, a drain on the Japanese economy that it simply could not sustain. A combination of the quake and the stock-market crash of 1929 led to economic collapse and depression and, as in Weimar Germany between the two world wars, to the rise of the military and a consequent, and unquenchable, thirst for empire and war.

The moving Earth

Every year the Earth shakes something like 500,000 times. Most of these tremors are, however, so tiny that they can be detected only by seismographs, and the amount of energy they release is very small. About 100 serious earthquakes greater than magnitude 6 on the Richter Scale occur every year, while, on average, only two major quakes in excess of magnitude 8 occur over the same period. Really great earthquakes are even rarer, but they are of major importance because they release nearly all of the seismic energy bound up in fault zones across the planet. Between the beginning of the century and the mid-1970s, it is estimated that there were over 7 million earthquakes. Well over 90 per cent of the seismic energy released over this period was, however, the result of 10 huge quakes larger than Richter magnitude 8 (see table below).

Earthquakes occur when two great rock masses spontaneously jolt past one another along a fault. In order to store up strain and then deform suddenly like this, the rock must be brittle. As a result of this, earthquakes do not occur in the soft, plastic asthenosphere, but are confined to the relatively cold and brittle lithosphere that incorporates the crust and the uppermost part of the mantle. Most earthquakes occur

Ten great earthquakes of the twentieth century.

Date	Location	Magnitude on Richter Scale
1906	Colombia and Ecuador	8.6
1922	Chile	8.3
1938	Papua New Guinea	8.2
1950	Assam, India	8.6
1952	Kamchatka	8.25
1957	Aleutian Islands	8.25
1960	Chile	8.3
1963	Kurile Islands	8.1
1964	Alaska	8.4
1965	Aleutian Islands	8.1

at shallow depths, usually less than 20km, and these are the most destructive. In subduction zones, where a cold, brittle slab of lithosphere is sliding into plastic mantle, quakes can occur down to depths of nearly 700km, although their effects are rarely felt at the surface. Over 75 per cent of the seismic energy released every year comes from earthquakes confined to the top 15km of the crust, and over three-quarters of all earthquakes occur within the uppermost 60km of the lithosphere.

Earthquakes are a world-wide problem, with the threat of potentially destructive quakes hanging over 40 or so countries. As explained on p. 24, however, earthquakes are not randomly distributed across the planet, but instead, along with volcanoes, are concentrated primarily along the boundaries between the plates. Although the ground regularly shakes in all five continents, most earthquake activity is focused in the subduction zones that surround the Pacific – which is one reason why the tsunami threat is also greatest here. A cursory glance at the list of great earthquakes in the table on p. 161 will show that eight of the ten occurred around the margins of the Pacific Ocean. Some of the most seismically active parts of the Pacific Rim are relatively poorly inhabited, however, and most earthquake-related deaths occur elsewhere in a band, again coinciding with a series of plate boundaries, that runs from the Mediterranean, through the Middle East and the Himalayan region, into China and South-East Asia. The high death toll here results from a combination of frequent earthquakes, high population density, poorly constructed buildings and often-mountainous terrain where quakes trigger lethal landslides. Two of the most devastating of all natural disasters resulted from earthquakes in China, with a quake in Shenshi Province taking as many as 800,000 lives in 1556, and another 250,000 deaths occurring in 1976 in the Great Tangshan Earthquake.

As discussed on p. 26, not all seismic activity occurs at plate boundaries. In the hearts of the continents, far from the plate edges, major earthquakes sometimes occur, albeit on a rather infrequent basis. The high-magnitude–low-frequency characteristic of these intraplate quakes actually poses a great problem for disaster managers in such regions. In Tokyo, where the last quake in 1923 killed perhaps 200,000 people, and where the Earth continues to shake on a regular basis, it is relatively easy to drill the population in ways of coping with a future quake. In New Madrid, Missouri, in the heartland of the USA, however, where the last great quake occurred nearly 200 years ago, few are interested in heeding warnings of future seismic catastrophes.

Measuring moving ground

Earthquakes are recorded in the Old Testament – remember the walls of
Jericho coming tumbling down? – and also in texts of Classical Greece
and Imperial Rome. Not surprisingly, the destruction of a city was big
news even then. Although there is no evidence that the ancient civilizations of Europe took any interest in the causes of earthquakes, it appears
that as long ago as AD 132 the Chinese were trying better to understand
what caused the ground to shake so violently. The Chinese developed
an earthquake-recording device that consisted of a circle of eight connected bronze dragons sitting above a corresponding circle of eight
bronze toads. Each dragon held in its mouth a metal ball, which could
be dislodged if the device was shaken by an earthquake. The idea was
that only the ball held by a dragon oriented in the direction of the
quake would be dislodged and fall into the mouth of the toad below,
and thus the toad that held the ball would point out the direction from
which the quake came. It is quite possible that this beautifully constructed piece was more in the way of a conversation piece to impress
visitors than a serious scientific tool. Firstly, seismic waves issuing from
the source of a quake travel by such circuitous routes and involve such
erratic shaking of the ground that the ball-swallowing toad would
almost certainly be pointing in the wrong direction. Secondly, a strong
quake would either drop all the balls into the mouths of all the toads or
hurl the device out of the nearest window!

After the dragons and toads we have to wait over 1,500 years for
the next instrument designed to measure earthquakes. The European
seismoscope consisted of a tube containing liquid mercury that would spill
out if the ground shook. Once again, this was a purely qualitative tool,
capable of indicating to the observer that an earthquake had occurred
but little else. Useful earthquake monitors did not appear until scientists
discovered that a pendulum could record the often tiny reverberations
coming from distant quakes.

In the middle of the last century, a pendulum attached to a pencil was
used to make a visual recording of seismic waves, and this was the first-
ever *seismograph*. The idea behind such a system is really quite simple. A
heavy pendulum and its recording pencil or pen is suspended above a chart
so that they just touch. When the ground shakes during an earthquake,
the mass of the pendulum causes it to remain still while the Earth moves
beneath it, causing the pen to trace the path of the movement on the chart.
Pendulum-based instruments were perfected in Italy and Japan during the

second half of the eighteenth century, enabling ground-shaking to be recorded in three directions: north–south, east–west, and in the vertical dimension. Consequently, by the time of the great San Francisco earthquake of 1906, sufficient numbers of seismographs were in place around the world to make a detailed study of the associated ground motions.

As you might expect, late twentieth-century seismographs are much more sophisticated, with the ground motions displayed on a screen and analysed by complex computer software. Not only are the different components of motion measured, but also the different characteristics of the seismic waves reaching the recorder, such as wavelength and amplitude. With a huge world-wide network of seismographs now in operation, the depth and location of any earthquake can be pinpointed within minutes. This is critical information, particularly where a damaging quake may have taken place in a poorly accessible region or where there is a widespread tsunami threat.

Measuring earthquake intensity

So far, the Richter Scale (see p. 27) has been referred to when discussing the strength of an earthquake. This, however, is not the only way in which the size of an earthquake can be determined, and indeed the alternative *Mercalli Scale* was devised 50 years before Mr Richter dreamed up his method. Giuseppe Mercalli based his scale on observations of the effects and damage resulting from an earthquake. In this sense, the scale is more subjective than that of Richter, but it does have its advantages. Firstly, it does not rely on the use of seismographs, and secondly the size of a quake can be determined even some time after it happened. Provided that there are reliable written accounts of the damage, the Mercalli Scale can even be used to assess the intensity of earthquakes that occurred far back in history. A major drawback of the scale, however, is that it works only for inhabited areas. With no buildings to demonstrate the impact of a quake, it is impossible to determine its intensity using the scale. Another problem lies in the fact that the Mercalli Scale tells you nothing about the strength of the earthquake at its source. For example, the damage experienced by a particular settlement would be the same whether it was caused by a medium-sized quake nearby or a bigger quake further away. Because Mercalli's original damage descriptions have been tinkered with on a number of occasions since he put the scale together in 1883, it is now normally referred to as the *Modified Mercalli Scale* (see table on p. 165).

Modified Mercalli Scale for earthquake intensities and comparison with the Richter Scale for earthquake magnitude.

Scale	Intensity on Modified Mercalli Scale	Effect or damage	Corresponding magnitude on Richter Scale
I	Instrumental	Not felt by humans	—
II	Feeble	Felt by some people at rest	—
III	Slight	Hanging objects swing; similar to heavy truck passing	<4.2
IV	Moderate	Doors, windows, and crockery rattle; felt by people walking	—
V	Slightly strong	Doors swing, liquids and pictures disturbed; sleepers wake; church bells ring	<4.8
VI	Strong	Windows and crockery broken; walking difficult; trees sway; masonry may crack	<5.4
VII	Very strong	Furniture broken, walls crack, and plaster falls; noticed by drivers; difficult to stand	<6.1
VIII	Destructive	Partial collapse of poorly constructed buildings; chimneys fall; steering of cars difficult	
IX	Ruinous	Some houses collapse; underground pipes break; obvious ground cracking; general panic	<6.9
X	Disastrous	Many buildings destroyed; landslides and soil liquefaction common; many ground cracks	<7.3
XI	Very disastrous	Most buildings and bridges collapse; railways, pipes and cables destroyed	<8.1
XII	Catastrophic	Total destruction; trees uprooted; ground rises and falls in waves; objects thrown into the air	>8.1

Instead of relying on subjective observations of damage, the Richter Scale is based on measuring the total amount of energy released during an earthquake. This can be determined, via some pretty basic mathematical jiggery-pokery, from the maximum shaking, or ground motion, as indicated by the pen-trace on a seismograph. Like the Volcanic Explosivity Index (see p. 74), the Richter Scale is logarithmic, which means that every increase in magnitude represents a 10-fold increase in the amount of ground motion experienced. A magnitude 6 quake is therefore 10 times more violent than a magnitude 5, while a magnitude 7 quake is 100 times more violent. Although the Richter Scale is open ended, it is very rare for a quake to exceed 8.5, and although they may have occurred in recent history, no magnitude 9 quakes have yet been recorded on a seismograph. The reason why earthquakes greater than about magnitude 9 do not occur probably lies in the fact that the brittle crust can accommodate only a finite amount of strain – an amount that corresponds to a magnitude 8.9–9 quake. At least, we hope this is the case, otherwise some city, somewhere, is in for a great shock.

Earthquake waves

Many of you may have seen, if only on the small screen or in books, the trace of an earthquake on the chart of a seismograph, but what exactly do all those little squiggles actually mean? What do they tell the seismologist about the earthquake? The first thing to recognize is that there are different types of squiggle, each caused by a different type of seismic wave (see figure on p. 167). When an earthquake occurs somewhere within the crust, shock-waves head out in all directions. Some of the waves travel through the atmosphere, generating the express-train or rumbling sounds often associated with earthquakes, while, if the quake is submarine, others travel through the water in the form of tsunami. The rest of the energy released during sudden movement along a fault radiates outward as waves through the solid Earth itself, and these are the ones that are picked up on a seismograph.

This energy is transmitted as three different types of seismic wave, known as *P-waves*, *S-waves* and *surface-waves*. Each travels at a different speed through the Earth, and each results in a different sort of ground-shaking and therefore a different trace on the seismograph. P-waves, or *push-waves*, travel the fastest, at about 5.5km/second and are, therefore, the first to arrive at a seismograph. They move by squeezing and

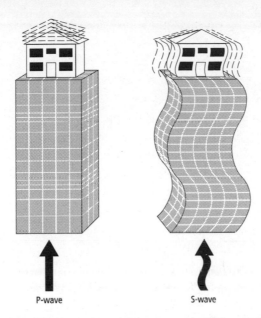

P-wave · S-wave

The devastating impact of earthquakes on buildings and other structures results from three different types of earthquake wave. The P-waves arrive first, stretching and squeezing the rock through which they travel, followed soon after by the S-waves, which cause the ground surface to shake from side to side. Finally, the surface waves appear, making the ground roll like the surface of an ocean. (Source: Zebrowski, 1997)

stretching the rock through which they travel, rather like a concertina being pulled and pushed, or like a row of wagons being shunted back and forth by a railway engine. These are followed by the slower moving but far more damaging, S-waves, or *shake-waves*, which cause the ground surface to shake from side to side. It is these shake-waves that turn bridges into waving ribbons and roads into slithering snakes. After the S-waves, the surface-waves arrive. These take longer because they have come by a more circuitous route; as the name suggests they travel along the Earth's surface rather than through the body of the planet. Like the S-waves, surface-waves are particularly destructive, causing the ground to roll like the surface of the ocean, setting tall buildings and bridges swaying, bringing down elevated highways and snapping communication and power cables.

Because the P- and S-waves travel at different speeds, the further away the earthquake that produced them, the greater will be the time gap between the arrival of the P-waves and the arrival of the S-waves. This is a particularly useful property because it means that the distance

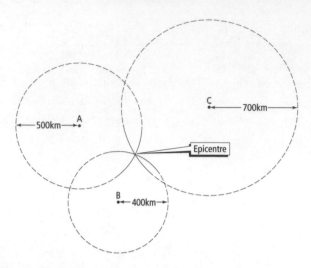

Once three seismological observatories have determined the distance to an earthquake, its precise position can be easily determined by combining the data as shown.

of the quake can be measured from the seismograph record. If three widely spaced observatories have determined their distance from the quake, it then becomes possible to locate the *epicentre* of the quake, the point on the surface directly above it (see figure above). Pinpointing the actual source of the quake itself – the *focus* – is a little more complex, but can now be successfully accomplished with the advanced computer software available.

Earthquakes as destroyers

As the magnitude of an earthquake is related to the amount of energy released, it provides a useful guide to the potential destructiveness of a quake. In terms of both the degree of damage to property and the casualty figures, however, many other factors are also important, and there are many cases of relatively small earthquakes causing terrible damage whereas quakes 100 times larger have very little impact. For example, while the magnitude 6.9 Loma Prieta earthquake that struck San Francisco in 1989 killed only 64 people, the magnitude 5.9 quake that rocked Agadir in Morocco in 1960 took more than 14,000 lives. Similarly, quakes of the same magnitude can have a hugely different impact. In Japan, the Great Hanshin Earthquake disaster of 1995, otherwise known as the Kobe earthquake, was about the same size as the Loma Prieta event, but the quake left over 6,000 dead, 35,000 injured, and nearly 500,000 homeless – an incredible contrast. At Loma Prieta injuries totalled less than 4,000, and just over 10,000 were made homeless.

The reasons for the extraordinary contrast are manifold. The Kobe earthquake was shallow – only 14km deep – and located only 20km from the city itself, while the Loma Prieta quake occurred almost 100km away from San Francisco, the nearest major population centre. Furthermore, while most of the Californian buildings were designed to withstand a quake of such magnitude, many of the older properties in Kobe, especially those belonging to poorer residents, were built to withstand typhoons rather than earthquakes. As soon as the ground started shaking, their timber frames could no longer support the heavy tiled roofs, which were designed to cope with strong winds, and the buildings came crashing down on the families within. As demonstrated by Kobe and Loma Prieta, the distance from the epicentre is obviously important, because generally the degree of ground-shaking falls off with increasing distance from the source of the quake.

This is not always the case, however, and in some circumstance, seismic waves may be amplified by local conditions far from the epicentre. In 1985, for example, ground-shaking associated with an earthquake 350km from Mexico City was amplified four or five times when the seismic waves entered the soft sediments of an ancient lake-bed that now underlies part of the capital. The enormously increased vibrations literally shook buildings apart, and over 10,000 lives were lost beneath collapsed homes, schools, hotels, and office blocks. The length of the quake, in other words the duration of ground-shaking, is also critical, and, all other things being equal, a quake that lasts longer will be more damaging. In fact, the Kobe earthquake was particularly short, little more than 20 seconds, otherwise the destruction would have been very much greater. Somewhat surprisingly, the time of day can also have an enormous influence on the number of casualties incurred during a quake. In the Great Kanto Earthquake described on p. 159, the huge firestorms that killed so many thousands and razed the cities of Tokyo and Yokohama to the ground would probably never have developed if the quake had occurred a few hours later. By then, lunch would have been over, and the thousands of braziers and stoves that stoked the firestorms switched off.

As demonstrated by the Mexico City example, the local geology can be critical in determining the destructiveness of an earthquake.

Generally speaking, buildings constructed on solid bedrock are much less likely to suffer damage or collapse than those located on soft sediments. This is because the seismic waves travelling through such unconsolidated material cause it to behave exactly as if it were a liquid, especially if it is saturated with water. As a result of this *liquefaction* effect, the material can no longer support the buildings above, which simply sink into it or topple over as their foundations begin to float free. Liquefaction was responsible for most of the deaths in the Loma Prieta quake, when an elevated section of the Nimitz Freeway in Oakland, which was constructed on mud, collapsed. Similarly, the Marina District of San Francisco, during the same quake, and the port facilities at Kobe in 1995 were severely damaged as a result of their construction on soft muds and sands. During the terrible Armenian earthquake of 1988, many of the 25,000 deaths resulted from the collapse of quite modern, concrete multi-storey buildings, 95 per cent of which were destroyed because they were constructed on soft sediments that amplified ground-shaking eight times and caused it to last three times longer.

Where earthquakes occur in hilly or mountainous terrain, much of the devastation is often the result of landslides triggered by the ground-shaking rather than collapsing buildings. For example, more than half of all earthquake deaths in Japan over the past 35 years have been due to landslides. Indeed, an earthquake also triggered the greatest landslide disaster on record. In 1970 a magnitude 7.7 quake offshore caused the overhanging face of the Nevados Huascarán Mountain in the Peruvian Andes to collapse, bringing millions of tonnes of rock and ice crashing down onto the settlements clustered on its lower slopes. Within 4 minutes of the collapse, a wall of mud and debris 80m high hammered into the towns of Yungay and Ranrahirca and several neighbouring villages at 350km/hour, burying them to a depth of 10m and killing virtually every resident – over 25,000 in all.

Preparing for the threat

Yet again that universal mantra of earthquake engineers – 'It is buildings not earthquakes that kill people' – holds true. There are only two ways of reducing the number of casualties incurred in earthquakes. Either do not build at all in quake-prone regions or build quake-proof properties. Given the billions of people who are now at risk, the former is clearly unrealistic, so we are left with the latter. The 1908 Messina quake, the

Kobe disaster and many, many other earthquakes have shown how inappropriate building construction can lead to an enormous increase in death and injury. So what can be done to improve the situation?

Earthquake-proof buildings

First of all, the building material is critical. Many of the casualties that result from earthquakes in developing countries are caused by the collapse of adobe (mud-brick) buildings that have very little resistance to even moderate ground-shaking. In a magnitude 6.9 quake, such as those at Loma Prieta or in Armenia, 100 per cent of adobe buildings will be severely damaged or destroyed. This compares with only 25 per cent of buildings constructed using reinforced masonry. Clearly, there is no question of the poor inhabitants of developing countries having the funds to construct high-quality, earthquake-proof, masonry homes, but there is no reason why low-cost housing should remain a death trap. Simple design changes can make a huge difference, such as avoiding breeze blocks in the walls and heavy lintels above doorways, and instead building a light timber frame with cane walls and a wattle-and-daub exterior.

In recent quakes that have hit major urban centres in developed countries such as Japan and the USA, buildings constructed in the last 20 years have fared pretty well, primarily because they have been constructed according to stringent earthquake building codes. The Marriott Hotel in San Francisco, for example, was opened on 17 October 1989, the very day of the Loma Prieta earthquake. Despite every glass in the hotel being smashed, bar one, which is now proudly displayed in a glass case, the building survived unscathed and relatively untouched. Like the San Francisco Marriott, modern buildings in earthquake zones can be made earthquake-safe in a number of ways. They can be built on large rubber shock-absorbers that allow the building to rock back and forth without shaking itself to pieces. Alternatively, the vibrations caused by ground-shaking can be minimized by resting a heavy counterweight on the roof of the building or by bracing of the walls.

The problem with earthquake building codes is that, in order to have any impact in reducing casualties during quakes, they must be rigorously enforced. In California this may not be too much of a problem, but even in Japanese cities many of the older buildings often do not come up to modern standards. In developing countries earthquake vulnerability remains very high, and there is still a long way to go before the poorest families in Colombia or Afghanistan will sleep safe and sound within earthquake-proof homes.

Education

Alongside the construction of earthquake-proof buildings, community preparedness is a critical element of programmes aimed at reducing the numbers of casualties incurred during a large earthquake. Civil authorities must have measures in place to ensure an effective and instantaneous response by the emergency services, while citizens must be educated in terms of what to do when an earthquake strikes. Having a better understanding of how people behave during an earthquake and exactly how casualties are sustained can help disaster managers to plan more effectively for future quakes. In this context, the 1976 Great Tangshan Earthquake in China provides some useful lessons. A quarter of the city's 1 million inhabitants lost their lives in this devastating quake, and more than 150,000 people were seriously injured. Virtually all buildings were destroyed or severely damaged, burying nearly 90 per cent of the population. Of these, however, 250,000 were able to pull themselves from the rubble and help with the rescue of others still buried. In all, only 20 per cent of those buried actually died. Of those killed, less than 20 per cent died as a result of being crushed in collapsed buildings or hit by falling debris. The rest all expired while awaiting rescue, succumbing either to suffocation caused by the huge quantities of dust generated by the pulverized adobe or to the effects of heat or thirst. Some deaths also resulted from a lack of medical attention following rescue. The survivors consisted largely of people who had hurled themselves under substantial pieces of furniture at the first sign of the ground shaking, while few of those who ran screaming outside lived to tell the tale. Unfortunately, the latter response is a common one, even in regions whose inhabitants experience earthquakes on a regular basis. After the Loma Prieta quake, a survey undertaken by the USGS showed that almost 70 per cent of the inhabitants of Santa Cruz froze or ran outside while only 13 per cent sought immediate protection – figures that do not bode well should the next 'big one' strike in southern California.

On the basis of the Tangshan experience, it would seem that the way to reduce casualty figures in a large earthquake that strikes a city of poorly constructed buildings is by educating the population to hide beneath furniture rather than head into the street, to ensure that they always have emergency supplies to hand and to await rescue if trapped.

The length of time taken for rescue teams to extract the living from the debris is critical, because after 48 hours of being buried few victims remain alive. As it takes at least this long for specialist rescue teams from the developed world to arrive on the scene, it is vital that local teams are trained in the difficult task of how to delve among the often precarious piles of debris in a way that does not threaten those trapped beneath.

Inevitably the moments immediately after a large earthquake are ones of chaos and a critical time for rapid and appropriate decision making. To minimize death and injury, an effective disaster plan must already be in existence, and all the major players must be completely familiar with their responsibilities and their lines of command. Without such pre-planning, confusion and disorganization will rapidly make the situation much worse. The emergency services in particular have a critical role to play in the hours following a large quake, and they must have the means to contact their staff even when communication lines are down. California is leading the way here, and emergency service workers have pagers linked to a computerized earthquake-monitoring network known as Earthworm, while a new computer system, called Readicube, will be able to relay details of a quake to the emergency services within 5 seconds.

In the immediate aftermath of a major earthquake, one of the biggest problems involves getting the emergency services quickly to where they are most needed. Telecommunications will inevitably be difficult, and many roads are likely to be impassable. The civil authorities must ensure, therefore, that emergency supplies are stationed beforehand at appropriate points around the city, while heavy lifting equipment must be available to create routes through the blocked roads. At the same time, survivors of the quake should be educated to fend for themselves in the days immediately following the quake in order to leave the emergency services free to concentrate on search and rescue.

As the citizens of San Francisco learned in 1906, and those of Tokyo and Yokohama in 1923, the fire following an earthquake may be even more devastating than the quake itself, and although there are now far fewer wooden buildings around, fire remains a potential problem. In the Great Kanto Earthquake of 1923, huge numbers of small fires started independently as cooking stoves and braziers were overturned. The inhabitants of Japanese cities now use fewer cookers, but fires starting from gas leaks in homes and fractured gas mains can be just as destructive. In an attempt to minimize their impact, the Tokyo Gas Company has developed an 'intelligent' gas-meter called the Miconmeter. This has a microcomputer attached that automatically cuts off the supply of gas when an earthquake of intensity 5 on the Japanese seismic scale strikes. The meter operated successfully during the magnitude 5.9 earthquake that hit Tokyo in 1992, although many householders had difficulties getting their gas supplies reactivated again afterward!

Earthquake forecasting

Constructing earthquake-proof buildings and preparing for the worst are all very well and, if executed effectively, can have a dramatic effect on reducing the toll of death and destruction during a major quake. But what about forecasting? Is it possible to tell when an earthquake is coming with sufficient accuracy and precision to evacuate the threatened area? This issue is probably the most controversial in seismology.

Achieving the ability to forecast earthquakes accurately and repeatedly is currently the Holy Grail of geophysics, guaranteeing a Nobel Prize to the successful discoverer. But just what exactly does forecasting mean? First of all it might be useful to distinguish between the terms 'forecast' and 'prediction', both of which tend to be used interchangeably to describe the efforts of seismologists to see into the future. Given the frequency with which so many of us have come home cold and drenched at the end of a day that the smiling television weather-forecaster has assured us will be one of warmth and brilliant sunshine, it should surprise no one that the term *forecast* is a relatively imprecise statement. In contrast *prediction* relates to something altogether more precise and accurate, which covers a shorter time period than a forecast. On the basis of these definitions we can already forecast earthquakes, in a manner of speaking, but it remains contestable whether anyone has yet been successful in predicting an earthquake. Chinese scientists do, however, claim to have predicted a quake in Haicheng in 1975, about 5 hours before the event.

Return times

Earthquake forecasting is all about looking at the past record of earthquakes for a particular region or for a specific fault in order to reveal some sort of regular pattern of events that can provide a clue to the size, timing and location of the next quake. For example, if a magnitude 6 quake had occurred on a particular fault in 1800, 1850, 1900 and 1950, it would be reasonable to forecast that the next earthquake in the sequence would take place in the first year of the new millennium. Unfortunately, things are never quite this simple. Although, like eruptions of a particular volcano, earthquakes occurring on a specific fault do have regular return times, they do not appear quite like clockwork. A more realistic sequence for our hypothetical quake might be 1800, 1847, 1911 and 1950. This gives an *average* return time of 50 years, but the actual gaps between the different quakes range from 39 to 64 years.

On the basis of this information alone, a seismologist making a forecast in 1950 would have to say that the next event in the sequence would be likely to occur sometime between 1989 and 2014 – not a particularly useful piece of information for the inhabitants and disaster managers of the threatened region. Furthermore, even this forecast might be of limited use, because four dates over 200 years might not accurately describe the true pattern of earthquakes, which could be determined only if the record went back much further. For example, if the quake prior to 1800 had taken place in 1620, the whole forecasting exercise becomes virtually meaningless. The lesson then is that, the longer the record, the more accurate a forecast based upon it is likely to be. For the Los Angeles area of California such a record is available from the dating of earthquake-related deformation over the past 1,500 years or so. This reveals that, since AD 565, there have been eight major earthquakes, spaced at intervals ranging from 55 to 275 years, and with an average return time of 160 years. The last time the Earth moved in a big way was in 1857, so LA has a reasonable chance of being faced with the next 'big one' sometime in the first few decades of the next century. Then again, it might not happen until 2132.

The reason why earthquakes on a specific fault occur reasonably regularly is that their purpose is to release strain that is accumulating in the rocks. If the strain is increasing at a constant rate – and there is a certain threshold, determined by the material properties of the rock and the nature of the fault and its surroundings, above which the strain is released by movement on the fault – then some periodicity in the earthquake record should not be surprising. The strain build-up on many faults relates directly to the rate of movement of the lithospheric plates, and most earthquakes occur on faults that coincide with plate boundaries that are moving past one another at several centimetres a year. If the annual rate of movement is known and constant, which it is for the Earth's plates, and the amount of fault movement that occurs during each earthquake is also known, then the frequency of quakes can be worked out. If the lithosphere on either side of a fault is moving at 5cm/year, and the fault jumps 5m during every quake, then the strain accumulating in the rock must be released every 100 years. So the fault is trying to move continually at 5cm/year, but frictional forces between the rock masses on either side prevent this. After a century the accumulated strain is great enough to overcome the friction, and the fault jumps 5m to make up for lost time and reduce the strain across it to zero. Then the cycle starts all over again.

Seismic gaps

A clue to the imminence of a larger than normal earthquake can be gained from studying this sort of pattern and looking for gaps. If, for example, a quake forecast to occur from strain and fault displacement data, such as that just described, fails to appear, then it is time to start worrying. Sometimes a fault becomes 'locked' for one reason or another, and the strain is allowed to build up over a much longer period. This means that, when the fault does eventually move, a greater displacement will be needed in order to take the strain back down to zero. This greater movement will mean a bigger and almost certainly more destructive quake. Locations where this behaviour is observed are known as *seismic gaps*, and they are often the sites of the biggest and nastiest quakes. The 1964 Alaska earthquake filled one of these seismic gaps, but worrying gaps still occur around Los Angeles, in Papua New Guinea, around much of the Caribbean and in Japan (see p. 187).

Stress transfer

Making any sort of earthquake forecast is further complicated by the fact that the faults on which quakes occur often do not exist in isolation. Typically they are connected to other faults that have their own characteristic rates of strain accumulation and earthquake records. Because of these complex links, a quake that releases strain on one fault may actually transfer that strain to a neighbouring fault, bringing forward the time when that also snaps and thus produces an earthquake. The importance of this *stress-transfer* phenomenon to seismology is becoming increasingly recognized, because a relatively small movement on a neighbouring fault may trigger a much larger displacement, and therefore earthquake, on a major fault close by.

In the Tokyo area, for example, studies of past earthquake records have revealed that some of the biggest quakes to hit the city have been preceded several years earlier by a smaller quake on a fault to the south-west, near the city of Odawara. Similarly, in California, seismologists are concerned that small displacements along associated minor faults might be just enough to trigger movement along a locked segment of the great San Andreas Fault, with devastating consequences. If the strain that has accumulated in a fault is at a critical level, only a small degree of added stress is needed to make the fault snap and trigger a quake. Even another earthquake thousands of kilometres away can do this, and the magnitude 7.3 earthquake that occurred near Landers, in the Mojave Desert east of Los Angeles, caused smaller quakes throughout California and as far away as Yellowstone in Wyoming, over 1,000km distant.

When a fault is poised to shift, even the Moon can have a role to play. As the Moon's gravity pulls the oceans to produce the tides, it also pulls at the solid rock that makes up the lithosphere. These *Earth tides* set up stresses within the rock that can be sufficient not only to trigger earthquakes but also to set off volcanoes that are in a critical state.

How useful are earthquake forecasts?

Earthquake forecasts, then, have a useful role to play in providing a general guide to roughly when the next quake might occur. For disaster managers and the emergency services, however, they are not particularly useful. Such people need something much more precise that will tell them, with sufficient warning, when and where the next earthquake will strike and, ideally, how big it is going to be. As mentioned earlier, the Chinese claim to have successfully provided such a prediction before an earthquake close to the city of Haicheng in 1975. Following several months of tilting of the land surface, water gushing from the ground and strange animal behaviour, over 90,000 citizens were evacuated from the city on 4 February. The next day, just over 12 hours later, a magnitude 7 quake hit the city, destroying over 90 per cent of the buildings but taking virtually no lives because of the timely exodus. Was this a true prediction, however, or did the scientists and authorities get the timing of the evacuation right more by luck than judgement? In fact, the latter is probably true.

Other factors, such as ground-surface movements, water bursts and unusual animal behaviour, may all indicate that an earthquake is on its way, but it has yet to be demonstrated that such events can provide information on the precise timing of a quake. It seems that, in Haicheng, the scientists correctly surmised that a quake was on its way, but were just lucky in terms of telling the civil authorities when to evacuate. Certainly the method of prediction was not transferable to other earthquake-prone areas, and the Chinese failed utterly to warn of the devastating Tangshan quake that occurred only 4 years later. Not to be outdone by their Chinese comrades, Soviet scientists made similar earthquake predictions for the Kuril Islands between Japan and the Kamchatka Peninsula, only to have to wait 8 years before the Earth shook.

Earthquake prediction

In countries of the West, little attention was focused on trying to accurately predict earthquakes until the 1970s, when increasing worry over the imminence of the next 'big one' in California led the USGS to devote more time and money to monitoring the San Andreas Fault System. Much of the work concentrated on using advanced instrumentation to measure the accumulation of strain along the various parts of the fault and to look for anomalous movements that might warn that an earthquake was on its way.

Like volcanologists, seismologists have at their disposal an impressive array of instruments to study faults and their activity, and in fact, many are the same as those utilized to measure volcano deformation (see figure on p. 179). *Strain-meters* are used to monitor stress changes in the rock around the fault, while small displacements across the fault can be detected using a number of different methods. These include laser and infrared electronic distance-meters, which bounce beams off reflectors located on the far side of the fault and can detect displacements as small as a millimetre, and *creep-meters*, which provide a continuous record of the tiny movements along the fault. Just as tilt-meters and levelling can be used to monitor swelling of a volcano, so they can be used to look for the ground-surface deformation that may warn of a forthcoming earthquake.

Radon gas

Some days before a major earthquake, the enormous strains that have accumulated along a fault can lead to cracking of the rock deep down. Because water quickly enters these cracks, the level of the water table may change prior to a quake, and this can be measured by monitoring the water levels in specially dug wells that penetrate into the top of the water table. The same cracks may also provide a passage to the surface for the naturally occurring radioactive gas *radon*, which is common in ground water. Special radon detectors, located in wells, may therefore be able to warn of a forthcoming earthquake by spotting an increase in the amount of radon gas coming from the well water. Detailed studies of water-table changes in China and elsewhere have revealed that, generally speaking, the larger the area affected and the longer the period before a earthquake that the changes are observed, the bigger the quake will be.

Fore-shocks

Many seismologists look to their own specialist instruments, seismographs, to warn of a future quake, believing that a major earthquake is often preceded by smaller quakes, known as *fore-shocks*. On a broad scale, a number of moderate quakes in a particular region may precede a major one, probably related to the stress-transfer phenomenon, and this appears to have been the case prior to the great San Francisco quake

A comprehensive range of techniques is available for monitoring active faults. Most rely on detecting small changes, e.g. in deformation and micro-seismicity, in the hope that they may provide warning of a future earthquake. (Source: Smith, 1996)

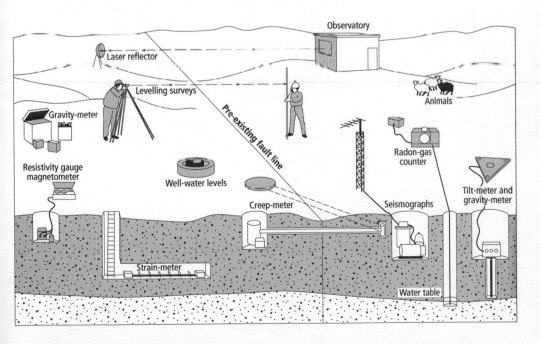

of 1906 that razed the city to the ground. On a smaller scale, tiny quakes, sometimes known as *microseisms*, may occur in the vicinity of a fault a few days to a few hours before it snaps. Unfortunately, they are not always seen before a big quake, so they cannot be relied upon. Furthermore, they may also occur in the absence of a larger, following earthquake, making them even less reliable predictors.

Electrical currents

In the last couple of decades there has been much debate about whether or not the stress variations that occur around a fault before a large earthquake can cause changes in the electrical or magnetic properties of the crust in its vicinity. Natural electrical currents, known as *Earth currents*, are constantly flowing through the crust, and some scientists claim to have detected small changes in the strength of these currents prior to a large earthquake. Similarly, the natural resistance of the crust to electrical currents has also been observed to change before a major quake. This property, known as the *electrical resistance* of the crust, can be monitored using an *electrical resistivity meter*, which shoots pulses of electrical energy into the crust and measures the resistance in the rock to their passage. Scientists working in various earthquake-prone parts of the world have reported detecting noticeable falls in electrical resistivity around faults prior to large quakes, although, once again, the changes remain too unreliable to be used as dependable predictors.

In 1981 three Greek scientists – Varotsos, Alexopoulos and Nomicas (collectively known as VAN) – published a paper that suggested that earthquakes were preceded by what they called *seismic electrical signals* (SES), and that these signals could therefore be used to predict earthquakes accurately. This VAN method of quake prediction remains, however, highly controversial, and its very mention can lead to much heated debate among its supporters and antagonists. The VAN supporters propose that SES are generated by stress changes in the crust and that they can be detected weeks before an earthquake and hundreds of kilometres away. They even claim to have used the method to predict earthquakes in Greece, although those scientists who hold the VAN method in contempt have described these so-called predictions as 'absurdly vague'. Clearly, this is a debate that will run and run. In the meantime, watch this space and don't whisper the term 'VAN' into the shell-like ear of a seismologist unless you want to send him into fits of apoplexy.

Animal behaviour

Enough then of high-tech methods of predicting earthquakes, what about getting back to basics? Is there a cheaper and simpler way of finding out if a major quake is on its way? It seems that in unusual animal behaviour there might be. The problem is that monitoring animal behaviour to predict an earthquake is extremely subjective and depends as much on what the observer defines as 'unusual' as it does on the behaviour of the animals themselves. There are, nevertheless, numerous accounts from all over the world of anomalous animal behaviour prior to significant earthquakes. Japanese fishermen have reported bigger catches just before an earthquake, the idea presumably being that, given a choice, the fishermen's nets seem preferable to the impact of an undersea quake. Japanese catfish are also said to become more active prior to an earthquake, leaping out of the water in an excitable state. Before the Haicheng quake all sorts of animals are reported to have gone wild, with pigs becoming unusually aggressive and birds flying into trees.

Notwithstanding this, however, the body of evidence does support the notion that some organisms can detect phenomena that warn of an imminent quake. This is a critical discovery because, if animals are able to do this, then we should be able to build instruments to do the same thing. Although much conjecture is involved, some scientists have suggested that some animals may be able to detect ultrasound or electromagnetic radiation emitted from the crust just before a fault moves. Others have suggested that electrostatic charges may be generated that give furry and feathery beasts repeated electric shocks – certainly enough to irritate an already aggressive pig! The answer remains, however, that we simply do not know what causes animals to react so strangely before a large earthquake. Perhaps, once we do, the Earth will become a much safer place.

The dangers of predictions

It is sometimes worth pondering what would happen if we could accurately predict a major earthquake many months, or even years, ahead. Imagine that, in 50 years time, seismologists have developed a technique that allows them to pinpoint the timing and size of an earthquake 2 years ahead with an accuracy of 2–3 weeks and that, in early 2048, the USGS issues a warning that a magnitude 8.1 quake will strike Los

Angeles in November 2050. The immediate effect would be a plummet in property prices and the collapse of the real-estate business, as buyers for property in the region evaporated. Insurance companies would pull out just as quickly, leaving those with unwanted properties on their hands without cover. Major companies would make plans to move elsewhere, offloading their workforces and creating a huge unemployment problem. It is not hard to believe that, even before the earthquake strikes, its prediction might have caused almost as much, if not more, damage to the economy of the region. Perhaps then it would be better if the Holy Grail of successful earthquake prediction – like the real thing – remained always just out of reach.

'Big ones' of the past and future

The accounts of seismic devastation given so far provide some idea of the terror, mayhem and destruction that will change for ever the lives of the inhabitants of the city, or cities, where the next 'big one' hits. Where, however, is this likely to be, and can we get some clue from looking at where great earthquakes have occurred in the past? Furthermore, is the next 'big one' likely to occur in a country that constantly lives under the threat of major quakes or in one that has experienced nothing so much as tremor for hundreds of years. The answer is that we just do not know, although there are many candidates in both categories. The occurrence of a major earthquake in a region that has not experienced one in recent times is particularly worrying, because the affected communities are likely to be totally unprepared for the shock. Let us look in a little more detail at the possibilities and examine some of the areas under threat.

USA

Ask any citizens of the USA which parts of the country are susceptible to earthquakes and they are certain to say California and, perhaps, also Alaska. Unless they just happen to be geologists, however, they are virtually certain not to think of Missouri as being earthquake prone, and definitely not New York or Charleston on the eastern coast. The problem is that, although major earthquakes have hit all these places, they did so in the last century – Missouri in 1812, New York in 1884 and Charleston, South Carolina, in 1886 – and therefore not in living memory. Consequently, their effects have been forgotten and the threat of

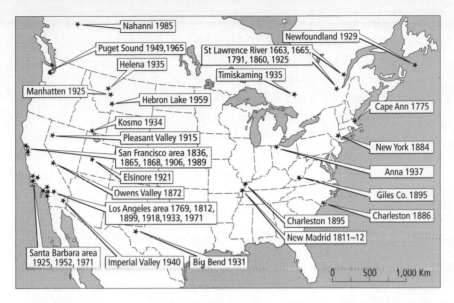

Earthquakes in the USA are not confined to California. Earthquakes causing significant damage have also occurred along the eastern coast and in the interior. (Source: Bryant, 1993)

earthquakes has been wiped from the communal memory. All three quakes shared a common characteristic: they were located far from the plate boundaries where most major quakes are concentrated. A typical feature of such large, intraplate earthquakes is that they have long return periods, usually several decades or even centuries, which has the effect of lulling the local population and often, it has to be said, the civil authorities, into a false sense of security. When the next quake in the sequence comes then, it is often right out of the blue, and, as a result, its effects are often devastating.

Between 16 December 1811 and 7 February 1812 three huge earthquakes approaching 8 on the Richter Scale shook New Madrid on the Mississippi River. Such was the force of the quakes that the land never looked quite the same again. Not only did the tilting and warping of the ground cause the Mississippi to change its course, but swamps and bogs were drained and new lakes formed. Near the epicentre, the intensity of the quake is estimated to have registered X or XI on the Modified Mercalli Scale, sufficient to destroy most buildings, no matter how well constructed. In the event, because of the sparse population at the time, little property was damaged and few lives were lost in the worst hit area. Even 1,000km away, in Pittsburgh and Washington DC, the quakes were strong enough to set doors swinging and church bells ringing, and minor damage was caused as far away as Richmond, Virginia. Ground-shaking associated with one of the quakes triggered tsunami on the Mississippi and also caused the river to reverse its flow for half an hour while it poured into earthquake-generated depressions to form new lakes.

On average, it appears that a quake of magnitude 6 or greater strikes the New Madrid area every 100 years or so, and in 1895 another quake that hit the area was sufficiently strong to be felt from Canada in the north to Louisiana in the south. Based on average return times then, the next earthquake can be expected some time soon, with seismologists forecasting significant damage if the quake is in the magnitude 6–7 range. In addition to injuries and loss of life, the next earthquake is expected to cost nearly US$4 billion in terms of property damage. Also, New Madrid will not be the only community to suffer. Because of their underlying geology, the cities of St Louis, in Missouri, and Memphis, in Tennessee, will experience ground-shaking just as severe as that felt close to the epicentre and will be badly damaged as a consequence. In fact, a quake the size of the Loma Prieta event at New Madrid is forecast to result in Modified Mercalli Scale intensities as high as XI up to 200km from the source, causing major structural damage over a wide area (see figure on p. 185).

You might be wondering why such earthquakes occur at all, well away from the agitation that is constantly taking place at plate boundaries. The reason is that the stresses caused by the movements of the plates relative to one another insinuate themselves, albeit more slowly, even into the hearts of the continents. As at plate boundaries, if the accumulated strains become too high, they must somehow be released. This happens along any available line of weakness, such as the crustal flaw that lies beneath New Madrid, where a fault zone intersects a huge mass of solidified granite magma. Sometimes, earthquakes occur on faults, known as *blind faults*, which do not actually reach the surface, and the Charleston quake of 1886, for example, probably occurred on a fault of this type. This is a general worry in seismology, and geologists are constantly on the look-out for evidence of new, deep and potentially dangerous faults. This morning, even as I write, a newspaper headline trumpeted the discovery of a previously unknown fault directly beneath Los Angeles. The new fracture, christened the Puente Hills Fault, is hidden 15km down and is believed to have been responsible for a magnitude 5.9 quake that occurred in the Los Angeles area in 1987, killing

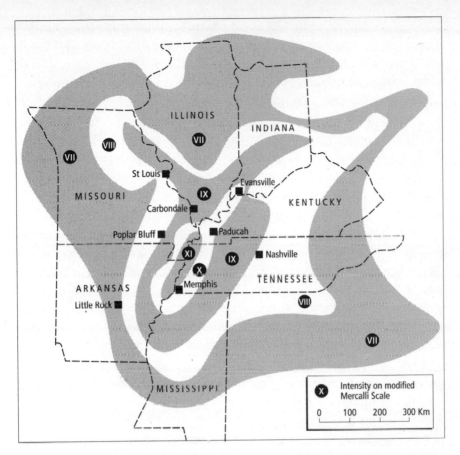

A recurrence of the New Madrid quake of 1811–12 is expected to cause damage worth US$4 billion, with the city of Memphis being particularly badly affected. (Source: Bryant, 1993)

eight people and injuring over 200. The new fault is also thought to be similar to that on which the magnitude 6.7 Northridge earthquake occurred in 1994, killing 57 people, leaving 20,000 homeless and causing economic damage totalling US$35 billion.

Without doubt California remains a prime candidate for the next 'big one': The state continues to be extremely seismically active, and in 1998 southern California alone experienced nearly 12,000 earthquakes, fortunately none large enough to cause damage. The state is nevertheless living on borrowed time, and a major quake is expected to hit within the next few decades. When it comes it will almost certainly be the greatest natural disaster in US history. Despite the 1989 Loma Prieta quake in the north of the state and the 1994 Northridge event in the south, California remains due for a magnitude 8 earthquake. This will occur on either the San Andreas Fault or one of its subsidiaries, which together threaten over 15 million people. Only a single earthquake in excess of magnitude 8 has struck the state this century: the magnitude 8.25 quake that brought San Francisco to its knees in 1906. In that event, 700 people died, either buried beneath debris or incinerated in the fires that raged for days afterward.

The San Andreas Fault, which passes right through modern San Francisco, is one of the most active faults on the planet. It has been in existence since dinosaurs roamed the Earth over 130 million years ago, and since this time the Pacific side of the fault has slid northward by 500km relative to the North American continent to the east. Ever since the ice started to leave its polar retreats 2 million years ago, the western side of the fault has moved north by 15km or so, and it continues to do so at 5cm/year, about the width of three fingers. Instrumental monitoring shows that, along much of its length, the San Andreas is continually creeping so that no strain is accumulating in the rock. At certain points, however, continual movement is inhibited, and it is these locked segments that threaten to release the next great earthquake. Where, then, can we expect this to occur? San Francisco is once again a candidate for destruction, and although many smaller quakes have occurred in the surrounding area over the past half a century, the city itself currently occupies a seismic gap. As mentioned earlier, Los Angeles also rests in such a gap, and a major quake here is also overdue. Scientists monitoring the situation in southern California worry about the swelling and subsidence of the crust at Palmdale, 50km north of the city, which may be related to severe strain accumulation in the area and may signify the imminence of a major quake.

Although many, if not most, people would name California as a part of the world that is vulnerable to large earthquakes, few are likely to point to the US State of Washington, 1,000km north of San Francisco. Nevertheless, recent research has indicated that the city of Seattle and its environs are in serious danger from a future major earthquake, probably more so than the major Californian cities, where earthquake building codes are stringently enforced. In Chapter 3 I briefly mentioned the earthquake threat to the northwestern USA in the context of the Pacific-wide tsunami triggered by the last big quake almost 300 years ago. To recapitulate, many US scientists now believe that geological evidence is overwhelming for major magnitude 8 or even 9 quakes occurring, albeit at infrequent intervals, in what is known as the Cascadia Subduction Zone. Here, where the small Juan de Fuca platelet is disappearing beneath the North American continent, strains currently accumulating in the crust will, in the future, be released in a devastating quake, although no one knows when.

The last earthquake, a magnitude 5.3, struck near Seattle in 1996, but something much larger is certainly in the offing. The impact of a major quake might be made worse by the underlying geology of the area, and both Tacoma and Seattle in Washington State, and Vancouver across the border in Canada, are built on sediment sequences that might well liquefy or amplify ground-shaking. Evidence of the strength of the last Cascadia earthquake is provided by spectacular, permanent changes in the topography of the area. When the Earth last shook, tracts of forest along the coast instantaneously subsided, killing the trees that found themselves with their roots in the sea and their supply of sweet water cut off. *Ghost forests* of dead red cedars still stand, providing an epitaph to the last episode of seismic violence and a warning of what is to come for all those who insist on burying their heads in the sand.

There are numerous other parts of the world where a major earthquake might occur in the near future; in fact, since two magnitude 8 quakes occur somewhere every 12 months, someone, somewhere will experience a 'big one' this very year. This is not, however, the issue. A magnitude 8 earthquake in the hinterland of China will not have the same impact as a similar-sized quake in southern California. There are one or two parts of the world, and southern California is clearly one of them, where a devastating earthquake can have an impact that stretches far beyond the borders of the region and indeed the country. The economies of individual nations are now so intertwined that a 'big one' in western Europe, the USA or Japan is capable of setting alarm bells ringing around the world and bringing an already teetering global economy to its knees, and the Tokyo region of Japan is particularly vulnerable in this context. Let us now take a closer look at the earthquake threat in Japan, a country where, quite literally, the Earth never stops shaking.

Target Japan

The four large islands and many smaller ones that make up the Japanese archipelago stretch for 3,000km from Taiwan in the south to the

Russian island of Sakhalin in the north. In less knowledgeable times, the Japanese thought that earthquakes were the result of divine shenanigans deep within the Earth. Here they believed that the god Kashima, the protector of the Earth, held down a giant catfish, or *namazu*, with a huge rock. Sometimes, however, Kashima would fall into a slumber or drop his guard, allowing the catfish to thrash about, causing the earth above to shake and tremble. In our more enlightened times we appreciate that the many earthquakes that strike Japan on a frequent basis are due not to the flailings of a hyperactive catfish but rather to the complex geology of the region.

The Japanese islands are located along the eastern edge of the Asian continent, where dense oceanic lithosphere is being subducted beneath the gigantic Eurasian Plate that stretches west as far as the middle of the Atlantic Ocean. The oceanic lithosphere that is pushing down beneath the lower density Asian continent belongs to not one but two oceanic plates: the great Pacific Plate in the north and the much smaller Philippine Sea Plate in the south (see figure on p. 189). In the vicinity of Tokyo, the Pacific Plate plunges beneath the Philippine Sea Plate, which, in turn, dips beneath the Eurasian Plate. It is this highly complicated and poorly understood geology that is the cause of the devastating quakes that strike the area with worrying frequency. So dynamic is the Japanese region that it accounts for something like 10 per cent of all the seismic energy released in the world every year. Although much of this takes the form of minor tremors detectable only by instruments, around three a day are powerful enough to be felt.

Since the Great Kanto Earthquake and fire of 1923 that obliterated Tokyo and the neighbouring city of Yokohama, Japan's capital has led a charmed life. Although the city has been gently to moderately shaken on occasion, most recently during a magnitude 5.9 quake in 1992, no major earthquake has struck the region since 1923. Everyone, including the Japanese government, knows that sometime soon the ominous silence must be shattered. When it is, the economic shock-waves will hurtle around the world, devastating country after country. Tokyo is the heart of Japan, and Japan is at the heart of the global economy. Over 20 million people live in the region, which is also the home to the national government, the stock market and most big businesses. Many believe that, if Tokyo stops working, so will the rest of the world. Probably the best way to get some idea of how a major earthquake will affect Japan's capital is to take a look at how the authorities coped in the mid-1990s,

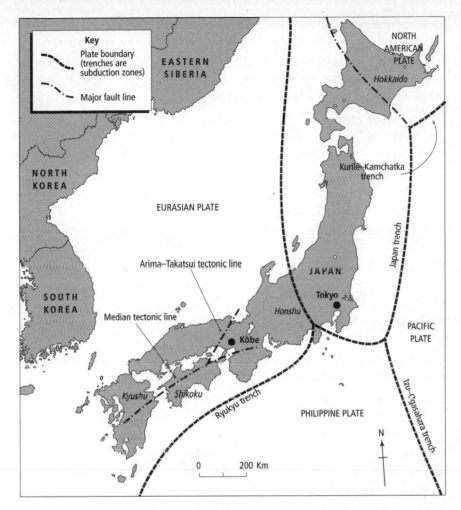

Tokyo is located in a region of particularly complex geology where the Pacific, Eurasian, and Philippine Plates converge. The last major earthquake, the Great Kanto Earthquake, occurred in 1923 and caused the near-complete destruction of Tokyo and Yokohama. Many experts believe that the next major earthquake is now imminent. (Source: Bishop, 1998)

when the Great Hanshin Earthquake ripped through the city of Kobe just over 400km southwest of Tokyo.

As we have seen, the Kobe quake of 17 January 1995, at magnitude 7.2, was virtually identical in size to the Loma Prieta quake that struck the San Francisco area 6 years earlier, but for a number of reasons the damage and loss of life at Kobe was many times greater. What surprised many people in the West, who regarded Japanese society as a model of efficiency, a view largely based on their astute business acumen, was the apparent inability of the authorities to cope with the aftermath of the quake. Appropriate plans were simply not in place to permit the movement of emergency supplies and equipment when most of the road and rail links were blocked by debris, and many of the hundreds of thousands of homeless received no help whatsoever for days after the quake. At least some of the problems at Kobe appear to have been rooted in the notoriously hierarchical nature of Japanese society, a trait that stifles independent thought and action and hinders rapid response in emergency situations. It remains doubtful whether any earthquake disaster plan devised for Tokyo could function effectively within the constraints imposed by such a deeply ingrained and restrictive social etiquette. The disaster managers will continue to try and plan for every eventuality, and the population will dutifully practise their earthquake drills every year, but when the next great quake hits the city the eyes of the whole world will be watching to see if anything has been learned from the Kobe experience.

The Tokyo metropolitan area is at risk from earthquakes occurring in no fewer than four different locations, all of which are widely regarded as being overdue. A quake of magnitude 6.5–7 near the city of Odawara, 75km to the southwest of the city, is thought to be imminent and capable of causing moderate damage to the capital and its environs. A so-called 'Tokai' quake, perhaps of magnitude 8, is also expected to occur beneath Suruga Bay 150km to the southwest. This is also not likely to have a major destructive impact on Tokyo, although the city of Shizuoka on the western coast of the bay will almost certainly experience severe damage and loss of life. The two greatest threats to Japan's capital come from a repeat of the Great Kanto Earthquake, beneath Sagami Bay, and from what is known as a *chokka-gata* quake directly beneath the city. Like the Odawara and Tokai quakes, a chokka-gata, possibly as strong as magnitude 7, is thought by many seismologists to be imminent, although a repetition of the Great Kanto event is probably a few decades off.

★ ★ ★

While the next chokka-gata will cause severe damage to Tokyo, the next Great Kanto Earthquake will devastate the entire Tokyo-Yokohama conurbation and have a truly catastrophic impact on the economy of the country and probably the world. Let us travel forward to the third decade of the next millennium to see what might happen in such an event.

Tokyo mega-quake, AD 2030

• *As you know, a magnitude 8 quake struck 25 years ago beneath Suruga Bay, causing severe damage.* The severity of the shaking locally registered 7 on the Japan Meteorological Agency Scale, or JMS as it is usually abbreviated (see table below), but only 5 in the Tokyo-Yokohama metropolitan area 150km to the northeast. The Suruga Bay event was what we call a 'Tokai' quake, after the name of the area in which it occurred, and it was the first to strike since 1854.

Japan Meteorological Agency Scale (JMS) and comparison with the Modified Mercalli Scale.

Intensity on Japan Meteorological Scale	Effects and damage	Approximate equivalent on Modified Mercalli Scale
0	Not felt; detectable only by seismographs	I
1	Faint tremor felt only by people at rest	II
2	Not detectable by all; lamps swing and water in bowls is disturbed; vibration similar to a passing truck	III
3	Detectable by all; houses shake, doors creak windows rattle, crockery disturbed	IV–V
4	Slight damage; felt by all; houses shake violently; loose plaster may fall and heavy furniture moved	VI
5	Notable damage; noticed by people driving cars; walls crack, chimneys damaged	VII
6	Major damage; fewer than 30 per cent of buildings collapse; ground fracturing and landslides occur; most people not able to stand	VIII–IX
7	Severe damage; over 30 per cent of buildings collapse; ground fracturing and landslides common	X–XII

The 2005 quake occurred offshore in the 2,000m-deep Suruga trough, where the basaltic oceanic lithosphere of the Philippine Sea Plate to the east is being subducted beneath the granitic continental lithosphere of which Japan is constructed. The Philippine Sea Plate moves at about 8 or 9cm/year and drags down the leading edge of the over-riding Eurasian Plate on which Japan is resting. Some 25 years ago, this plate edge sprang back up again, triggering the quake that destroyed over 90,000 buildings and damaged another 130,000. Another 300,000 were destroyed or damaged by fire and, along the coast, by tsunami. The death toll was over 16,000 with more than 100,000 people injured.

In Tokyo, the effects were not great, with damage mainly confined to the reclaimed land around Tokyo Bay, where liquefaction was a problem. There were only 300 deaths, mostly resulting from glass and other debris falling onto pedestrians. Tokyo escaped lightly in 2005, but it is now over 100 years since the capital was last hit by a really severe earthquake. When it comes, and many of us think it is now far overdue, the impact will be devastating.

Part of a lecture by seismologist Noboru Narita to Western journalists based in Tokyo, Disaster Day, 1 September 2030.

The world in chaos

It was almost midnight on New Year's Eve 2029, and all across the planet revellers were counting down the final seconds of the Old Year in traditional manner. It is perhaps understandable if some counted a little faster, desperate as they were to forget an appalling year for planet Earth. Virtually no country had been left untouched by the chaos, both natural and man-made, that had reigned across the globe during the past 12 months. As global warming really began to take hold, floods devastated China, the USA and Europe, while millions died in the great African drought and famine, caused by rains that have held off for over 4 years.

For months now, the world's economy had teetered on the edge of collapse, never really recovering from the hammering it took 5 years earlier when the Indo-Pakistani war went nuclear and threatened to draw in the United States of Europe (USE) and China. With the latest land war in the Balkans entering its sixth year, and Chinese officers for the first time acting as advisors to the Serb forces, the markets had reached their lowest ebb, expecting a major super-power conflict to break out at any time. So much of the optimism that had gripped the planet as the new millennium dawned exactly 30 years earlier had now been lost, and never before had there been such a general feeling of despair for the future. Like a great pile of junk in a breaker's yard, the whole infrastructure of global society was wobbling and ready to crash to Earth. All it needed was one tiny push.

After the 2005 Tokai earthquake, there had been considerable argument among Japanese seismologists about whether or not the quake should have been expected on the basis of another earthquake that occurred in the area beforehand. Some believed that another smaller quake in 2002, at Odawara on the northwestern coast of Sagami Bay, may have transferred crustal stresses onto the fault beneath Suruga Bay, which then eventually ruptured 3 years later. The same school looked with great concern on a series of relatively small, magnitude 4 or 5 quakes, that had struck the Tokyo metropolitan area in the quarter of a century since the Tokai quake, equating them with a similar, if longer, series of small to medium quakes that preceded the devastating Great Kanto Earthquake of 1923. Other seismologists and geologists felt, however, that the interaction of faults in the Tokyo area was too complex to permit such simple linkages and dismissed the ideas as pure speculation bordering on scaremongering. Although every Japanese seismologist knew that a major quake must hit the capital at some time, the majority still held to the views that, firstly, there was no hard evidence for its imminence, and secondly, and very optimistically, that they would be able to detect signals in the rocks that would allow its successful prediction.

Following the Tokai quake, the 15 million people of the Tokyo area lived in constant fear of the next 'big one' to hit the city, with the most nervous going to bed at night wondering if they would ever again see another sunrise. Others, however, were more optimistic, having dutifully practised their earthquake drills every Disaster Day and having listened to the comforting words of the government and state geologists, who assured them that they would receive a warning before the Earth next shook violently. Despite over 50 years of fruitless research, the Japanese government continued to pour money into efforts to predict earthquakes. The USA and other quake-prone countries lost faith in earthquake prediction in the 1980s, concentrating instead on seismic research related to making buildings safer and ensuring better preparedness. In the 1990s and the early years of the new millennium it looked as if at last Japan would follow suit. Loss models constructed for insurance companies forecast such utter devastation as a result of the next major earthquake to hit Tokyo, however, that an increasingly nervous national government was persuaded to look again at earthquake prediction research. The Tokai quake was the last straw, and a decade later three-quarters of the Japanese earthquake research budget was being spent on attempting to predict the next great quake to hit the capital.

• *Kaora Mizoguchi looked carefully at the radon gas data telemetered from one of the deep-water wells on the northern coast of Sagami Bay. His young technician Yukio Yamaguchi, worried about a consistent rise over the previous 3 weeks, had drawn his attention to them a few days ago. The reading was certainly up again, as it was in two other wells in the area. Radon gas is derived from radioactive minerals contained in the rocks that make up the Earth's crust, and an increase can sometimes be explained by the growth of tiny fractures in the rock that often precedes an earthquake. These allow more of the gas to travel up through the crust and into the ground water. Normally he would be concerned at the readings, but the water levels in the wells had not changed unexpectedly, and he had already checked the bore-hole strain-gauges and gravity-meters, neither of which recorded increasing deformation of the crust in the area.*

Doctor Mizoguchi input the data into a spreadsheet and incorporated it into the weekly report that he would e-mail to the Japan Meteorological Agency, which coordinated all data collection relating to earthquake pre-diction. The report, dated 3 October 2030, would indicate that activity was normal and the radon gas readings would be explained away in terms of nor-mal fluctuations.

Deep beneath Sagami Bay, everything was far from normal. The Tokai quake a quarter of a century earlier had reduced strain in the region of the Suruga trough to the west, but at the same time it had transferred stresses to the Sagami trough. Although the land on the northern coast of Sagami Bay had been undergoing uplift at the rate of a few millimetres a year for the past cou-ple of decades, there had been no increase in recent months and no other signs that a quake in the trough was imminent. So much, then, for the huge and opti-mistic expenditure of the government on earthquake prediction. Already it was too late. The destruction of the Japanese capital was only hours away.

• ***Professor Masatada Hori rummaged under the piles of paper that littered his desk at the University of Tokyo Earthquake Research Institute, trying to find and silence the beeper that had been going off for the past minute or so.*** *As far as he knew there had been no unusual geological activity to indi-cate that a big quake might be on its way, so he assumed it was just another drill. Why did they always happen at such inconvenient moments? He was due to give a seminar to staff and postgraduate students that evening, and he had not even started getting his notes together yet. Finally locating the beeper in an overflowing wastebasket, Professor Hori switched it off and talked quietly to his wrist videophone.*

Within minutes he heard the familiar sound of a police-car siren – the third time in as many months – and grabbing his coat, he headed for the door. The car screeched to a halt outside the main entrance to the building, and the harassed professor was bundled unceremoniously into it by a burly officer. Within seconds, the car was moving off, siren wailing, heading for the specially designed bunker in the Japanese Meteorological Agency's building. Historically the JMA had led Japanese earthquake research, and it continued to play the major coordinating role in earthquake research and prediction.

At the bunker, the five fellow members of the Earthquake Assessment Committee would join Professor Hori, there to be faced with a hypothetical pile of data relating to a possible imminent earthquake scenario. On the basis of these data, the Committee would have to decide whether or not the Prime Minister should go on television to inform the nation that a major earth- quake was on the way. If the committee decided that a quake was imminent, the PM would have to consult all his cabinet members and get their agree- ment before issuing the televised warning. In immediate response to the warning, citizens of the threatened area would be expected to switch off all electrical and gas appliances, make sure that water and emergency supplies were to hand and look for a relatively safe place to ride out the quake. Millions of workers would head for home according to a staggered time- table, hoping that the quake did not strike while they were out in the open. Professor Hori knew that in reality such an announcement was likely to trigger widespread panic, and in any case he had a strong suspicion that the next 'big one' would strike with no detectable warning signs.

Just as Professor Hori and his eminent colleagues took their seats at the big circular table in the dimly lit room and reached for the piles of seismo- grams and other geophysical and geological data stacked on its heavily polished surface, they became aware of a faint but distinct vibration. Within a few seconds this strengthened, tipping the table sideways and hurling the carefully arranged papers onto the floor. One of the older members of the committee tried to stand but was catapulted backward into the huge holo- graphic projection screen on which the Prime Minister was supposed to announce an imminent quake.

This would never happen now, because at that very moment the PM was staring with disbelief at the blood pouring down his chest from the great shard of stained glass that had penetrated his neck. Two fellow members of his party slowly stretched out the dying first minister on the floor, while deadly splinters of glass and other debris from the stained glass ceiling above continued to rain down onto the unfortunate honourable members of the Diet. The ceilings had always been envisaged as posing a problem in a large earthquake, and they had broken and collapsed in a similar manner during the last Tokai quake. Although the members of parliament had been issued with protective headgear for just such an event, most had left it in their offices. They therefore cut vaguely comical figures as they staggered desper- ately for the safety of the exits while holding their jackets protectively over their heads. Outside the parliament buildings all hell had broken loose.

The mega-quake

At 12.32p.m. Tokyo time, on 4 October 2030, the strains that had been accumulating for decades between the two great masses of lithosphere that met
beneath Sagami Bay were released in just over a minute of devastating violence,
as one thrust itself beneath the other. Out in the bay the waters boiled as the
sea-bed jolted explosively upward, transferring a gigantic pulse of energy to the
sea. Within minutes the waters began to withdraw from shores all around the
bay, gathering themselves at its centre for a terrible onslaught. On land the
impact of the magnitude 7.9 quake was almost unimaginable. For 72 seconds
the citizens of the Tokyo-Yokohama conurbation, together with those of many
other towns in the region, found themselves occupying a living hell.

The quake started off as a low, rumbling vibration, of the sort to which
the inhabitants of the region had got so used over the years that they hardly
noticed it. This was no minor tremor, however, and within 10 seconds windows
were smashing, walls cracking and chimneys tumbling to the ground. A few
seconds more and it was impossible to walk or even drive in a straight line.
Thousands of older buildings in the *Shitamachi*, or 'low town', started to collapse, their heavy tiled roofs instantly crushing those just sitting down to their
mid-day meal below. There were few automated gas supply cut-offs here, and
hundreds of fires started even before the ground had stopped shaking, as pans
of boiling oil for cooking tempura were overturned onto gas-burners.

In downtown Tokyo, total panic reigned in office blocks as plate-glass windows shattered and filing cabinets hurtled across rooms. Some sought shelter
beneath heavy items of furniture while many, despite their indoctrination, ran
screaming into the street. Here they came under sustained attack from huge
chunks of falling glass, pieces of giant advertising hoarding and masonry. On
the gridlocked highways, it was impossible for drivers to pull over as the earthquake drills recommended – there was simply no room – and under the
worsening bombardment from above they left their vehicles in the middle of
the road and looked in desperation for cover.

Half-way into the quake the severe ground-shaking cut power lines to
shreds, and much of the Tokyo metropolitan area was plunged into gloom.
Darkness reigned throughout much of the subway network, where hysterical
passengers tried to keep their feet while hunting desperately for the nearest
exit. As the shaking continued, much of the soft, water-saturated soils around
the Ara and Tama rivers, along the waterfront, and under much of the downtown area started to liquefy, offering no resistance to the buildings above,
which simply sank or toppled into them. At the height of the quake, muddy

water squirted out of the ground in great spurts to flood the precariously lean-
ing buildings. After just over a minute of utter horror, the shaking stopped
abruptly, and for a few moments perfect silence held thrall across the ruins of
what were once the great cities of Yokohama and Tokyo. The end of the quake
marked the beginning of even greater devastation, however, as flames began to
lick at the remains of millions of wooden buildings, and the sea out in Sagami
Bay waited in the wings to play its part in the mayhem.

Aftermath

Within a few minutes of the end of the quake, the waters of Sagami Bay hurled
themselves at the waterfront in downtown Tokyo, wave after wave up to 6m
high pounding the factories and port facilities to pieces. Elsewhere around
Tokyo Bay, over a dozen oil refineries, many constructed on reclaimed land,
took a severe pounding, from either the tsunami or the liquefaction of the
underlying soil. Around Chiba City across the bay from Tokyo, dozens of the
thousands of storage tanks were fractured by the severe sloshing of the oil or
gasoline inside them, and fires raged across the area, both on land and sea, fry-
ing alive refinery workers desperate to escape. As in the 1923 quake, fire took a
much more devastating toll on the cities of Tokyo and Yokohama than the
quake itself, and within hours conflagrations began to take hold across the
great conurbation.

The 4 October was another warm, dry autumnal day, although with a bit of
a chill wind coming up from the south. Following a miserably damp and humid
summer, the last month or so had been gorgeous, fresh and not too hot, and
with hardly a drop of rain since August. As a result, the 8.5 million wooden
buildings in the Tokyo metropolitan area were tinder dry. Despite automatic gas
cut-offs in many homes, it was inevitable that thousands of fires would start
after such a violent shaking, some from overturned stoves, some from fractured
gas mains or exploding cars, and others from oil or chemical spills. Once the fires
had started, especially in the poorer districts of the *Shitamachi*, they soon took
hold and spread through the narrow, debris-filled streets. Fanned by drying
winds of increasing strength, the fires merged to form huge conflagrations that
occupied entire city blocks. It was 1923 all over again.

Desperately trying to find a safe haven, tens of thousands of terrified men,
women and children were herded this way and that by the fire-storms, whole
crowds sometimes becoming trapped and roasted alive by the fast-moving
flames. In many districts there was no one to fight the fires at all; debris in the
streets prevented fire-fighting vehicles from reaching the flames, and damaged
water mains meant that there was nothing to fight them with. Many who

sought sanctuary in the sea or rivers faced an even more appalling end, being slowly boiled alive or fried to a crisp by burning slicks of oil.

For over 6 days the fires raged out of control and when, on 10 October, they had all but burned themselves out, an area of nearly 1,000km², larger than Greater London, was a smoking wreck. Japan's capital was a ruin: over 4 million buildings had been destroyed in total, a quarter of these by the quake itself and the rest by the great fires. The death toll amounted to almost 200,000, with a further 300,000 injured. So great was the devastation that the emergency services simply could not cope, and for weeks the sick and wounded wandered the streets, trying to find food, shelter and drinkable water. Months later bodies were still being exhumed from collapsed buildings, while the authorities desperately tried to cope with the millions of traumatized homeless. Most significantly, the bubble of Japanese economic supremacy burst overnight as the country's financial markets collapsed and the nation ground to a halt. Japan had stopped working – and now so would the rest of the world.

Economic depression

To a world poised on the brink of economic collapse the Great Kanto Earthquake of 2030 was the final straw. The staggering economic cost was estimated to be around 7 trillion euros, or 70 per cent of the gross domestic product of the country. Of this, about 3.5 trillion euros resulted from property damage, while a similar sum resulted from losses due to the interruption of business. As the Japanese financial market ceased to function on the day of the quake, economic as well as seismic shock-waves headed out across the planet. Stock markets elsewhere in Asia, in the USE and in the North American Economic Zone went into freefall. Within 2 days the markets had plummeted by an average of 40 per cent, with no end in sight. The last Great Kanto quake, little more than a century earlier, had had virtually no effect on the world's stock markets; this time, however, the situation was very different.

With both the Europeans and the North Americans distracted by dramatic changes in their political situations – the former by the Indo-Pakistani and Balkan wars – the Japanese market had become even more powerful. Before the quake struck, it handled three times the business of New York and twice that of Frankfurt. Now it handled none. As the global economic situation steadily deteriorated and the Japanese government became aware of the tremendous cost of reconstruction, the new prime minister called a cabinet meeting to discuss the future. After closeting themselves away for 3½ days, during which time they called before them the country's top financial and economic experts, they emerged to stagger the world with an announcement almost as devastating as the earthquake: Japan would retreat temporarily from global investment. In order to focus their immense resources on regenerating the economy of the Tokyo region, the Japanese began to dump government bonds in Europe and North America. As bond values plummeted, interest rates outside Japan went through the roof. At the same time, Japanese companies who had suffered badly in the quake began to sell foreign assets and to close plants across the world in order to concentrate on rebuilding their home base.

While the West struggled to operate in the drastically changed financial climate, many of the stock markets in the East went under without much of a fight. Already weakened by over-inflated economies, the stock markets of China, Singapore and Malaysia crashed within weeks of the Japanese initiative, triggering rampant inflation and a dash for cash among savers. Rioting in the streets followed soon after, as savers and small investors demanded funds that no longer existed. The same thing was happening in Central and South America and parts of the African continent, where Japanese investment was the only thing keeping the local economies afloat. At one fell swoop, the rest of the world was being deprived of a huge chunk of its debt-financing and investment capital, and it simply could not cope.

The impact of the quake on Japan's industrial base was devastating and explained the need to withdraw from foreign investment. In 2030 nearly 75 per cent of Japan's biggest companies had their headquarters in the Tokyo region, with the production of industrial goods and services in the capital being almost double that of the UK. The cost of replacing the industrial infrastructure of the region was unprecedented and required all those companies badly hit by the quake to look to their foreign assets to finance regeneration. While Japan concentrated all its attention on a massive programme of reconstruction in the years following the quake, the situation in the rest of world went from bad to worse. The deepest recession since the 1920s led to unemployment on an unprecedented scale in the USE and the North American Economic Zone, leading to a deterioration in the social fabric and the rise of extremist groups. Unable to fund peacekeeping in the Balkans, the USE ground troops pulled out, leaving a free-for-all bloodbath in which millions died as the warring parties gave vent to centuries of repressed hate. The withdrawal of similar international mediation forces from Northern Ireland, southern Turkey and several African countries led to savage fighting on an appalling scale and a new Dark Age in many parts of the world.

Five years after the destruction of Tokyo, much of the city had been rebuilt; shining, spanking new and, in theory at least, earthquake proof. The Japanese were ready once again to take their rightful place at the helm of the global economy. Now, however, the world economy was very, very different. Still in deep recession, and understandably mistrustful of the capriciousness of a capitalist market that effectively existed for so long to make money for financiers and their friends, many countries had retreated behind the perceived safety of rigid state control. The Japanese industrial machine was ready to go, but where? Unsurprisingly, former friends paid back their withdrawal from the global market 5 years earlier by refusing to drop barriers to trade and investment. Never again would a single country, or worse, a single city, be allowed to hold such power over the world's economy. Eventually the paranoia would fade and the barriers to international trade fall, but not for a very long time yet.

CHAPTER 5

GOD'S ANVIL:
HELL ON EARTH

The third angel sounded his trumpet,
and a great star, blazing like a torch,
fell from the sky on a third of the rivers
and on the springs of water.

Revelation 8:10

Jan Van der Eems tried once more to pull his shattered limb from beneath the huge wooden beam, but it just wouldn't budge. The earthquakes that followed the impact 300km to the south had brought the old house crashing down into the basement, the rubble protecting Jan from the rain of hot debris, but crushing and trapping his left leg. Sweat poured down his face, not only from the excruciating agony but also from the sweltering heat that trickled down from above. Listening out for the first crackle of the fires he knew must eventually come, Jan failed at first to hear a different noise. A quiet susurration to begin with, then a rushing sound like an express train, and finally a roar like the jets that swooped over the house to land at Schiphol. Today, however, there were no planes. At once Jan recognized the noise, smiled in resignation and slumped back against the basement wall. It was not the fire that would get him, it was that age-old combatant of every Dutchman, the North Sea, back at last to reclaim its own.

Two twentieth-century impacts

Consider early autumn in the English countryside. As the mornings dawn chilly and spiders' webs drape themselves across the hedgerows, leaves begin to take on the bright and varied hues of red, yellow and brown that herald the winding down of the year. Imagine walking along a forest path as the many-coloured leaves lose their grip and begin to float to earth. Sometimes it is like walking through a storm of coloured snow, only the flakes are 100 times larger. Although there are thousands of leaves in the air around you, most miss as you pass by, falling to the ground unimpeded. Occasionally, however, one will score a direct hit, bouncing off your head or shoulder on its way to join next year's mulch.

Such a walk through the autumnal forest is a little like the passage of planet Earth through a dangerous and debris-filled solar system (see figure below). It is estimated that something like 150 million, and perhaps as many as a billion, chunks of rock larger than 10m hurtle across

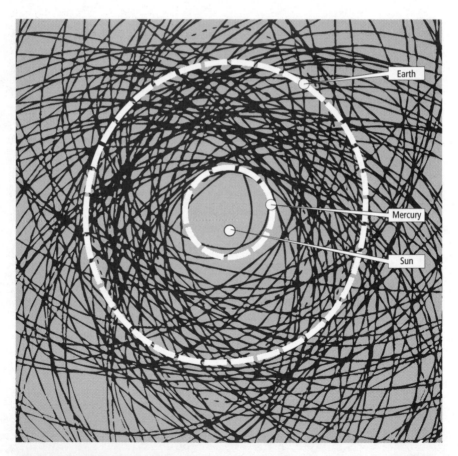

A plot of the orbits of the 100 largest earth-crossing objects (probably only about 5 per cent of the total) provides a disturbing picture of how congested our region of space really is. The Sun (central dot) and the orbits of Mercury and Mars (dotted lines) are visible. The orbits of the Earth and Venus are, however, hidden. (Source: In Steel, 1995, by courtesy of Rick Binzel, MIT)

our planet's orbital path around the Sun. Worryingly, between 150,000 and 1 million of these are over 100m across, big enough to take out a major city should they hit, while between 2,000 and 4,000 are larger than 1km across. Should one hit, these largest objects are capable of instantaneously wiping out billions of people, drastically altering the global climate and returning our advanced technological civilization to Dark Age squalor and mayhem.

Of course, the Earth has been pounded from space by chunks of rock and ice throughout its history and, as already explained, it was this collision process that led, through accretion, to the formation of our planet in the first place and, later, to the excavation of the Moon from the primitive Earth. As we shall see, large collisions with cosmic objects can have terrifying consequences, including wiping out the bulk of all life on the planet (see p 224). The dinosaurs learned this to their cost some 65 million years ago when a gigantic object, at least 10km across, ploughed into what is now the Yucatán Peninsula of Mexico, and the Age of Reptiles was finally brought to a violent conclusion. No impact of similar magnitude has occurred since, although, on the basis of the number of rocks hurtling about in the Earth's vicinity, it is likely that many 1km-sized objects have collided with the planet since the demise of the dinosaurs. Unfortunately, because of the extraordinarily active surface of the Earth, it is often difficult to track down, identify and study the scars of these events, and therefore to surmise accurately what will be the effect of the next 1km impact on the planet and our modern society.

During this century, however, we have had two opportunities to study impacts as they happened, or at least soon afterward. The first involved the arrival of a large lump of rock that blew itself apart above the Siberian taiga in 1908; the second was a disrupted comet that blasted into the planet Jupiter as recently as 1994. Examining the effects of these two remarkable events can tell us much about what the next big impact will mean for the human race.

Tunguska, Siberia, 1908

At just after 7.17a.m. on 30 June 1908 the peace and calm of a sparsely populated region of northern Siberia was shattered by a gigantic explosion that literally sent shock-waves around the world. Despite the fact that the area of the explosion was virtually uninhabited, there were numerous eyewitness reports that left little room for doubt that the Earth had collided violently with an object from beyond its atmosphere. Russian peasants from nearby villages reported seeing in the sky a blue-white fireball that was too bright to look at. The fireball took the form of a cylindrical pipe and was apparently visible for 10 minutes before approaching the ground. The object exploded with a noise like heavy gunfire, sending flashes of flame upward into the cloud. The event terrified the villagers, who took to the streets weeping, thinking that it was the end of the world.

Eyewitnesses in the Tunguska river area provided even more extraordinary accounts of the blast, particularly a herdsman called Ilya Potapovich Petrov, whose brother was probably the closest to the event. Ilya's brother reported a terrible explosion that flattened the forest over a great distance and destroyed his house, carrying the roof off in hurricane-force winds. The noise was sufficient to deafen him, and the shock caused him a long period of illness. Alongside Ilya Petrov's brother there were perhaps 20 people within 50km of the explosion, many of whom were injured and two reportedly killed. The short-term effects of the blast were to be seen all over Europe over the next several nights, as the gas and dust raised by the explosion glowed with enough strength to be seen even from the UK. Apocryphal stories abound, including one that reports a night sky so bright that games of cricket were played in London after midnight. Another purports to describe the mass desertion of a Polish army unit who, believing that the bright night sky foretold the end of the world, are said to have all joined a monastery. Seismographs thousands of kilometres distant picked up the blast, as did barographs across the planet, which showed the passage of the pressure-wave as it circled the globe three times.

Because of the utter remoteness of the Tunguska region and the minor diversion of the Russian Revolution, and despite great curiosity among the scientific community in Moscow and elsewhere, it was nearly 20 years before a full scientific expedition was organized to visit the site. The palates of the expedition leaders had already been whetted by further eyewitness accounts, gleaned from the locals by geologists working in the area in 1924 – 16 years after the blast. From these reports, the enormous scale of the event became apparent. The sound of the blast was heard loudly over an area of over 1 million square kilometres as the fireball was observed to plunge earthward. When the scientific expedition, led by Leonid Kulik, headed for the Tunguska basin in 1927, they knew that something from space had arrived in deepest Siberia, and they fully expected it to have left its mark in the form of a huge crater. What they found on their arrival in this desolate part of the world was even more astounding and completely unexpected.

As the expedition members neared their objective they began to encounter flattened and burned trees, first only on the tops of hills but later everywhere. When they reached the centre of the devastated area they soon realized that there was no sign whatsoever of a crater or of any pieces of meteorite debris. Instead, there was a 60km-wide, roughly circular zone of flattened trees, all pointing outward, away from the centre. All the trees were charred as if they had been exposed to extreme heat, and although those in the very centre of the zone still stood, all their branches had been sheared off. The expedition members were dumbfounded and perplexed.

So what exactly happened over Tunguska in the early years of the twentieth century? The accepted explanation is that a small asteroid, probably about 50m across, exploded in the atmosphere between 6 and 10km above the Siberian wastes. The blast was vertical directly beneath the explosion, allowing the trees there to remain standing while ripping off their branches. Elsewhere the blast had a lateral component that was sufficient to push over the trees, so that they all pointed away from the point on the surface directly beneath the explosion. As the object blew itself apart it generated sufficient heat to char the vegetation, although the hurricane-force winds that followed put out many of the fires before they had time to get a grip. The area affected by the blast, over 2,000km^2, can be used to provide a reasonable estimate of the energy of the blast, which must have been the equivalent of somewhere between 10 million and 20 million tonnes of TNT – equivalent to at least 800 Hiroshima bombs.

Although the 1927 expedition members were disappointed to find no trace of the impacting object, later detective work by scientists recovered small glass and metal fragments from the soil, confirming that the object was completely pulverized and partially melted during the explosion. Considering the amount of energy released in the impact, the death toll was remarkably small and entirely the result of the very low population density. If the object had struck at the same latitude little more than 4 hours later, the story would have been very different, and the beautiful city of St Petersburg would have been wiped off the face of the Earth.

Planet Jupiter, 1994

As we approached the end of the century that opened with the great Siberian blast, we had the first opportunity directly to observe an impact event, and one much more spectacular than that which devastated the Tunguska basin. Fortunately, however, the impact did not take place on Earth but on the planet Jupiter. The king of the planets, Jupiter lies in the outer solar system, beyond the orbit of Mars and the asteroid belt. With a diameter of over 140,000km, Jupiter has a volume large enough to contain over 1,300 Earths, although, because it is largely composed of hydrogen and helium gas, it has a much lower mean density. With a mass over 300 times that of the Earth, it has a particularly strong gravitational field, which explains its large retinue of moons. This field is also particularly effective at capturing any rogue asteroids or comets that happen to pass within its clutches, and this is exactly what happened to Comet Shoemaker-Levy 9, or more simply SL9. When the comet was discovered in 1993 by the late Eugene Shoemaker, his wife, Carolyn, and their colleague David Levy, it was realized very quickly that this was no ordinary comet. Firstly, it had fragmented into 21 different pieces, and secondly it was actually in orbit around Jupiter. Calculations showed that the comet's orbit would take it to within 50,000km of the centre of the planet sometime in July 1994. The problem − for the comet − was that Jupiter has a radius of over 70,000km. This meant that, the following summer, astronomers were going to get a grandstand view of the first known collision between a comet and a planet.

There was a good deal of argument about the size of the original object before it was pulled apart by Jupiter's gravitational field, ranging downward from 10km. An object of this size would be capable of wiping out the human race if the Earth was the target instead of Jupiter. As impact day approached, telescopes all over the world were trained on the planet, and the event caught the imagination of anyone with even an inkling of interest in science. To provide maximum coverage of the event, cameras on both the Hubble Space Telescope in orbit around the Earth and the *Galileo* spacecraft *en route* to Jupiter were trained on Jupiter's gaseous exterior. The first fragment struck the planet on 16 July, coincidentally the twenty-fifth anniversary of the launch of *Apollo 11* − the first moon-landing mission − sending up a great plume of gas and debris surrounded by an expanding shock-wave. Fragment after fragment hammered into the planet, some perhaps only 50m across, others much larger. Fragment G proved to the most spectacular, crashing into the gaseous giant just 2 days after the series of impacts began. This 4km object generated a flash so bright that it blinded many telescopes in the infrared waveband, and formed a huge dark spot on the planet that was larger than the Earth.

Fragment G would have hit Jupiter with a velocity of around 60km/second, releasing the same amount of energy as 100 million million tonnes of TNT or 8 billion Hiroshima-sized atomic bombs. Imagine the energy generated by the Tunguska impact and multiply it over 10 million times and you will get some idea of the devastation that Fragment G would have caused had it collided with the Earth. Eventually, on 23 July, the remaining pieces of the comet plummeted into Jupiter's atmosphere, and one of the most spectacular astronomical events of the century was over.

A huge mass of data remains to be analysed, however, and the implications for our safety here on Earth need to be reassessed. If nothing else, the SL9 impacts have brought home to many the fact that, if Jupiter can be hit, so can we. Just what are the chances, however? Should we be watching the skies constantly or is it a question of making a mountain out of a molehill?

The devil's billiard table

As we have seen, the space through which our planet travels on its eternal passage around the Sun is full of debris – perhaps a billion chunks of rock over 10m across and somewhere between 150,000 and 1 million with diameters greater than 100m (see table below).

Estimated numbers of Earth-crossing asteroids.

Object size (diam.)	Probable number	Possible numbers
>1km	2,000	1,000–4,000
>500m	10,000	5,000–20,000
100m	300,000	150,000–1 million
>10m	150 million	10 million–1 billion

We cannot see all these objects, however, and their numbers are estimated from extrapolation based on the power-law distribution introduced in Chapter 1. We can better estimate the number of the larger bodies because we can see them more easily with powerful telescopes, and this number is used to calculate how many smaller objects there are. Even so, estimates of the population of those deadly bodies larger than 1km across varies by 400 per cent, and those of objects larger than 10m across by 10,000 per cent. These great discrepancies are important because they affect our estimates of how often objects of these sizes hit the Earth and, after all, this is what we really want to know. The population of objects that cross the Earth's orbit is not fixed but will change over time as some rocks hit the Earth or other larger bodies that they encounter or become diverted into different orbits that do not threaten our planet. The numbers may also be added to through the break-up of larger bodies and the capture of new objects, such as comets, from elsewhere within the solar system or beyond.

On the basis of the available data, the best guesses for asteroid strike rates range from 1 a year for 10m objects to about 1 in 100,000 years for objects of 1km or more in size. Huge 10km planet-shakers, such as the dinosaur-killer that struck Mexico 65 million years ago are, fortunately, much less common and can be expected every 50 million to 100 million years or so. When the next one arrives, however, it is likely to wipe out

Estimated strike rates of different-sized objects on planet Earth.

Object size (diam.)	Frequency of impact on Earth
Pea	5 minutes
Walnut	1 hour
Soccer ball	1 month
50m	50–100 years
500m	10,000 years
1km	100,000 years
2km	500,000 years
10km	50 million–100 million years

something like 65 per cent of all living species, including us, or at least our distant and evolved descendants. Because of their huge kill rates, the chances of any individual dying in an impact event is twice that of being killed in a plane crash. Comparisons with some recent public health scares are even more impressive, and you are 100,000 times more likely to die in an asteroid or comet strike than from eating beef on the bone. The table on p. 208 gives a more detailed breakdown of the estimated strike rates of different-sized objects.

The billiard balls

So far I have referred to the blocks of debris hurtling across the solar system as chunks of rock, but are they all the same and where exactly do they come from? Although an occasional itinerant visitor may travel across the solar system and never reappear, most of the objects we observe are in relatively close orbit about the Sun. They can be broadly divided into two types: *asteroids* and *comets*.

Asteroids

The asteroid family consists of bodies of rock or metal, ranging in size from a few metres to 1,000km across, most of which roam the solar system on fairly circular orbits between Mars and Jupiter, that is between two and six times the distance of the Earth from the Sun. This material is probably debris left over from the early history of the solar system, when Jupiter's powerful gravitational field constantly disrupted the attempted formation of a planet in what we now know as the *asteroid belt*. Over 20,000 asteroids have been discovered in the belt, and there may be mpre than 500,000 in all.

Of much greater relevance from a hazard point of view are what are called the *near-Earth asteroids*, or NEAs. These have more elliptical orbits that bring them much closer to the Sun, crossing the Earth's orbit on the way. Three classes of NEAs have now been recognized, known as the Apollo, Amor and Aten asteroids. The Apollo objects orbit the Sun along paths that cross the Earth's orbit, but they remain beyond it most of the time. Some of the Amor asteroids also cross the Earth's orbit, but their paths are much more elliptical than those of the Apollo class, so they extend beyond the orbit of Mars. This makes them especially unpredictable because the strong gravitational influence of Jupiter may alter their orbits over time so as eventually to put one on a collision course with our planet. The Aten asteroids are a new class, the first of which was discovered only in 1976. These objects also cross the Earth's orbit, but their paths are primarily closer to the Sun. This means that they are particularly difficult to spot and therefore pose a second unpredictable threat to our planet.

A special class of NEAs, known as the *small Earth-approachers*, or SEAs, have been discovered even more recently, during the early 1990s. The few dozen SEAs found so far are small objects, less than 50m across, that have orbits that are almost identical to that of the Earth. This has suggested to astronomers that they must represent bits of the Moon that have been blasted off by large impacts. Since 1991 alone, three SEAs have passed within 400,000km of the Earth – a distance that is closer than the Moon.

So far it is unlikely that the NEAs would have survived in their current anomalous orbits if they had been around since the formation of the solar system, and it is probable that interactions with Jupiter's gravity have ejected them from the main asteroid belt. An alternative explanation, favoured by increasing numbers of astronomers, proposes that many of these so-called 'asteroids' are actually the remains of old comets.

Comets

Comets constitute the second group of objects to pose an impact threat to the Earth. They differ from asteroids in containing a higher proportion of ice. In fact, it is the evaporation of this ice as a comet approaches the Sun that leads to the characteristic tail, seen most recently in 1997, at least to the naked eye, on Comet Hale-Bopp. When Halley's Comet paid its last visit just 13 years ago, its unimpressive appearance proved a major disappointment to sky-watchers world-wide. However, things were very different during its previous visitation, or *apparition* as such events are traditionally called, in 1910, when its spectacular visage caused panic across the planet. On that occasion, the Earth passed right through the comet's gaseous tail, experiencing dramatic meteor showers as it did so. This, together with astronomers' identification of the deadly compound cyanide in the comet, led to widespread concern, but in the end the Earth and its population survived the ordeal unscathed.

Comets can be huge, perhaps hundreds of kilometres across, with a structure that has long been a matter for heated debate. Two theories competed for many years, one advocating the idea that comets could be likened to a 'flying sandbank', made up of a great mass of sand-sized particles of rock loosely bound together, and the other proposing a composition more along the lines of a 'dirty snowball'. This last opinion has proved to be the closest, and both recent telescope studies and information gathered from unmanned space probes have revealed that comets have a core, or *nucleus*, that is a mixture of rocks and ice. When comets are far out in the solar system beyond the orbit of Jupiter, their appearance is typically faint and unspectacular, and they may look pretty similar to a normal rocky asteroid. As they approach the Sun and begin to heat up, however, they undergo a wonderful metamorphosis. Gas and dust particles begin to be evaporated by sunlight off the cometary nucleus, forming a brightly glowing *coma* that envelops the comet's rock and ice core. Together, the nucleus and the coma constitute the comet's *head*, from which the tail can stretch across space for perhaps as far as 100 million kilometres. The tail we see consists of glowing gas that is blown away from the comet's head by the *solar wind*, the continuous stream of particles emanating from the Sun. This is why a comet's tail always points away from the Sun, even when it is heading away from it on its return voyage to the dark outer reaches of the solar system.

Three different types of comet have been recognized, based upon their *orbital periods* – the time they take to complete an orbit around the Sun. Generally speaking these periods are much longer than those for the NEAs, and the orbits themselves are much more elongated, bringing the comet close in to the Sun and then hurling it back out into the depths of the outer solar system or beyond. *Short period comets* take less than 20 years to complete a full circuit, while *intermediate-period comets* can take up to 200 years. Halley's Comet, with an orbital period of 76 years, comes into this latter category. Because comets of both types have been observed many times, in some cases going back thousands of years, their orbits are very precisely known. This means that their paths can be predicted far into the future in order to determine whether they will ever collide with the Earth. For example, calculations of the future orbital path of Halley's Comet shows that it will not come anywhere near Earth until at least the year AD 3000. For this reason the short- and intermediate-period comets are regarded as much less of a threat to our planet than those belonging to the third category: the *parabolic comets*. These have orbits about the Sun that take them so far away that they may have been seen only once, or perhaps not at all. This means that their orbital characteristics are only very poorly known, if at all. In fact, a parabolic comet that we have never observed may be on a collision course with the Earth at this very moment, and we would never know until it came closer to the Sun and showed its true colours.

The link between asteroids and comets

So far, I have talked about asteroids and comets as if they were different and mutually exclusive objects. It appears increasingly likely, however, that this is not the case, and many astronomers now think that asteroids are either dead or dormant comets. If a comet has made many visitations to the inner solar system, all its ice may have been evaporated by the Sun's heat, making it impossible for a tail to develop. At the same time, the immensely powerful gravitational attraction of Jupiter may gradually pull it into a more circular, asteroid-like orbit about the Sun. To an observer on Earth such an object would be indistinguishable from a normal rocky asteroid. In some cases, a comet's surface ice may be vaporized, leaving ice trapped within that is not released until thousands or millions of years later, perhaps as the object is broken up as a result of getting a little too close to giant Jupiter. Over this period, the dormant comet would be unable to develop either a coma or a tail and would appear asteroid-like, but the exposure of new ice to the Sun's heat would once again promote a spectacular metamorphosis.

Recently, two observations have provided even more conclusive evidence of a link between comets and asteroids. In the 1990s an asteroid with the rather unmemorable label 2060 Chiron began to lose its sharp, star-like appearance in the telescope and take on a fuzzy form. Clearly, the object was degassing – the result of frozen water vaporizing and venting into space – which indicated a significant ice content, just like a comet. Furthermore, in 1986 the unmanned European spacecraft *Giotto* approached close to Halley's Comet and was able to take spectacular photographs. These revealed a great chunk of cratered rock that was shedding a huge volume of gas and dust, which partly obscured it and contributed to its tail. Take away the gas and dust, however, and the image could be one of any straightforward, common-or-garden asteroid.

Earth-crossing asteroids: the search and the threat

We now know that the solar system is full of debris and that, during its travels about the Sun, the Earth has to run the gauntlet of perhaps a billion asteroids and a smaller number of comets (see figure on p. 213). Because of the huge numbers of *Earth-crossing asteroids* (ECAs) and

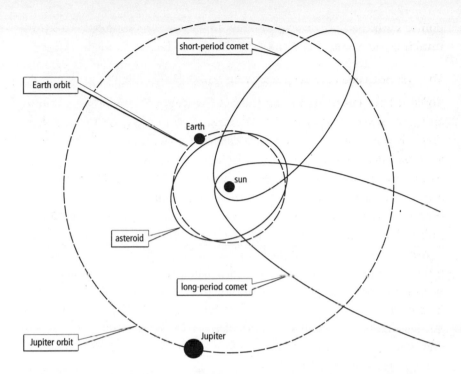

short-period comet

Earth orbit

Earth

sun

asteroid

long-period comet

Jupiter orbit

Jupiter

Asteroids and comets have very different orbital characteristics. Asteroids have near-circular orbits, similar to those of the Earth and other planets. Comets, on the other hand, have much more elliptical orbits which bring them close to the Sun and carry them out into the far depths of the solar system.

because only a few have been spotted, of which the orbits of most are still poorly known, these objects pose a greater threat to the Earth than the less frequent comets. Ballpark estimates suggest that between 2 and 30 per cent of potential impacts may result from collisions between the Earth and a comet, while the rest are attributed to impacts with asteroids. It makes sense that we should be devoting considerable time and energy to locating the rest of the ECAs and plotting their orbits into the future so as to look for possible collisions.

The need to know more about 'what is out there' really began to dawn on scientists in the early 1980s, when news of the Chicxulub dinosaur-killer impact began to spread. The idea rapidly took hold in the media world, and soon the public and even some politicians began to recognize that our world would never appear so safe and cosy again. At a stroke, we realized that our lives were being played out on a much bigger stage than we had previously thought and that the lights could go out at any time. More recently, a near miss by the asteroid Asclepius, which passed within 650,000km of the Earth, helped to further concentrate the global consciousness on the threat of impact. This awareness was heightened even more when, in 1992, initial calculations suggested that the recently rediscovered Comet Swift-Tuttle, which should have reappeared in the early 1980s, would collide with the Earth on 14 August 2126. A flurry of recalculations have shown that Swift-Tuttle will probably not hit, but it will be a close-run thing.

A similar sequence of events took place in March 1998 when newspapers reported that a 2km asteroid, discovered only a year earlier, would crash into the Earth in October 2028. Again, recalculations showed that the object would pass us by. Even more worryingly, on 10 August 1998 a 1.6km-wide chunk of rock missed the Earth by just 6 hours. In other words, if our planet had been just 6 hours further along its orbit around the Sun, you would probably not be reading this. Such temporary panics and close shaves have ensured that the threat of impacts from space is now well and truly in the spotlight, where it is likely to stay if the plethora of books and Hollywood blockbuster films on the theme are anything to go by.

If the danger is so real, presumably it is safe to assume that mapping the orbits of threatening asteroids and comets has priority status? Wrong! Only minimal funding is available for what is generally viewed, at least within the science, as an unglamorous occupation on a par with train-spotting, and few scientists are involved in this crucial task. As David Morrison of the NASA Ames Research Center once pointed out, the number of people involved in hunting for Earth-threatening objects is probably less than the staff of a McDonald's restaurant. Although the first ECA was discovered in 1932, serious searching for such objects did not begin until the 1970s, and by the 1990s sky-watchers had barely begun to scratch the surface in terms of the number of objects lurking in Earth-inhabited space. Even in the late 1990s only 160 ECAs are known, about half of which are 1km or more across, and the orbits of many of these remain only poorly defined. Remember these figures compare with a total estimate of maybe a million or more ECAs with diameters greater than 100m – big enough to devastate a major city – and up to 4,000 objects larger than 1km across.

The first comprehensive attempt to search the skies for ECAs was initiated in 1972 by Eugene Shoemaker, the co-discoverer in 1993 of Comet Shoemaker-Levy. Cruelly, on the third anniversary of the comet's collision with Jupiter, Dr Shoemaker was killed in a head-on car-crash while looking for impact craters in the Australian outback. Given the very small numbers of automobiles in the region, this tragic event was perhaps on a par with the chances of a minor asteroid hitting the Earth. Shoemaker's 1970s search, known as the *Planet-Crossing Asteroid Survey* (PCAS), was driven primarily by a need to develop our appreciation of the impact threat by getting a more accurate idea of how many objects were actually out there. Over the succeeding 10 years, searches by Shoemaker and his colleague Eleanor Helin resulted in a doubling of the number of known ECAs.

So successful was the survey that it spawned further similar initiatives in the 1980s: at the Mount Palomar Observatory in California and at the Anglo-Australian Observatory in New South Wales. These new surveys led to the discovery of dozens of new ECAs throughout the 1980s, although the numbers remained tiny compared with how many were actually estimated to be lurking out there. The problem was that, even using a particular type of telescope known as a *Schmidt*, which was designed to take photographs of a wider area of space than a conventional telescope, the area covered was still much too small even to make a dent in the problem.

In 1989, however, a new survey, entitled Spacewatch, came on-line at Kitt Peak Observatory near Tucson, Arizona, and dramatically improved the discovery rate of ECAs. Rather than spotting new asteroids by plotting their movement across a series of photographic plates taken one after the other, the telescope at Kitt Peak had been fitted with an electronic light-detector, known as a *charge-coupled device*, or CCD. This was much more effective at detecting the very faint appearance of small or distant asteroids, and since Spacewatch started in 1989, it has taken credit for almost half of all new ECA discoveries. The Spacewatch telescope has been particularly good for spotting smaller objects that pass very close to the Earth, such as the SEAs mentioned earlier, but because it can look only at a tiny part of the sky at any one moment, it is inevitable than most such objects hurtle past our planet unobserved. Indeed, the general detection programme for ECAs remains woefully inadequate and is proceeding at a snail's pace, and a slow snail at that. So far, only 5 per cent of all ECAs of 1km and above have been found, and at the current rate of detection it could take another 1,000 years to locate the remaining 95 per cent. The simple fact is, we may not have that long.

There is, however, some hope on the horizon. For one reason or another, governments around the world, at least in the developing countries, are beginning to sit up and take notice of the potential threat posed by impact events. In 1990 the US House of Representatives directed NASA to undertake a study designed to focus on improving detection rates of ECAs and on the feasibility of diverting or destroying any object that threatens the Earth. To some extent this latter initiative was a sop to advocates of the Star Wars anti-ballistic missile defence system. The break-up of the USSR and the end of the Cold War had left many US government scientists and engineers looking for something new to zap. Three years later, in 1993, NASA submitted its report on asteroid detection to the US House of Representatives. This proposed that six new, large telescopes should be constructed at selected points around the planet, dedicated entirely to searching the skies for Earth-crossing asteroids. For a total of about US$300 million, such a programme would be able to detect 99 per cent of all objects of 1km and above in about 25 years. A year later, the spectacular Jupiter impacts added impetus to the report's recommendations, and the House of Representatives directed NASA to identify and catalogue the orbits of all ECAs – within 10 years! Notwithstanding the unrealistic time-scale, serious funding to accomplish this task is still awaited.

Interest in the impact threat to Earth is now widespread throughout the world's scientific community, and in 1996 led to the establishment of the Spaceguard Foundation, an international initiative designed to promote the search for potentially dangerous asteroids and comets and to raise general awareness of the impact threat. Although NASA and the US Department of Defense are providing around US$2 million a year for Spaceguard-related research, progress continues to be hindered by a tight hold on the purse strings by governments too unimaginative or short-sighted to appreciate any threat that lies beyond the date of the next election. The US$300 million cost of the proposed NASA study works out at around US$20 per head of the Earth's population. On the basis of the estimated worth of a human being in the developed world, this compares with the potential cost of a 1km impact of US$1 trillion in the value of human life alone, not counting damage to the economy and the environment. In order to spend the same amount per head of population on impact studies as the UK spends on road safety, the international community should be earmarking US$0.5 billion a year. It seems likely, however, that we will have to wait for a Tunguska-sized object to wipe out New York or Paris before governments even consider paying out this sort of money.

Countering the impact threat

So far, most impact studies have focused on getting a better idea of how many objects are out there and finding out more about their orbits. Fewer scientists have concentrated on what we could do in terms of diverting or destroying an asteroid or comet should we find that one is headed our way. This is a complex issue that goes far beyond blasting the object to bits. Because this would not significantly change the orbit of the disintegrated object, all it means is that the Earth would find itself at the receiving end not of a single chunk of rock but of a potentially more destructive shotgun blast of debris. Given sufficient time, however, and provided that the object is not too large, it should be possible gradually to nudge an asteroid or comet that is on a collision course into a path that will miss the Earth. The best time to do this is when the asteroid or comet is at its *perihelion*; this is the point where it is closest to the Sun, and when just a small nudge can make a huge difference to its path when it reaches the Earth's orbit over 144 million kilometres further out.

Just how could this nudge be imparted, however? A number of possible methods, some more feasible than others, are considered in the 1993 NASA report to the US House of Representatives on near-Earth object (NEO) interception. The most straightforward diversion method involves exploding 'stand-off' nuclear devices close to the threatening object, thereby heating up one side of the asteroid or comet so as to give off a blast of gas and debris that would push the object into a new orbit. Other possibilities include strapping rocket engines to the object, or using explosives to open cracks in the rock, through which jets of escaping vaporized ice would do the same diversionary job. Such discussion of the various ways in which an asteroid or comet might be deflected could quite well become academic, however, if the threatening chunk of rock is either too big or discovered too late to modify its orbit. In both cases, all we could hope to do is perhaps use powerful nuclear weapons in an attempt to reduce the size of the object, taking the risk that it might be preferable to be hit by more, smaller objects than by a single, huge, planet-shaker.

One of the problems besetting all proposals to divert an asteroid or comet, or blast it to bits, is that we know nothing about how such objects will respond to impact or explosion. In an attempt to find out, an unmanned spacecraft, *Clementine 2*, due for launch in 1999, will fire probes at two ECAs. These probes will smash into the chosen asteroids at the incredible velocity of 70,000km/hour and provide invaluable data on their strength and internal structure. Other follow-up missions are planned in order to find out more about asteroids and comets, partly through scientific curiosity but mainly because we need to know more about this potentially devastating adversary if we are not to go the same way as the dinosaurs.

Is the impact threat constant?

Perhaps the greatest current debate in what I will call 'impact studies', involves the rate of impact events and whether or not this is uniform over time. Many scientists accept that this rate is constant and unvarying. Others, however, are more sceptical of such impact *uniformitarianism* and propose that there have been times in the past when asteroids or comets plummeted into the Earth with much greater frequency. These essentially British advocates of impact clustering, or *coherent catastrophists* as one might call them, even suggest that budding Bronze Age civilizations across the planet were destroyed during a period of increased impact activity just over 4,000 years ago. If we are to determine the threat to the Earth from future impacts, it is critical that the argument between these two groups be resolved. Clearly, if impacts are clustered, we need to try to identify the timing of future clusters as soon as possible if we are accurately to assess the threat to our planet. The frequencies with which different-sized objects are likely to hit the Earth (see table on p. 208) are based upon estimates of the numbers of these objects currently hurtling around our Sun. What, however, if there are periods when the Earth, or even the entire solar system, passes through a region of space containing much more debris than normal? Plainly, in this situation, collisions with objects of all sizes would be considerably more common for a time.

Many ideas have been put forward to explain the passage of our planet through clouds of debris, on time-scales ranging from a few thousand to tens of millions of years. Starting at the top of the scale first, in the early 1980s, soon after it was first proposed that an impact event killed off the dinosaurs and many other species, a number of palaeontologists claimed to recognize major mass extinctions on Earth every 30 million years or so. Mike Rampino of New York University, who was involved in studies of the Toba super-eruption (see Chapter 2), and his colleague Richard Stothers proposed a model to explain the periodicity. They suggested that, as the solar system, including the Earth, travelled about the centre of our galaxy (the Milky Way), it moved up and down in a wave-like motion. Every time it passed through the plane of our disc-like galaxy, the extra gravitational pull exerted by the great mass of stars toward the galaxy's centre disrupted a great cluster of comets, known as the *Oort Cloud*, which lurks far beyond the boundaries of our solar system. The result of this disturbance, they suggested, would be an influx of new comets into the solar system, dramatically increasing the frequency of large impacts on Earth.

Still on the theme of disrupting the Oort Cloud, a very few scientists advocated that our Sun was part of a binary star system and that a dark, much cooler twin, known by some as Nemesis, orbited at a great distance beyond the solar system. According to the supporters of this model, every 30 million years Nemesis came close to the Oort Cloud, where its gravitational field caused sufficient mayhem to send many comets speeding toward the inner solar system and the Earth. A modification of this idea has also been proposed, whereby the disruption of the cometary cloud is caused by the infamous Planet X that supposedly orbits far beyond Pluto. So far, we have no hard evidence for the existence of either Nemesis or Planet X, and indeed the whole idea of a regular periodicity in mass extinctions on Earth remains to be confirmed.

Of more relevance to us, from the point of view of an impact threat in the medium term, is a proposed clustering of impact events that occurs every few thousand years. It is this idea, put forward by British astronomers Victor Clube and Bill Napier, and increasing numbers of supporters from around the world, that has been invoked by others to account for impact mayhem on Bronze Age Earth. This 'coherent catastrophist' school of thought advocates what I will call a *comet fragmentation model* to support episodic increases in impact rates on our planet. I will look more closely at the model and its implications on p. 229–30. For now, suffice it to say that it relies upon the break-up of new, giant comets that every now and then enter our solar system from the depths of space.

Past impacts

Given the manner in which the planets formed during the early history of the solar system and the amount of remaining debris that is still hurtling about in our small corner of space, it would be surprising if there was no evidence of past impacts. The Earth certainly bears the scars of such encounters, although erosion has taken its toll, rendering them mostly unrecognizable. However, there is plenty of evidence on our nearest neighbour, the Moon.

Craters of the Moon

We have only to take a look at the lunar surface through a powerful telescope to see that it is covered with literally millions of craters of all sizes. It has taken a considerable time, however, for it to become generally accepted that these craters were produced by collisions with other bodies, and for almost 150 years a volcanic origin was preferred by most scientists who gave the problem any real consideration. The volcano theory almost certainly stemmed from a report by the famous astronomer William Herschel, who, in 1787, claimed to have observed volcanic eruptions on the surface of Moon. Some 40 years later another scientist named Gruithuisen pronounced that the Moon's craters had been formed as a result of what he called a 'cosmic bombardment in past ages'. This statement, however, was taken by his contemporaries with a rather large pinch of salt, perhaps because at the same time he reported that he had also found evidence for the existence of humans, animals and an ancient civilization on the lunar surface.

Over 60 years later, the American geologist Grove Karl Gilbert became the first scientist seriously to consider an impact origin for the Moon's craters. Gilbert performed laboratory experiments to simulate the impact of objects into powder or mud. These experiments produced a range of crater shapes, from circular to highly elongate, depending on the angle of entry. This confused Gilbert because it revealed that the angle of entry of the impacting object had to be vertical to form a circular crater. Because the lunar craters were virtually all circular, even though the impacting objects must have come in on a range of trajectories, many of which were not vertical, he began to have doubts about their impact origin. What Gilbert did not know, however, is that, at the extremely high velocities involved when an asteroid or comet hits the Moon, the crater produced is nearly always circular, whatever the angle of entry. This is because the gigantic explosion that occurs at the instant of impact always blasts a circular hole in the lunar crust. Only very rare, low-velocity objects coming in at particularly low angles produce elongate craters. In 1928 W. M. Smart categorically excluded the fact that lunar craters could be impact related because 'the craters are round' and 'there is no *a priori* reason why meteors should always fall vertically', and this misconception continued to be held right up to World War 2.

At around the same time, Thomas Chamberlain refused to accept that the craters of the Moon could have been generated by impacts because of the absence of objects within the solar system that could have caused them. This was, of course, before the general acceptance of the accretion model for the solar system, which involved intense bombardment in its early stages, and before any ECAs had been detected. After World War 2, it gradually dawned on those scientists studying the Moon that, like the billions of bombs dropped in the previous few years, asteroids and comets hitting the Moon would generate enormous explosions that would blast out material equally in all directions, thereby forming circular cavities. Slowly, more and more scientists began to accept that lunar craters represented a thorough pounding of the Moon's surface by countless chunks of rock and ice. Incredibly, it took another 25 years before this idea gained complete acceptance, and even in the late 1970s there were still a few geologists around who espoused the notion that the craters of the Moon were mainly volcanic in origin.

Craters on the Earth

Because planet Earth is as dynamic as the Moon is dead, most signs of the pounding it has taken from space throughout it history have been obliterated; nevertheless, look closely and they can still be found. Some of the more recent impact craters are actually very obvious, but for many decades they were not recognized as such. Again a failure of imagination meant that a considerable struggle was required to convince scientists, even those who accepted an impact origin for the lunar craters, that the Earth had also taken a pounding and that we could see evidence of it (see figure on p. 222).

Despite the fact that, because of its larger size, the Earth must have experienced up to 30 times as many impacts as the Moon, we see many fewer craters. There are two reasons for this. Firstly, we live on an incredibly active planet, the surface appearance of which is very much controlled by plate tectonics. Remember, because of subduction, the two-thirds of the planet's surface that lies beneath the oceans is only a few hundred million years old and therefore will show no signs of the battering from asteroids and comets during the first 90 per cent or so of the Earth's history. In consequence, signs of very old impacts will be revealed only in continental rocks that are billions of years old, where

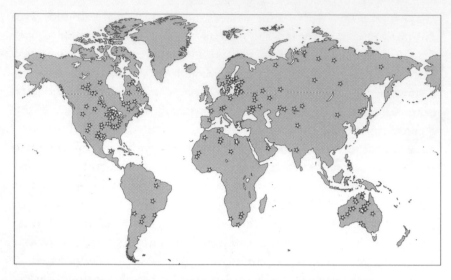

Around 150 impact craters have so far been identified on the Earth's surface. Many hundreds – perhaps even thousands – remain to be discovered, however, and, to some extent, the current geographical distribution reflects those areas that have been intensively studied. (Source: In Steel, 1995, by courtesy of Richard Grieve and Janice Smith, Geological Survey of Canada)

they are likely to have been largely obliterated by weathering and erosion (see figure on p. 223). More recent impact craters should be more obvious, but these will be much less common than those formed by impacts during the early history of the planet, because of a gradual reduction over time in the amount of debris hurtling around the solar system.

The first crater on Earth to be accepted as resulting from the impact of an object from space was the Barringer Crater in Arizona, USA, about which the physicist Benjamin Tilghman wrote in 1905: 'The formation at this locality is due to the impact of a meteor of enormous and hitherto unprecedented size.' Convinced that there lay millions of tonnes of meteoritic iron and nickel beneath the crater, Tilghman and his mining engineer colleague, D. M. Barringer, spent over 25 years drilling into the crater in an attempt to find it. Sadly, they never did – because it was never there. As we now know, the enormous energies released in these huge impacts simply vaporize the impacting body, leaving little to find except a few metal fragments and a lot of fused desert sand caused by the incredible temperatures generated. The Barringer Crater resulted from the impact of a small asteroid, probably around 40m across, that blasted into what is now the Arizona desert about 50,000 years ago with the energy of 50 million tonnes of TNT – the equivalent of 4,000 Hiroshima bombs. This Barringer object was about the same size as the one that exploded over Tunguska in 1908, but was made up of iron and nickel rather than rock. For this reason it survived its passage through the atmosphere to excavate a crater over 1km across and 200m deep. It is a sobering thought that an object of this size, sufficient to obliterate a major city, strikes the Earth at least once a century.

Since an extraterrestrial origin was established for the Barringer Crater, nearly 150 other impact craters have been identified on Earth, many much larger in size, although considerably more difficult to spot because of their great age. Most of these craters are found in the old hearts of the continents, particularly in Canada, Siberia and Australia, and many are buried by more recent sediments and/or very strongly degraded by weathering. However difficult they are to discern, a close examination of the geology of a possible impact site should be able to confirm its origin with some certainty. If an asteroid or comet has struck the Earth, the enormous energies released will have melted and shocked the surrounding rock as no other terrestrial event, such as a volcanic eruption, could do. The presence of such intensely shocked and melted rocks clinches an impact origin wherever the actual form of a crater is less convincing.

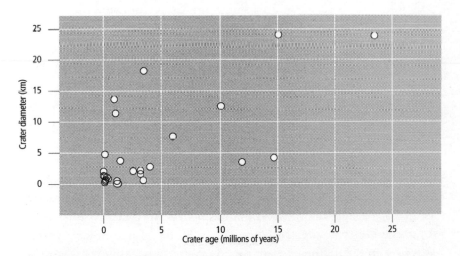

A plot of crater diameter against age for all dated terrestrial craters less than 25 million years old shows that most are relatively small and young. This is not surprising because small craters are rapidly degraded by weathering and erosion and soon become unrecognizable. No craters smaller than 5km across have been identified prior to 15 million years ago. (Source: Steel, 1995).

The relatively small number identified so far is likely to increase quite rapidly, with up to five new impact sites being identified each year. As more and more are discerned and dated, an interesting relationship is beginning to become apparent, which has major implications for the nature of a future impact. Pairs of craters of the same age, at least within the constraints imposed by current dating methods, have been identified, often in very different parts of the world. For example, the famous Ries Crater in Germany and another less than 50km distant are both 15 million years old, while the two craters that now form the Clearwater Lakes in Quebec, Canada, are also the same age, both dated at just under 300 years. Many other crater pairs are now being identified, suggesting that multiple impacts may be common. Bearing in mind the 20 or so fragments of Comet Shoemaker-Levy that hammered into Jupiter, this should not be surprising, although it does provide for an even more worrying scenario with regard to the next impact on our planet. The tendency for single objects, particularly comets, to fragment during their passage through the solar system, and the increased threat that they pose to us here on Earth are examined on pp. 229–30.

Chicxulub: the dinosaur-killer

Sixty-six million years ago, dinosaurs roamed the surface of the Earth as undisputed lords of the animal kingdom. Sixty-four million years ago they were gone, and the small, furry mammals that were our distant ancestors emerged from their burrows and lairs to begin the long evolutionary struggle that would eventually put *Homo sapiens* at the top of the tree. But what exactly happened to the dinosaurs? For many decades their disappearance constituted one of the great mysteries of geology, and countless ideas were put forward to explain their demise, some more likely than others, but none particularly convincing. Climate change was a favourite, with the dinosaurs being wiped out because the Earth became too hot or too cold, while another suggestion advocated death by constipation as a result of changes in the vegetation that formed the staple diet of those dinosaurs that were herbivorous. There is little doubt that, after dominating the Earth for 150 million years or so, many of the dinosaurs were already on their way out for one reason or another, but something catastrophic happened 65 million years ago that finished them off in short order – and not only the dinosaurs were affected. Whatever happened also wiped out over 60 per cent of all species then living, including three-quarters of those in the ocean.

In 1980 the American physicist Luis Alvarez and his colleagues published a paper that split the academic world and offered a very different
cause for the death of the giant reptiles. Alvarez and his co-workers
announced the discovery of a thin layer of clay in northern Italy that
was particularly rich in the rare element iridium. Because iridium, in the
sort of concentrations found in the clay, occurs only in space debris,
the Alvarez team proposed that it had been derived from a major collision between the Earth and an asteroid or comet. Furthermore, as the
iridium-rich layer was formed at exactly the time when the dinosaurs
disappeared, they proposed that it was this huge impact that wiped the
giant reptiles from the face of the Earth. The clay layer separates two
geological periods, the Cretaceous and the Tertiary, and is therefore said
to mark the *K/T boundary*, the rather confusing K coming from *Kreide*,
the German word for Cretaceous. Similarly the postulated impact is
known as the *K/T event*.

The Alvarez announcement was welcomed by some scientists, but
given little credence by many, particularly palaeontologists. Because
they studied the evolution of life forms through examination of the fos-
sil record, most of them were used to change occurring incredibly
slowly and could not adjust to the idea that a single catastrophic event
could have such astonishingly widespread ramifications for life on Earth.
Furthermore, and probably just as importantly, they were none too
keen on physicists meddling in their pet subject. Soon, however, the
evidence for the impact became overwhelming. Iridium was found at
more and more sites across the planet, along with *shocked* quartz crystals,
battered by the enormous pressures generated by the gigantic blast associated with the impact. Soot was also found at many of the sites,
providing evidence for global fires ignited by the impact fireball and by
molten debris raining down all over the Earth. Slowly, the climate of
opinion began to change as increasing numbers of scientists began to
accept the growing mass of evidence that supported a huge impact at
the end of the Cretaceous period.

Some even began to link other mass extinction events in the geological record to giant impacts, including the greatest of all at the end
of the Permian period some 245 million years ago. At that time over 90
per cent of all species were obliterated in the greatest disaster to hit the
planet since complex life forms first appeared over 600 million years
ago. A small group of geologists offered a terrestrial explanation for
the iridium, suggesting that it was derived from deep within the Earth

during a gigantic eruption of basalt magma that occurred around the time of the dinosaurs' demise. Unable satisfactorily to explain many of the other features, such as the widespread soot and shocked quartz, the idea attracted few followers and soon lost ground.

In 1989 new evidence became available that shed light on the nature of the impacting object, suggesting that it was a comet rather than an asteroid. Complex organic molecules, known as *amino acids* and of a type found only in space debris, were found at the K/T boundary. Clearly they had something to do with the impact, although there was a problem over how these delicate molecules had survived the incredible pressures and temperatures of the collision. Somewhat surprisingly, the answer lay in the fact that they had probably not been involved in the impact at all but had been derived from the dust and gas cloud that accompanied a comet. While all or part of the comet hammered into the Earth with the force of at least 2 million of the most powerful atomic bombs ever built, the amino acids drifted slowly down through the atmosphere, possibly for many thousands of years before and after the impact itself.

Despite gaining general acceptance, the K/T impact model still suffered from one drawback. Where was the 'smoking gun'? In other words, where was the crater left by the impacting comet? Given the global devastation caused by the collision, the crater should be huge and pretty easy to spot. The scar should be around 200km across and 20km deep, and although it took a while, it was eventually identified straddling the coast of the Yucatán Peninsula in Mexico, beneath the town of Chicxulub. In fact the crater-like structure was already known, and the Mexican oil company PEMEX had drilled in the area as early as the 1940s although, not entirely surprisingly, no oil was found. Several geophysical surveys since have revealed a great circular feature with a central peak, clearly an impact crater, but now buried beneath a 1,000m-thick layer of sediments. Although, during the 1980s, many scientists proposed that Chicxulub was the site of the K/T impact, it was not until the presence of shocked quartz was confirmed in rock samples in the early 1990s that the scientific community finally accepted that here was the very point where the dinosaur-killer collided with the Earth. By this time, however, some researchers were talking of further 'smoking guns' and considering the idea that the Chicxulub impact was not the only one that occurred around this time. Now it is thought that our planet was struck a number of hammer blows at the end of the

Cretaceous, of which the Chicxulub crater represents only the largest. It really hardly seems to matter, however, as this impact alone would certainly have been sufficient to send the dinosaurs on the road to oblivion.

Impacts in myth and legend

So far I have talked about asteroids and comets that left their mark on Earth tens of thousands to thousands of millions of years ago. We have also examined recent arrivals, such as Tunguska. But what about the intervening period? Ancient texts, and to some extent the myths and legends of the past, may provide convincing evidence of catastrophic events in the early history of our civilization (see Chapter 1). Such accounts provide clues to major floods and earthquakes, but do they mention any phenomena that could realistically be interpreted as resulting from an impact event? Certainly there are descriptions, such as those in the Book of Revelation in the New Testament of the Bible, that could be related to impacts (for example, the opening quotation of this chapter). The problem is that so much interpretation of the descriptions of disastrous events from the Bible and other ancient texts is subjective that, while some see evidence for impacts everywhere, others see none. In studying such texts we must always be aware that, although the descriptions of doom and disaster they contain may provide clues to great natural catastrophes of the past, this is all they are – clues.

In order to confirm without doubt that such events occurred we must look hard for incontrovertible archaeological and geological evidence. When looking at ancient texts and studying myth and legend for signs of past impacts, it might be worth thinking about how many such events occurred over the period. Assuming a constant impact rate and taking the generally accepted frequencies for impacts by objects of different sizes, we can expect something of the order of 50–100 strikes by objects the size of those at Tunguska or the Barringer Crater over the last 5,000 years. Taking into account the fact that, statistically, two-thirds of these are liable to have occurred over the ocean, and that civilizations with the capability to record accurately such events occupied only a few per cent of the land area over much of this period, it is likely that few, if any, would be observed and recorded by ancient societies. The alternative view, introduced on p. 218, is, of course, that the number of objects hitting the Earth follows a cyclical pattern, and that there were very many more impacts during the early stages of human civilization.

Let us then take a closer look at this blast from the past. What exactly is the evidence for a real pounding of the planet just a few thousand years ago and does it stand up to critical analysis in the cold light of day?

Much of the recent work involved in gathering together evidence for a period of devastation across the globe during the early Bronze Age and linking it to a period of increased impacts has been undertaken by Benny Peiser, a social anthropologist at Liverpool John Moores University in the UK. Peiser has brought together archaeological and geological information to paint a picture of environmental carnage that he and like-minded colleagues suggest led to the collapse of early civilizations during the third millennium BC, something over 4,000 years ago. Peiser and others have linked collapses in Asian, African and European urban societies in around 2350 BC with tsunami, wildfires, atmospheric blasts, earthquakes and climate changes caused by repeated strikes from 'super-Tunguska' objects. In support of this thesis, Peiser cites accounts from ancient Egypt's First Kingdom, the period when the inscrutable Sphinx was built, that talk of a bustling agricultural region being reduced to desert by floods and an intense blast of heat. At the same time stories of flood and fire accompany the desertification of the Dead Sea region of the Middle East, while floods devastated the civilizations of the Indus Valley in India and pounded the coasts of the Greek mainland. Other urban centres that appear to have collapsed at about the same time are found as far apart as Spain, Turkey, Afghanistan and China. In northern Syria, an unusual soil layer may provide the first physical evidence of an impact at this time. Here, a horizon containing a mixture of pulverized mud bricks, burned surface material and ash-like debris has been tentatively interpreted as resulting from a devastating air blast associated with a Tunguska-like explosion

A similar series of impacts may have taken place much more recently, toward the end of the twelfth century AD. In 1178 contemporary reports of strange activity on the face of the Moon may have been triggered by a major impact event that formed the crater known as Giordano Bruno. At about the same time, Maori legends of great wildfires that destroyed forests and wiped out the moa bird have been linked to the formation of two impact craters near the town of Tapanui, in Otago Province on the South Island of New Zealand. Evidence for the extent of the damage caused by the strikes is provided by the orientations of fallen trees from the same time, which point radially away from the craters. Intriguingly, one interpretation of the Maori name

Tapanui is 'the great explosion'. Aboriginal stories from New South Wales in Australia talk of a falling star that brings fire and death, which appears to support the notion that a number of smallish objects may have hit the Australasian region at this time. As often happens with a new discovery, however, these likely impacts have now been given, by some at least, a central role in all sorts of cultural changes that affected the Pacific region around this time. These include the Polynesian migrations, flooding in Peru, the birth of the Incas and the westward march of the hordes of Ghengis Khan.

Much of this is completely unsubstantiated speculation and is largely unhelpful to those trying to unravel the effects of such impact events for which there is hard evidence. Unfortunately, this type of speculation is rife within the currently trendy study of impact effects, and all sorts of human events are now being attributed to 'lights in the sky' Some have even attributed episodes of social upheaval, such as the English Civil War and the French Revolution, to increases in the numbers of large bright meteors known as *fireballs*. The idea is that populations take such activity as a sign that the end of the world is nigh and devote what they see as their final hours to an orgy of civil unrest. Clearly, too much can be, and is, being, read into the role that impact events have had on the roller-coaster history of human civilization over the last few thousand years. Nevertheless, there is growing evidence that the early Bronze Age was characterized by more impacts than normal. Dating of impact craters on the Earth's surface indicates that it is not unusual for the Earth to be struck by more than one object at one time or, at least, over a relatively short period. Such a clustering of impacts seems to have occurred around the time of the early Bronze Age, with seven impact craters, as far afield as Australia, Estonia and Argentina, now having been dated as 4,000–5,000 years old. What then could be the cause of such bursts of impact activity? The coherent catastrophists think they have the answer.

Every now and again, perhaps ever 20,000–200,000 years, a new comet from the Oort Cloud enters the solar system. For one reason or another, perhaps through getting too close to the Sun or to Jupiter's strong gravitational pull, the comet is captured and broken apart. Over thousands of years the many fragments of rock and dust spread out along the whole of the comet's orbit, forming a ring of debris just waiting for something to hit. A large comet, when fragmented in this way, might 'seed' the inner solar system with a million 1km-sized chunks of rock, each one capable of killing billions if it hits the Earth. Victor Clube, Bill

Napier and their coherent catastrophist colleagues claim that such a giant comet entered our solar system as recently as 20,000 years ago, breaking up soon afterward to form a trail of debris that pummels our planet every few thousand years.

It is common for comets to fragment when they get too close to Jupiter or the Sun, as shown by the fate of Shoemaker-Levy, and other historical comets have also been observed to break up. The most famous example is probably Biela's Comet, which broke in two during its 1846 apparition. On the occasion of its forecasted return in 1865, observers could spot no trace of either fragment, and 7 years later it became apparent why. At that time the Earth passed through one of the most spectacular meteor showers ever seen, with over 150,000 meteors per hour being recorded at some locations. Clearly, the comet had broken up entirely, and the Earth was passing through the trail of resulting debris. This has now spread out along the whole of the original comet's orbit and visits our planet every year in the form of the Andromedid meteor shower.

The coherent catastrophist school proposes that the giant comet that entered our solar system toward the end of the last Ice Age broke up to form a mass of debris, called the *Taurid complex*, circling the Sun. The gravel-sized fragments, boulders and smaller chunks of rock of the complex make up at least four, and perhaps as many as twelve, clouds of *meteoroids* that regularly encounter the Earth and form meteor storms, including the *Taurid meteor stream* that lights up the night sky a couple of weeks before Christmas every year. This meteor shower is, however, on the edge of the Taurid complex, the core of which contains heftier chunks of debris that pose a much greater threat to our planet, including an Earth-crossing comet known as Encke, which is a good 5km across, and nearly 40 asteroids. There are probably many more potentially dangerous objects in the complex, but no one has any idea how many and, more worryingly, exactly where along the orbit the biggest chunks of rock are to be found.

Fortunately for us, the orbit of the main mass of Taurid complex debris does not intersect that of the Earth every year. Because its orbit wobbles, the trail of debris sometimes crosses the Earth's orbit a little closer to the Sun and most of the time a bit farther out. When the orbit of the debris stream intersects the orbit of the Earth exactly, we may see spectacular meteor-storms; sometimes, however, we may collide with much bigger debris fragments. If you think of the Taurid complex orbit as a Grand Prix racetrack, with the cars representing the debris spread out all along it, then in places the track will be almost empty, with perhaps one or two isolated cars. Elsewhere along the track, however, a bunch of cars might be clustered together. On most occasions, the orbit of the Earth intersects that of the complex at a point where it is free of large fragments. Every now and again, however, the orbits intersect exactly at the point where the space-debris equivalent of the bunch of racing cars is gathered together. When this happens, our planet might take a pounding from objects ranging upward from Barringer- or Tunguska-sized to vastly more destructive chunks of rock up to 300m across. The coherent catastrophists claim that the Earth is on the receiving end of such a barrage every 2,500–3,000 years or so and propose that the Bronze Age mayhem was the result of the last big volley of debris, when hundreds of super-Tunguska objects may have smashed into the our early world over a period of a few days to a few years.

The last time our planet is alleged to have passed through the dense part of the Taurid complex was around AD 400–600, the period known as the Dark Ages, which followed the collapse of the Roman Empire. The coherent catastrophists also recognize increased numbers of impacts at this time, their evidence being largely gleaned from legends and contemporary texts. Some even suggest that fireball-storms, formed as numerous boulder-sized rocks burned up in the atmosphere, may have promoted the social upheavals in Europe that led to the collapse of an already crumbling Roman state. Going further back in time, the Australia-based astronomer Duncan Steel has even proposed that the great megalithic monument of Stonehenge was built to predict meteor-storms associated with a much earlier Taurid complex-related bombardment during the fourth millennium BC. There does seem to be a tendency, among some of the coherent catastrophists at least, to explain virtually every war, riot or natural catastrophe in terms of increased numbers of impacts, and it must be stressed that their ideas are very much in a minority within the impact-studies community. Having said this, however, if they are correct, then we have only 1,000 years respite before the Earth suffers its next pounding at the end of the coming millennium.

A choice of annihilation

Clearly a great chunk of rock or metal hurtling into the Earth with a velocity of several tens of kilometres a second is going to cause a huge amount of damage as the *kinetic energy* – the energy of motion – is converted into heat. Even a small object, such as the 40m hunk of metal that excavated the Barringer Crater in Arizona, will generate an explosive blast sufficient to devastate a major city. When the Barringer object struck, it is estimated that an instantaneous atmospheric shock-wave moving at over 3,000km/hour pulverized every living thing within 3km of the point of impact. Hurricane-force winds from the blast would have extended as far as 40km from the impact site, devastating the prevailing ecosystem – lush grasslands and forest at the time – over an area of 1,500km².

If a similar-sized object, not much bigger than a large back-garden, were to strike Manhattan today, it would devastate the entire New York metropolis, including all of Staten Island and the eastern half of Long Island, reaching beyond the Watchung Mountains to the west. The death toll could easily reach 10 million or more, and any buildings or people surviving the initial blast would probably succumb to the huge fires generated by the tremendous heat of the impact, while the shock-waves would reverberate around the planet for days afterward.

New York, or any large city, would fare no better if it were hit by an air blast caused by the explosion above it of a stony Tunguska-like object. No crater would result, but the devastation would otherwise be just as complete. Such an explosion over central London would obliterate everything within the M25 orbital motorway. If you double the size of the rock, the resultant destruction is multiplied manifold. An asteroid 100m across would obliterate an area of around 10,000km², about half the area of Massachusetts. If it struck in one of the major ocean basins – and an impact of this size can be expected every 4,000 years or so in the Pacific, for example – the death toll from the resulting tsunami could run into tens of millions.

Let us increase the size of the impacting object and consider what will happen when a 500m rock collides with our planet. Although not much more than 10 times bigger than the Barringer or Tunguska objects, the devastation caused by a rock of this size will be millions of times greater. If it were to strike Birmingham, the UK's second-largest city, it would annihilate England and Wales, and leave little of Scotland, Ireland, northern France and the Low Countries untouched. If the impact occurred in the sea, the resulting gigantic tsunami could be 100m high in the deep ocean, but would build to an even greater height as it sped into shallow water at 800km/hour. Should the next 500m object hit the Pacific, and the chance of this happening is actually as high as

1 per cent in the next century, then every coastal city in the hemisphere would be obliterated within 20 hours or so. The death toll resulting from such an impact could easily exceed 500 million souls.

The effect of a future 1km comet-fragment impact is described in the fictional account that concludes this chapter. Here, however, let us examine in more detail the horrifying consequences of a 10km impact – the true dinosaur-killer (see figure below). Based upon the size of the crater it left behind, which is around 180km across, the Chicxulub comet or comet fragment is thought to have been at least 10km wide. With a velocity of 90,000km/hour, fast enough to cross London in a single second, the Earth's atmosphere would have offered no resistance whatsoever. So large was the object that, while the leading edge burrowed into the crust of what is now the Caribbean Sea, its tail-end may still have been out in the cold and dark of space. It is impossible to describe in mere words the cataclysmic release of energy during the few seconds following collision.

A survivor of one of the atomic bombs dropped on the Japanese cities of Hiroshima or Nagasaki might well think that nothing could be more devastating, but these man-made devices were less than

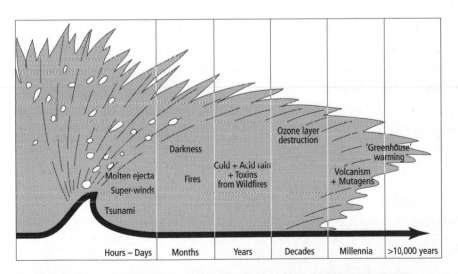

The impact of the Chicxulub 'dinosaur-killer' on the planet and all life would have been devastating, and its effects may have lasted for tens of thousands of years. The immediate mayhem resulting from tsunami, super-winds and molten ejecta raining down from the skies would have been superseded by global fires, acid rain, darkness and freezing cold, and later by destruction of the ozone layer, deadly chemicals and 'greenhouse' warming.

firecrackers compared to the incomprehensible power of the K/T impact. The energy released 65 million years ago at Chicxulub was equal to 8 billion Hiroshima bombs set off simultaneously. Within seconds the explosion would have generated a gigantic fireball, hotter than the Sun, that sliced through the ocean and blasted a cavity over 100km across and 15km deep in the underlying crust, vaporizing the comet almost instantaneously. At the same time the blast would have temporarily stripped away the atmosphere above the impact site, hurling over 100 trillion tonnes of mainly molten rock into space.

So fast were these molten fragments travelling that some would have escaped into space, never to be seen again. Most, however, would have rained down across the Earth – heating up again as they re-entered the atmosphere – in a firework display that would have turned the whole sky into a gigantic grill. Animal life would have been roasted alive before the raining hot fragments hit the surface, starting global fires that raged across the planet for months, incinerating forests and grasslands and turning to soot a quarter of all living material. Titanic shock-waves would have levelled mountains and torn rocks apart across the world, focusing at the opposite side of the planet to wreak geological havoc at the Antipodes. One of the loudest sounds ever heard would have shattered animals' eardrums as the atmosphere exploded into the vacuum created by the fireball, while a shock-wave would have headed outward to flatten everything over an area greater than Europe. Within seconds of the impact, super-winds five times more powerful than the greatest hurricanes would have swept much of the planet, fanning the flames of the conflagrations, tsunami many kilometres high would have poured across the continents, and lava would have burst from the great scar in the Earth.

In the following weeks, as smoke and dust from the impact accumulated in the atmosphere, the Sun would have been blotted out, utter darkness would have fallen, and temperatures would have dropped by 15°C, precipitating the world into a *cosmic winter* in which plants died for lack of sunlight and the few remaining herbivorous dinosaurs not already fried starved to death for lack of food. As the long night continued, poisons generated in the global conflagrations and acid rain, formed from sulphur blasted into the atmosphere from rocks at the impact site, would have drenched the battered landscape and poured into the oceans, destroying three-quarters of all marine life. As the soot and dust cleared, the surface would have been fried again as the Sun's ultraviolet rays blasted with little hindrance through an ozone layer left in shreds by the action of huge quantities of nitrogen oxides produced in the fireball.

After the period of intense cold the planet would slowly have begun to heat up again, only this time temperatures would have just kept rising. Gigantic quantities of carbon dioxide, released from the limestone into which the comet smashed, would have acted like a great blanket around the Earth, keeping it overheated for perhaps tens of thousands of years. The K/T impact would have so upset the natural balance of our world's geology, oceans and atmosphere, that it may have been as long as 500,000 years before anything approaching normality returned. By this time the giant reptiles had long gone. Only their descendants, the birds, remained, together, of course, with those innocuous, primitive mammals whose descendants in the far future would someday look back on this episode as one of the most critical in determining the evolution of life on planet Earth.

★ ★ ★

As explained earlier, comets come in three types: short period, intermediate period and long period, or parabolic. Because members of the first two types return on a regular basis, we know their orbital characteristics pretty well and can forecast with some accuracy if and when they will approach close to the Earth. Parabolic comets are, however, a very different matter. These take at least 200 years to make a complete orbit of the Sun and so may have been observed only once or twice in recent times, if ever. Consequently, their orbits are very poorly known, and the threat they pose to our planet and our civilization is difficult to assess. Some parabolic comets have orbits that take them far out into deep space, way beyond the edge of the solar system, and they may take thousands of years to return. Never having been observed before, such objects are great unknowns, whose appearance may spell death and disaster for our race, as the following fictional account will show.

Armageddon!

• *How much better can it get for Australia this week?* After coming out top of the medals table with that Men's High-jump Gold on the last day of the Olympic competition, another Aussie has gone even higher. Jim Farrier who, when he is not running a sheep station in New South Wales, spends his time *staring out into space, has just been confirmed as the sole discoverer of a new comet. Jim, using just a pair of powerful binoculars, found the object 6 days ago, and immediately informed the International Astronomical Union's Central Bureau for Astronomical Telegrams in Cambridge, Massachusetts.*

Yesterday, the IAU reported that the Spaceguard-dedicated Schmidt camera at the Anglo-Australian Observatory had picked up the object and confirmed it as a new comet, designated 2000s – the nineteenth of the year – or more simply Comet Farrier. Although precise details of the comet's orbit remain to be worked out, astronomers report that it is of the 'parabolic' type. This means that it has an orbit that takes it so far from the Sun that it has never been observed in the solar system before. Already within the orbit of the planet Jupiter, the comet is forecast to be a tremendous sight as it closes on the Sun and is expected to put on an even more spectacular display when it crosses the Earth's orbit on its return journey to deep space.

ABC News Report, 3 October 2000.

The new discovery

In most other countries reports of the discovery of Comet Farrier did not make the main news headlines but were hidden away in science-magazine pro-grammes and in the 'World in Brief' slots of national newspapers. Amateur astronomers eagerly polished their telescopes and looked forward to many a sleepless night later in the year as the comet drew closer. The general reaction in Western countries inured to the wonders of scientific discovery was, as might be expected: so what? To billions of the poor struggling to survive in the devel-oping world, the message did not even get through and would have meant little if it had. In the world of professional astronomy, however, the discovery had a devastating effect.

Following the acquisition and tracking of Comet Farrier by staff at the Anglo-Australian Observatory, its location was rapidly disseminated via the Web to astronomical institutions across the world. Soon observatories in Chile and South Africa picked up the object, and astronomers beavered away to calculate an orbit. It quickly became apparent that this was going to be no ordinary cometary apparition. Firstly, the object was large, perhaps 50km across, and it was moving fast. Having been accelerating for several centuries at least, the comet was now hurtling sunward at over 70,000km/hour, and its velocity could well exceeded 1,000,000km/hour as it swung around the Sun on its way out of the solar system once more. Secondly, preliminary calculations suggested that it just could be on a collision course with the Earth. Two forecasts for the comet's path had it almost grazing the Sun on its inward journey before heading out into deep space again, directly across the Earth's path. It looked as if it would miss the planet by something like 500,000km, less than a hair's breadth in astronomical terms, although changes in the comet's orbit due to explosions caused by vaporizing ice could bring it much nearer. Even if it did miss, the Earth could expect some spectacular meteor activity from the dust and smaller fragments of rock and ice that accompanied the comet on its eternal journey. It might even suffer a cooling of the climate if sufficient quantities of cometary dust were deposited in the atmosphere, thus reducing the level of solar radiation reaching the surface.

Following a flurry of e-mails and telephone conversations, those scientists involved in studying the comet agreed not to go public until they had more information. Two weeks later the Hubble Space Telescope was trained on Comet Farrier, confirming its likely size as around 50km. Seven days later, a group of astronomers from the USA, UK, Chile, Holland, Russia, South Africa and Australia, met incognito at NASA's Jet Propulsion Laboratory in Pasadena to discuss their next move. More rigorous calculations of Farrier's orbit had confirmed initial estimates that the comet would probably just miss the Earth, although it could feasibly hit it. Just as the meeting was ending, an Australian mathematician involved on the periphery of comet research announced that, on the basis of the preliminary orbital data accessible on the Web, he estimated that the comet would hit the Earth on 1 May 2001, a little less than 6 months away.

The threat

Within hours, chaos had broken loose, both within the astronomical community and throughout all walks of life. Such cosmic catastrophes had been forecast before and proven to be false, but always centuries hence, never within the lifetime of the average human being and certainly never only a few months ahead. As governments debated, religious leaders ranted and survivalists bought in even more guns and provisions, the IAU called a press conference at the UN headquarters in New York. Under the sweltering glare of 100 television cameras, a spokeswoman reported the facts without comment.

  • *Ladies and gentlemen, if you will please come to order. I would like to get this over with as soon as possible, so I can try to answer some of your questions. I am required to read the following statement, prepared with the help and support of the principal research groups involved in monitoring Comet Farrier and under the auspices of the International Astronomical Union. Comet Farrier was first spotted by the Australian amateur astronomer James*

Farrier on 27 September, using only binoculars. It belongs to the long period, or parabolic, type, which means that it has a very large orbit that brings it close to the Sun only on rare occasions.

Determination of the orbit of Farrier indicates that it last visited the inner solar system about 4,000 years ago. The orbital characteristics of the comet also reveal that there is a chance that it, or part of it, will collide with the Earth sometime on or around 1 May next year. I cannot stress too strongly, however, that the consensus opinion of scientists currently working on the comet's trajectory is that the most massive part of the comet, known as the nucleus – which seems to be about 50km across – will probably miss. Nevertheless, even if this is the case, there is a high probability of rock or ice fragments in the 10–100m size range penetrating the Earth's atmospheric shield, with the potential to cause severe damage on a local to regional scale.

*The comet is currently just within the orbit of Jupiter and will continue to accelerate toward the Sun into next year. It accelerates across the Earth's orbit in March, but the Earth will be near the other side of its orbit so there will be no threat of collision. Farrier's velocity will accelerate to over 1,000,000km/hour as it passes closer to the Sun than Mercury, the innermost planet, and it will then begin its outward journey. On 1 May, at approximately 07.25a.m. GMT, the comet will encounter the Earth. I have no further information to report at this time. **Thank you, ladies and gentlemen, for your attention. If you will bear with me I have time for one or two very quick questions.***

As expected, virtually everyone in the press-conference audience wanted to know the answers to the same two questions. What would happen if the comet did hit? And could we do anything to prevent it? In the circumstances, the spokeswoman could add little to her statement, beyond saying that a direct hit from a fragment 1km or more across would probably ensure the end of modern civilization as we had come to know it. On the prevention side, she explained that theoretical studies had been undertaken on how asteroids might be deflected by setting off nuclear devices in close proximity, but comets were such complex objects that this strategy would probably not be an option. Two days after the press conference, the government heads of the UN Security Council countries met, together with their advisors, for a briefing by scientists at the UK prime minister's country retreat at Chequers just outside London. The news they received was not good.

Although the impact threat had been taken seriously for some years, particularly after the spectacular collision between Jupiter and Comet Shoemaker-Levy in 1994, studies on impact avoidance remained rudimentary and largely theoretical. The only practical research had been undertaken a few months earlier, when the unmanned asteroid probe *Clementine 2* had fired probes into the earth-crossing asteroid Toutatis, with surprising and rather uncomfortable results. The 1m-long probes had smashed into the 3km rock at nearly 80,000km/hour, breaking off several large chunks tens of metres across and revealing the rock to be surprisingly weak and strongly susceptible to break-up. The last thing that anyone wanted at this time was for Comet Farrier to go the same way, thereby presenting an even larger target to the Earth as it hurtled into the comet's vicinity at over 100,000km/hour.

The scientists, together with representatives of the US Space Command and Spaceguard, presented the government heads with an unexpected consensus of opinion. With neither the knowledge nor the expertise to destroy or divert Comet Farrier in the time available, any attempt to do so in the light of their ignorance could very well make the situation worse by breaking up the comet's nucleus and increasing the chance of impact. If there was nothing they could do in terms of stopping the comet, they might at least be able to find out a little more about its composition. A NASA representative informed the heads of state that the *Clementine 2* back-up spacecraft was being readied for a launch window in the next few weeks that would permit a high-velocity encounter with Farrier's coma a few weeks before it reached the Earth. In response to a wry question about whether or not the spacecraft had yet been named, the NASA man replied no, but that in the circumstances they had been considering 'Marvin', after the notoriously pessimistic robot in Douglas Adams's *The Hitch Hiker's Guide to the Galaxy*. Things certainly looked bad enough to justify this.

The end of November 2000 saw the launch from space shuttle *Endeavor* of *Clementine 3*, or *Marvin* as it had now become fondly known throughout NASA and, indeed, in the international media. An additional powerful booster slowed the craft sufficiently to send it dropping sunward. Because of the limited time available and the greater energy required, the probe could not be fired directly toward the speeding comet. Instead it would have to swing around the Sun and catch Farrier on the far side, just a few weeks before it encountered Earth. At least we would get a close-up view of our potential nemesis. As winter deepened in the northern hemisphere, a sullen depression settled across the planet. Few, even in the most sparsely populated areas of the poorest countries, had not heard of the imminent arrival of the rock from space that, in a few short months, might bring their lives to a terrifying end.

To start with, national governments and international agencies tried to carry on as usual: planning for a future that might never arrive. Despite considerable familiarity with short-termist thinking by only having to look as far ahead as the next election, many governments found it difficult to live with the idea that they might have only another 5 months in power. In the poorest countries, living one day at a time had always been the norm, so little changed as people went about the business of ensuring that there was enough to eat for themselves and their families. In the developed countries, however, the social malaise was soon replaced by one of devil-may-care impetuosity and increasing levels of violence. New Year's Eve rioting in New York's Times Square left 300 dead, while, in Northern Ireland, Protestant and Catholic celebrated perhaps their last year on the planet with a return to full-scale hostilities. Churches across the world were packed to over-flowing, and recruitment to cults and minor religious groups reached an all-time high. In the USA survivalist groups, which had in some cases waited for many years for just such an eventuality, found themselves fighting the hordes of frightened refugees that streamed daily out of American towns and cities and into the wilder-ness. As society began to crumble, so did the global economy. Production slumped as many workers left to spend what they saw as their last few months on Earth with their families, while the financial markets collapsed utterly. Nobody was going to gamble on the future of stocks and shares in this climate, while insurance became a product entirely without a market.

By the end of January the comet was faintly but clearly visible to the naked eye as a smudge of grey light in the early morning sky. As a small tail became visible, *X-Files* fans gathered on freezing hillsides, convincing one another that they could see a gigantic spacecraft following along in Farrier's wake – a desperately sought-for lifeline for a doomed race. Once into March the comet's tail began to grow brighter, the constant gale of particles streaming away from the Sun and trailing out into space for 10 million kilometres. Now visible in both hemispheres, the sight could not be ignored, and all over the world eyes turned constantly to the ever-growing cosmic visitor. By now the whole planet seemed to be caught up in a dream. Few workplaces remained open, despite government incentives to continue in employment. Public utilities struggled to provide a service, while shops were emptied within hours of new supplies arriving as hoarders descended like locusts to strip the shelves of everything they could carry. The media provided little relief because the comet filled virtually every column inch and every second of air-time. Astronomers and geologists talked themselves into exhaustion as they explained what comets were made of and what sort of damage they could do if they hit the Earth.

Eventually the messages – of molten rock from the skies and towering tsunami – began to get through, and slowly but surely the great exoduses away from the coasts and into the mountains began. Caves were like gold dust and were fought over to the death time and time again, despite the scant protection they afforded against the potential devastation to come. In some countries, governments, the armed forces, and the emergency services attempted to plan for every eventuality barring the utter destruction of all life on the planet, and in the West the bunkers constructed for nuclear war were put to good use. Here the good and the great, and those who could afford to pay, would sit out the worst of the encounter, while the rest of humanity could put bags over their heads and kiss the world goodbye. Generally speaking, however, authority had lost control, and community was quickly replaced by selfishness and greed as 'every man for himself' became the mantra for survival.

As Farrier crossed the Earth's orbit and appeared bent on crashing into the Sun, its tail became even longer, blazing out into space for nearly 20 million kilometres. In the brightening sky of dawn, however, the tail became dimmer, until by the end of March it was barely visible as it sped behind the Sun at over 1,500,000km/hour. Right across the planet people breathed a collective sigh of relief at the few weeks respite from the sight of their possible nemesis. Ten days later, however, it was back, this time stretching out across the evening sky just after sunset. But something was wrong: it looked more irregular in shape, and there were two tails. Something had indeed happened to the comet. While out of sight of Earth, *Clementine 3* had been closing on Farrier, sending back the first rather blurred pictures in early April. What these showed was bad news for the inhabitants of planet Earth. As the comet grazed the Sun, the enormous gravitational forces had literally pulled the nucleus apart, splitting it into three large chunks and several smaller ones. These were already beginning to spread out, enlarging the area of the comet and making it more likely that at least one substantial fragment would hit the Earth. It was impossible to forecast the precise paths of each of the new chunks of rock because blasts of vaporized ice and dust tugged and pulled them this way and that. As mission controllers prepared to send *Clementine 3* into the coma of gas and dust enclosing the nucleus, a small pebble travelling at several hundred kilometres a second sliced off the high-gain antenna, cutting communications with Earth – just seconds before the side of the craft was obliterated by a house-sized hunk of ice. As its *Hitch Hiker's Guide* namesake Marvin might have said at this time: 'Oh God, I'm so depressed!'

On the night of 29 April, 2 days before encounter, Comet Farrier blazed across the sky, a gigantic veil of gas and dust stretching from horizon to zenith. Brighter flashes marked the advance guard of doom as smaller chunks of debris flashed across the sky as blazing fireballs, burning up before they could penetrate the Earth's atmospheric shield. This was not enough, however, to stop the larger fragments that now began to encounter our world ahead of the main mass of the comet. Over the bleak wastes of northern Canada, families of polar bears were blinded and then broiled alive as a Tunguska-sized lump of ice and rock exploded directly above them, causing fires to rage across thousands of kilometres of forest. A similar-sized rock smashed into the Pacific off the coast of the Philippines, generating tsunami 50m high, which devastated much of the eastern coast, drowning hundreds of thousands and reducing their homes to matchwood. Amid the fear and shock, however, there was new hope. Radar signals, bounced off the comet's nucleus from the great Arecibo radio telescope in Puerto Rico, confirmed the existence of three huge chunks of rock, each around 10km across, surrounded by a swarm of smaller fragments up to 1km in size. The good news was that the most recent calculations showed that the largest fragments looked like missing the Earth, although the Moon might take a serious pounding. Across the world, 6 billion pairs of fingers were crossed.

Encounter Day minus 1: Detroit, Michigan, was not the place to be. Soon after dawn, while early risers were brewing coffee and fitness freaks were already pounding the park lanes, the city and its population ceased to exist. A 150m hunk of stone buried itself in the northern suburbs with the force of 30,000 Hiroshima bombs. Within seconds, skyscrapers were blasted into nothing, while every living thing within the city and its suburbs was instantaneously incinerated before being blown away in a hurricane of cinders. Motor Town, USA, was gone forever, transformed into a wasteland of melted steel and fused glass. Over the next 12 hours, fireballs blazed across the sky, bright enough to be seen even in full daylight. The world was quiet and empty as families huddled together in their homes or in hastily built shelters beneath their gardens. Across all five continents, thunderous reports shattered the silence as chunks of ice blasted themselves to bits attempting to burst through the Earth's protective atmospheric shield. Tunguska-sized fragments exploded above Iran, India and the Pacific and Atlantic Oceans, but nothing else on the scale of the Detroit killer got through.

Just after 6a.m. GMT, on Encounter Day, Comet Farrier's nucleus passed within 200,000km of the Earth. Telescopes trained on the Moon recorded the first collision of two bodies in the solar system since Shoemaker-Levy struck Jupiter 7 years earlier, as one of the comet's 10km fragments smashed into the Mare Serenitatis. A blinding flash dazzled watching astronomers as the chunk of rock punched its way through the Moon's crust and vaporized itself in milliseconds. A great cloud of melted Moon rock was blasted into space, some to fall on the Earth a few days later, but most raining down all over the lunar surface to form countless new craters. In Serenitatis a hole wider than Belgium glowed a burning red as the heat of the impact radiated out into the bitter cold of space. Several more chunks of ice and rock struck the Moon, our nearest neighbour, two over 1km across blasting new craters in the barren landscape, but radar confirmed that the two remaining 10km-sized fragments had missed both the Moon and our own planet. Billions who were clustered around radios and television sets across the planet almost collapsed with relief when the announcement was made, and parents cried with joy as they realized that their children would have a future after all. But the jubilation was premature. Comet Farrier had, quite literally, a sting in its tail and its target was Europe.

Impact

• *On the chilly, misty morning of May Day 2001 over a hundred men, women and children were shoe-horned into the caves and tunnels that honeycombed the chalk cliffs near the English Channel port of Dover, anxiously awaiting news of the comet amid the damp rock and rusting World War 2 gun emplacements.* *As BBC Radio 5 reported the last-minute reprieve for the Earth, the tinny sound from the two small radios was drowned out by a great roar of relief, and Eddie Krafft hooted, screamed and shook his fists at the sky with the best of them. Desperate to get out of the smelly heap of humanity with which he had been sharing the old wartime dug-outs for the last 18 hours, he pushed his way through the crowds, stopping to hug friends and shake hands with complete strangers.*

He emerged onto the narrow rocky platform above Dead Man's Beach and, peering eastward across the Channel to France, he revelled at the sight of the calm, blue sea and breathed deeply of the salt-tanged air. The bustling ferry- and container-port was as quiet as the grave, and the great ships lay idle, slowly rising and falling on the almost imperceptible swell. Eddie could just see the King Arthur, on which he had worked as an engineering technician for the past 5 years. Stepping off the platform, Eddie took the narrow, winding path up the cliff face to the lush-green Kent downland above. He reached the cliff top, panting a little, and turned to look at the sun rising above his beloved home town.

Half a second later a second sun appeared – right on the horizon and a billion times brighter. His eyes, face and hands burning terribly, Eddie turned away and slumped to the ground behind a chalky outcrop. A second later an atmospheric shock-wave blasted him to pieces and exploded into the cave system below, obliterating everyone within. Hard on its heels an unimaginable blast of superheated steam and molten rock completed the job of wiping all trace of life from this part of the Kent coast, before a mighty crack of doom warned those many thousands of kilometres distant that a swift death was on its way.

The Earth was struck at 08.05a.m. GMT, on 1 May 2001. A 1km rocky fragment trailing behind the main body of the nucleus caught the celebrating planet unawares. Hitting the atmosphere at 60km/second, the rock punched its way through in the blink of an eye and struck the sea 20km east of Dover. In three-quarters of a second, temperatures many times hotter than the Sun blasted a hole through the sea and into the crust beneath. For fractions of a second a gigantic chasm gaped in the sea, filled with a mixture of superheated, high-pressure steam, vaporized comet and melted crust. Within milliseconds this material blasted upward into the stratosphere and outward across Britain, France and the Low Countries with a force many hundreds of times that of the world's nuclear arsenal. Southern England, northwestern France and western Belgium were instantly obliterated beneath a rain of molten debris, while further afield an atmospheric blast many times more powerful than the strongest hurricane razed virtually everything to the ground. Seismic shock-waves, snaking out from the impact site, finished the job, heaving the land surface this way and that, from Oslo in the north, to Budapest in the east and Nice in the south.

As condensing boiling water rained down on the steaming remnants of the British, French and Belgian coasts, gigantic waves 100m high poured across eastern England. Holland eventually lost its long battle with the North Sea as most of the country and its population disappeared beneath the devastating waves, while Denmark fared little better. Between the French and English coasts a gigantic boiling maelstrom marked the impact site, where temperatures hotter than the surface of the Sun continued to hold back the water, transforming it to live steam before it had a chance to flood the 20km-diameter, lava-filled crater on the sea-bed. Twenty-four hours later the sea still boiled and bubbled in the English Channel, but over northwestern Europe utter silence reigned. Two hundred million were dead, boiled alive or blasted to smithereens in an instant, drowned by the great waves or crushed beneath the rubble of cities shaken to the ground. Further afield, even New Zealand, as far away as you could get from the impact, had not escaped. Here, at a point exactly opposite the site of the collision, the seismic shock-waves generated by the impact met up once again to send convulsions through the distant country and shake Auckland, the capital, to pieces. Europe was dead and the rest of the world was helpless, but for the survivors worse was yet to come.

Legacy

In the days after the impact, fires continued to rage across the blighted wastelands of western Europe and the British Isles, and the sky was dark with soot, dust and heavy cloud. Across the planet, a pall of pulverized rock from the bed

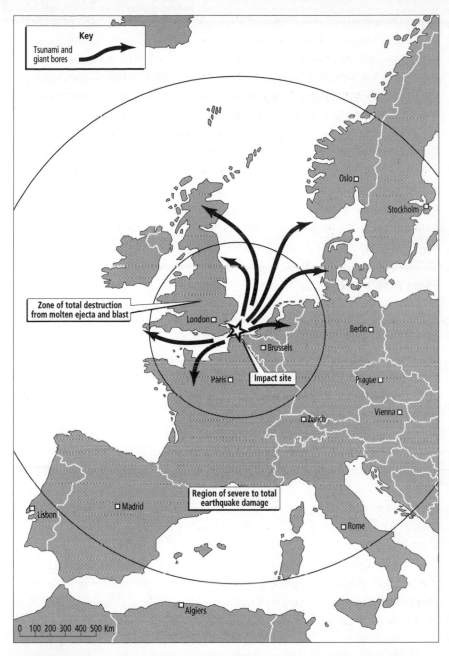

Key
Tsunami and giant bores

Zone of total destruction from molten ejecta and blast

Impact site

Region of severe to total earthquake damage

Oslo
Stockholm
London
Berlin
Brussels
Paris
Prague
Vienna
Zurich
Madrid
Lisbon
Rome
Algiers

0 100 200 300 400 500 Km

A 1km impact in the southern North Sea would bury much of Great Britain, northern France and the Low Countries under a blanket of molten debris, while the whole of western Europe would be devastated by catastrophic earthquakes. Tsunami and giant bores would flood the coasts of the North Sea and English Channel, while the huge quantities of dust pumped into the stratosphere would rapidly lead to global cooling and the onset of a cosmic winter.

of the English Channel acted like a heavy veil, blocking the life-giving warmth of the Sun's radiation and plunging the Earth into bitter cold. Within 2 weeks, global temperatures fell by 8°C and snow and biting winds raged across much of the planet. Slowly the atmosphere began to clear, and within 5 months temperatures crept back almost to normal. But it was too late. In the cold, the dark and the wet, harvests had failed all over the world. Cities had emptied as their starving populations headed for the countryside to hunt for food that simply did not exist. In a world where a few grains of rice meant the difference between survival and oblivion, life was cheap and death came swiftly and easily. At a few isolated locations in North America, Russia and Australia, all under military rule, some semblance of normality remained, although food was scarce and life was hard. Elsewhere, society had broken down completely, and law and order no longer existed. In a few short months the human race had been reduced to the near-animal existence of scavenging and fighting from which it had hoisted itself a mere 10,000 years earlier.

EPILOGUE

If you have managed to read this far you may well by now be feeling like throwing yourself out of the nearest lofty window. Please don't, because there is still hope. In this book I have attempted, through a combination of hard scientific fact and what I hope is reasonably authentic dramatization, to get across the message that a natural catastrophe is not always something that happens to somebody else. The world is a dangerous place, as it was even before we appeared on the scene; so much so that Nature has the potential to place the whole race in a perilous position with the blast of a single volcano or a brief shiver of the Earth's crust.

In appreciating that such global natural catastrophes are not just possible but certain, we will already have made a start on the long road toward coping with their effects. The threat of impacting asteroids and comets on our planet has, in recent years, attracted sufficient concern from some national governments to encourage them to provide funding for research into the subject or even to debate it in the national legislature. I am optimistic enough to hope that the potentially devastating global impact of the other mega-catastrophes that I have introduced in this book will also eventually be recognized by the movers and shakers, and that measures will be taken, at the very least, to limit the scale of their awful legacies.

As I am sure others in the disaster business have also found, I am often regarded as a doom-monger – a circling vulture just waiting for the next catastrophe to strike. This is, of course, untrue; those of us who study geophysical hazards, such as earthquakes, hurricanes and volcanoes, are fascinated by them and are drawn to them in order to discover why they occur and how they work. This interest is not, however, driven entirely by curiosity and, in my case at least, I want to know what I can do about reducing their impact on our society and our environment. I hope that the publication of *Apocalypse* will go at least some way toward doing this through engendering a fascination with geophysical mega-hazards and their effects. In the meantime – keep smiling!

FURTHER
INFORMATION SOURCES

There is now an abundance of information sources on geophysical hazards, both on and off the World-Wide Web. Below is a small selection of the best.

Off-line

Abbott, P. L., *Natural Disasters*. Wm. C. Brown. 1996

Alexander, D., *Natural Disasters*. UCL Press Ltd. 1998

Bell, F. G., *Geological Hazards: Their Assessment, Avoidance ond Mitigation*. F. & F. Spon (an imprint of Routledge). 1999.

Bishop, V., *Hazards and Responses*. Collins Educational (an imprint of HarperCollins). 1998

Bryant, E. A., *Natural Hazards*. Cambridge University Press. 1993

Hamilton, R. M. & Johnston, A. C., *Tecumseh's Prophecy: Preparing for the Next New Madrid Earthquake US Geological Survey Circular*, No. 1066.

Institution of Civil Engineers, *Megacities: Reducing Vulnerability to Natural Disasters*. UK. 1995

McGuire, W. & Kilburn, C., *Volcanoes of the World*. Promotional Reprint Company. 1997

Newson, L., *The Atlas of the World's Worst Natural Disasters*. Dorling Kindersley. 1998

Smith, K., *Environmental Hazards*. Routledge. 1996

Steel, D., *Rogue Asteroids and Doomsday Comets*. Wiley. 1995

Zebrowski, E., Jr., *Perils of a Restless Planet: Scientific Perspectives on Natural Disasters*. Cambridge University Press. 1997

On-line

Benfield Greig Hazard Research Centre. (Information on cutting-edge hazard and natural disaster research.) http://www.bghrc.com

Discovery Channel Online – Earth Alert. (Daily updates on the state of the planet.) http://www.discovery.com/news/earthalert/earthalert.html

Earthwatch. (Information on storms and extreme weather.) http://www.earthwatch.com

NOAA Websites: Hurricanes. http://www.websites.noaa.gov/guide/sciences /atmo/hurricanes.html

Seismo-Surfing the Internet. (Information on earthquakes around the world.) http://www.geophys.washington.edu.seismosurfing.html

Tornadoes Theme Page. http://www.cln.org/themes/tornadoes.html
Tsunami! The WWW Tsunami Information Resource.
   http://tsunami.ce.washington.edu/tsunami/intro.html
USGS Earthquake Information Centre. http://quake.wr.usgs.gov/
USGS National Landslide Information Centre. http://landslides.usgs.gov
Volcano World. http://volcano.und.nodak.edu/

INDEX